Two and Two

ALSO BY RAFE BARTHOLOMEW

Pacific Rims

Two and Two

McSorley's, My Dad, and Me

Rafe Bartholomew

LITTLE, BROWN AND COMPANY

New York   Boston   London

Little, Brown and Company
Hachette Book Group
1290 Avenue of the Americas, New York, NY 10104
littlebrown.com

First Edition: May 2017

Little, Brown and Company is a division of Hachette Book Group, Inc. The Little, Brown name and logo are trademarks of Hachette Book Group, Inc.

The publisher is not responsible for websites (or their content) that are not owned by the publisher.

The Hachette Speakers Bureau provides a wide range of authors for speaking events. To find out more, go to hachettespeakersbureau.com or call (866) 376-6591.

Unless otherwise noted, all photos are from the collection of the author.

ISBN 978-0-316-23159-6
Library of Congress Control Number: 2016959023

10 9 8 7 6 5 4 3 2 1

LSC-C

Printed in the United States of America

For my dad and my sister, Becca

Contents

Two and Two

INTRODUCTION

SATURDAY MORNINGS WERE MY TWISTED version of heaven. I was five, six, seven years old, and every weekend I got to spend a few hours hanging out with grown men. Not just any men, but characters—workingmen, old men, homeless men, policemen and firemen. Men who cursed and spat and groaned, who broke each other's chops and answered insults with a "Right here!" and a handful of crotch. (They were also doting fathers, occasional criers, and poets, but those things didn't seduce me back then.) Men with names like Frank the Slob, whose last name, Slovensky, was itself slovenly; names like Fat Sal and Johnny Wadd, Dead Eddie and the Buggerman; if I was lucky, I might catch a glimpse of Bunghole Thompson.

I worshipped them all, sometimes in small ways and sometimes in every way, and the man I most wanted to be like was also the reason I was there. Where? McSorley's Old Ale House, New York's landmark saloon on East Seventh Street, open in the same spot since Old John McSorley founded the place on February 17, 1854. My father, Geoffrey Bartholomew—but at the bar it's just Bart—has worked at McSorley's since 1972.

Throughout my childhood, he brought me to the bar, partly because he and my mother had nowhere else to put me. Saturday mornings and early afternoons belonged to my mom. They were her time to attend antialcohol twelve-step meetings, to get lunch with friends, to study for her degrees in food studies. I was a few years too young to be left alone in our Manhattan apartment, so my dad took me to work. But my trips to McSorley's were always about more than simple necessity. My dad wanted to bring me, to show me his world of drunkards and lunatics, neighborhood sages and men in uniform. It was the late 1980s, when New York felt a little bit less like the playground for plutocrats it does today, and probably the last handful of years when you could get away with calling the East Village gritty.

We'd arrive at the bar between nine and ten in the morning, a little more than an hour before opening. While the waiters and barmen prepared for a seven-hour shift that usually meant serving ten to twelve kegs of McSorley's light and dark ale, the guys would toss a couple of bucks my way to buy coffee, Danishes, and an occasional bialy. I'd memorize the order and scurry down the block to Kiev, the Ukrainian diner on the corner of Seventh and Second Avenue. The change was mine, a tip for my trouble, but the real reward came when the staff sat down for breakfast together. This was when the guys traded stories, bullshitting about palms gashed on broken mugs and laughing over customers who had to be eighty-sixed. One morning, there was talk of a fight the night before that had cleared out the bar, and my father dusted off a pair of homemade brass knuckles that a waiter he'd worked with in the seventies had given him. It was a thin strip of metal that had been bent into a rectangular loop and wrapped with layers of black electrical tape, with space in the middle to slide one's fingers through and make a fist. "Thank God no one ever needed to use 'em in the bar," my dad said. "But the guys in

Zory's day must have been rough if they were carrying these." He tossed me the weapon to try on—it was so big that I could almost slip it over my wrist and wear it like a bracelet. I imagined being grown enough for my hand to fill it, not because I wanted to crack some skulls, but just to close my fist and feel that power, to join them in manhood.

Just as powerful as the flesh-and-blood characters of McSorley's was the bar's history. I grabbed bar mops and wiped down tables under the eyes of Theodore Roosevelt, JFK, former New York governor Al Smith, and a slew of other public figures of Irish heritage or Roman Catholic background or just plain New York stock whose framed portraits lined the walls. I hauled blocks of cheddar cheese up from the basement refrigerator for my father to load into the same eight-foot-tall nineteenth-century icebox Old John had installed behind the bar when he opened McSorley's. (The iceman stopped delivering in the middle of the twentieth century, and although the icebox's ancient façade was preserved, its guts were converted to a refrigerator.)

Between tasks, I'd daydream, gazing at the ceiling, where Harry Houdini's handcuffs dangled a few feet from a medieval-style mace and a pair of Civil War–era shackles from the Confederate prison camp at Andersonville. I already knew better than to reach up toward the sacred turkey wishbones hanging from the busted gas lamp above the ale taps. With steel in his voice, my father told me that first Saturday he brought me to work: *Those belong to the neighborhood guys who fought in World War One and never came back. Nobody touches them.* I scanned the newspaper clips and photographs and posters, absorbing the lore of heavyweight champs Jack Dempsey and Gene Tunney, Yankee legend Babe Ruth, and champion racehorses whose names and exploits might only still be remembered on the walls of McSorley's. John McSorley himself, with his intense, prideful eyes and white mutton-chop whiskers, stared down at me from various paintings and snapshots. Reminders of his legacy were everywhere: Signs in the bar's front and back rooms reminded staff and customers to heed one of Old John's original mottoes—BE GOOD OR BE GONE—while newspaper headlines from the day in August 1970 when female customers were first served at McSorley's marked the death of Old John's other founding creed—GOOD ALE, RAW ONIONS, AND NO LADIES.

The object that I came to love most was a framed certificate—about the same size as the bar's yellowed replica of the Declaration of Independence—that honored my father's first twenty years of employment. It hung from a spot high on the wall, looking down on the taps where my dad spent the majority of his shifts, pumping light and dark ale, surveying the floor, and barking orders to the waiters. I would mouth the words on his certificate while watching him work:

CONGRATULATIONS TO McSORLEY'S
PERSONABLE BARTENDER,
GEOFFREY BARTHOLOMEW

The sentence was terse and not all that eloquent and the document wasn't even correct. It recorded the beginning of my dad's career as 1973, when he actually worked his first shift in 1972. But it didn't matter. That piece of paper meant I was part of this place. McSorley's had been there for a century and a half. That was forever to me, and in my wide eyes, it seemed like the bar would last another forever. I got to occupy a sliver of that history.

CHAPTER 1

The Company of Men

I HAD MY FATHER'S SATURDAY routine memorized before I learned my multiplication tables. He'd roll out of bed around 9 a.m., two hours before the bar opened. I'd be ready long before then, waiting on our living room couch, pushing the last few Frosted Flakes around a bowl of cereal-sweetened milk until I'd hear him groan or sometimes fart from the other side of my parents' bedroom door. Moments later he'd emerge and take his first knock-kneed, half-stumbling steps into wakefulness. Saturday was his hump day, the middle of his work week, and it meant one more grueling haul behind the bar before the relative calm of Sunday and Monday night. So as eager as I was to start bugging him about McSorley's on those Saturdays, I knew to wait—at least long enough for him to hit the bathroom and then pour a mug of coffee.

After he'd taken a couple of sips, though, I couldn't help

but start harassing him. Who's working the bar with you today? Which waiters are on the floor? Is there a doorman? Is Henry in the kitchen? Or Eddie or Jackie Ng? What about the shithouse? How long can I stay?

"What's your mother say?" he'd ask.

"I'll get lunch with Mimi and then pick him up around two," she'd answer without looking up from the *Times* Metro section.

I was in. After two cups of coffee and a couple of spoonfuls of yogurt, my father would grab a worn-out sock and a small tin of mink oil and start waterproofing his work boots. They came waterproof when he bought them, but my father preferred extra protection. With his hand inside the sock, he'd scoop out a mound of mink oil with his index finger and spread it over the toe of his boot, working back toward the heel. Each week he'd apply a fresh layer, and each week he could count on being soaked with ale and water from the knees down by shift's end.

Then he'd pull on a long-sleeved thermal undershirt and start buttoning a white dress shirt over it. McSorley's bartenders have been wearing white button-downs since the tavern opened, and my father always had a stack of them — washed, starched, and folded — ready for work. He'd leave the top open at his neck, fasten the two small buttons at the tips of his collar, and then tuck the shirt into a pair of faded blue jeans. He'd pull a pair of heavy wool socks up to his calves, then squeeze a shot of talcum powder into his boots before working his feet inside. Next, he'd roll the sleeves of both shirts up to his elbows and spend a few moments rubbing a small growth on his wrist.

He'd given the gumdrop-sized ganglion (a kind of cystic fluid tumor caused by inflamed tendons) a name: the knob.

It had formed on the inside of his right wrist, some kind of repetitive-use injury from his years of pumping ale and grabbing giant handfuls of mugs. But to hear my father tell it, the knob never hurt much. Still, he thought it an eyesore, so he would strap a leather brace with three buckles and a zipper around his wrist for extra support.

"You ready?" he'd ask, and since I had spent the previous half hour watching him suit up, I never was. It didn't matter, though. I'd say yes and scramble to my room to pull on a sweatshirt and chase him out the door.

Normally, my father would bike to work. But I was too young to ride alongside him, and the days of seeing hip New York dads pedal their kids around in custom bike seats wouldn't arrive for another fifteen years. So we'd either walk the half hour to McSorley's from our apartment in the far southwest corner of Greenwich Village, or, if we were running late or my father's knees were hurting, we'd hail a cab.

By the time we set foot in the bar, around ten, the door would be unlocked, with a wooden chair blocking the entrance to dissuade unknowing customers from moseying in before eleven. Richie the King, the back-room waiter, would already be inside, setting up along with the chef, who'd be chopping vegetables and warming chicken stock for the day's soup. Frank "the Slob" Slovensky, a longtime customer turned informal employee, would be there, too, sitting at the table next to the women's restroom, slumped over a crate of onions and peeling them to make slicing easier for the chef.

"Hey, Rafe, you wanna work?" Richie would ask. I never thought of saying anything but yes.

"Run downstairs and grab a bag of coal for the stove."

I knew the route by heart: into the back room, between Frank the Slob's table and the one next to it, through the emergency exit that opens into the ground-floor hallway of the tenement building at 15 East Seventh Street, and down the steps into the cellar. The room was filled with rolls of duct tape and hammers that looked old enough to have been swung by Old John McSorley. Broken chairs were scattered throughout, waiting for someone to replace their missing legs. Behind the staircase was a mound of white burlap sacks, each filled with a fifty-pound load of coal. I'd grab one, drag it back into the bar, and watch Richie build a fire in the blackened potbelly stove that had been in use at McSorley's since the nineteenth century.

"Jimbo!" my father called. (It was a term of endearment that, along with its derivatives Jim and Jimmy, he and other bar employees constantly flung back and forth.)

"Quit pulling your pud and get over here! You know what to do." He'd hold out a tin can filled with steaming water and a pair of long-necked pliers. It was time to extract nickels and dimes and quarters from the tables in the front room. Over the years, customers had adopted the tradition of hammering coins between the seams of McSorley's hundred-year-old tabletops. My job was to remove the change from the tables and hopefully dissuade drinkers from committing copycat crimes. If customers didn't look down and see coins wedged into the cracks of their tables, they might not decide to smash their own little ten-cent bits of history into the establishment. The practice did just enough damage to the sturdy old tables to cross the Be Good or Be Gone line. As payment, I was allowed to keep whatever money I retrieved.

My game plan with the pliers was simple: First, I'd scan a table, searching for the coins that looked to have been hammered in most recently. Those came out easy. If a large enough sliver of the coin was protruding from the tabletop, I'd just latch on to it with my tool and wiggle back and forth until it popped out. Sometimes I'd use my fingertips to roll a bit of the coin up from the table—just enough so the pliers could grip it. I targeted quarters first; then nickels, then dimes. Nickels came before dimes because although they were worth less, they were harder to mistake for pennies. A dime is obviously slimmer and more silver, but imagine how being lodged inside an ale-soaked table for a couple of decades might alter that appearance.

That's where the can of hot water came in handy—to soak away whatever grunge had grown on the coins over the years. Just about every Saturday I'd manage to pry loose a quarter that had been encased long enough to turn green and grow fuzz.

"Make sure you get the *feduh*, Jimbo." *Feduh*, pronounced "feh-DUH" with the emphasis on "duh," is what grows in dank corners of hundred-year-old bars. It was there when my father first started bringing me to McSorley's, and it's still there now, almost thirty years later. *Feduh* is another word for the Yiddish *schmutz*. The term comes from a Ukrainian immigrant one of the other bartenders would bring to McSorley's on weekday mornings to help clean and set up the bar. This guy's name was Fedyuh (or something like that—my dad's ability to render Cyrillic-to-English phonetic spelling is probably far from perfect), and he complained about wiping the slime from behind the bar. Naturally, my father named the gunk after him, and the term stuck.

Feduh isn't simple grime, but something more primordial.

It's no longer recognizable as plain old dirt. It becomes cheese-like, sometimes gooey, and working at McSorley's can make you a connoisseur of the stuff. Feduh tends to inspire a gross, corporeal fascination. You can't just wipe it off and forget it. You feel compelled to examine it, play with it, show it to the guys.

Once, I decided to share it with my father. "Jimbo," I called out to my dad, eager to use his lingo, "look at this one." Then I flipped a mossy coin at him, freshly pulled from a table, knowing that his reflexes would force him to catch it. When it landed in his palm and he felt his fist close around the slimy metal, he let out a retch and a laugh. "You little fucker!" he said, tossing the coin into a sink full of hot water and dishwashing solution behind the bar. "You're gonna get it now."

He wasn't kidding. That morning, I saw how quickly feduh pranks can escalate into all-out warfare. I also learned that my father's knowledge of the place left me hopelessly outgunned in this arms race. There's more unseen gunk growing behind that ancient bar than in the rest of McSorley's combined. Over the next fifteen minutes, while I helped Richie spread a fresh layer of sawdust over the saloon's smooth hardwood floor—"toss it in handfuls like you're throwing out chicken feed," Richie advised—my father went on a schmutz expedition. He scooped feduh from the damp shelf beneath the ale taps; he fished crud from the drainage hole in the corner of the bar where the waiters pick up overflowing orders of twenty, forty, one hundred ales at a time; he lifted the rubber mats on the tile floor behind the bar and wiped what lay below. Then, once he'd assembled the feduh smorgasbord and collected it all in a single bar rag, he got his revenge.

"Jimbo!" I looked up to find the rank ball of cloth hurtling through the air at my head. Before I could think to dodge it, my arm shot up and snatched it from the air. And as soon as I did, I felt ages of accumulated New York filth grease my palm. It was grainy and slick and smelled like rot. My dad was laughing his balls off behind the bar, and I couldn't help but join him.

By half past ten the bar was ready for business. Richie had emptied a bottle of bleach into the urinals to freshen up the men's room. McSorley's weapons-grade spicy mustard had been mixed—the condiment was made every morning with mustard powder, water, and suds from newly tapped kegs, then decanted into beer mugs to be left on the tables and spread over saltine crackers and squares of cheddar cheese. The phalanx of mugs that had been lined up atop the bar when we arrived had been washed, scrubbed, rinsed, and stacked on shelves behind the taps, ready to be rinsed again and then filled with ale. The coal inside the potbelly stove was glowing, and the staff sat around the table next to it, five men in white undershirts and blue jeans, reading the *Daily News* and the *Post*, cursing about George Steinbrenner and the dismal late-eighties Yankees, and sipping coffee from blue cardboard cups before work.

Most of their banter was shop talk—barman's gossip about fights and scams and sex, shot through with gallows humor and cynicism. I was too young to understand much of it, but just sitting there allowed me to soak in their world and absorb a communication style that felt like a way of being—all dismissive chortles, knowing nods, belly laughs, and surprised grunts.

You should have seen the fucking disaster in here Thursday night. Aussies at one table, bikers on the other side of the front room, and cops in between. It was the cops we had to throw out first, and I'm still finding bits of the Aussies' puke in the shitter.

Did you guys hear about Ronnie, the manager of one of the Irish pubs out in Sunnyside? His entire building flooded at six in the morning after he got home from work because the crazy prick tried to flush the tape from the bar's cash register down his toilet!

After a few minutes of story time, I'd usually wander the bar, looking at the framed photos and drawings on the walls, revisiting the faces of historical figures and McSorley's misfits before the customers arrived and made it impossible to climb on chairs and press my face up against the wall to get a good look. My father had me playing baseball at age five and started taking me to recreation centers to teach me basketball a couple of years later, so my Saturday tour of McSorley's inevitably focused on sports artifacts.

Behind the bar, I'd reach up and palm the weathered softballs sitting atop a row of old ceramic McSorley's mugs. The softballs had accumulated over the years, brought in by guys from local firehouses at the end of their rec-league seasons, until an entire section of wall behind the bar was given over to their display. Some of them remained fairly unmarked by time, so it was still possible to make out the engine company numbers the firefighters had inked onto the leather orbs. Some had been there so long that their exteriors had dried and darkened and shriveled and cracked.

Down the bar from the softballs, I'd take a moment to pay my respects to the Babe. High in the ranks of treasured McSorley artifacts, along with the wanted poster for John Wilkes Booth, a signed letter from President Franklin Delano

Roosevelt, and others, is a print of Nat Fein's Pulitzer Prize–winning photograph, "The Babe Bows Out." Fein captured the image of Babe Ruth two months before his death in 1948, as he climbed out onto the field for his final curtain call at Yankee Stadium. The story goes that Fein himself made the print, signed it, and gave it to then-manager of McSorley's Harry Kirwan, and customers who've been to Cooperstown have sworn that the framed photo behind the bar is larger than the one on display at the Baseball Hall of Fame.

Next I found my way to the boxers. McSorley's has been around long enough to encompass much of the history of American prizefighting, and it's no coincidence that a New York watering hole opened by an Irishman in the mid-nineteenth century would favor the sport's great Irish champions. Just above the Babe, next to a bust of John F. Kennedy, is a bronze figurine of John L. Sullivan, the Boston-born fighter who was boxing's last bare-knuckle heavyweight champ. Just beside the taps, affixed to the wall that separates McSorley's front room from the back, there's a signed portrait of Jack Dempsey, framed in the center of a collection of Mecca Cigarettes boxing trading cards. The Mecca cards dated back to the early 1900s, and I loved to circle around to the other side of the wall, which had a hole cut in it to display the descriptions on the cards' backs.

Joe Gans, lightweight champion: *Fought over 150 battles winning all but 5. . . . He died of consumption in Baltimore, August 10, 1910.*

Gentleman Jim Corbett, heavyweight champion of the world: *Won the heavyweight championship from John L. Sullivan, who had held the title for 12 years. . . . Lost the title to Bob Fitzsimmons in 14 rounds at Carson, Nevada, March 17, 1897.* (That would have been the forty-third St. Patrick's Day at McSorley's.) *Retired from the ring and is now an actor.*

Back then, I had no real understanding of what Dempsey meant to the sport. Nor did I really know a thing about Joe Gans—that he's among the greatest lightweights of all time or that he was the first African-American world champion. But the boxers still mattered to me. They were another part of McSorley's that invited me into a past and a tradition I might never have discovered otherwise, and they made a twelve-year-old in 1994 feel like he could step back into 1906.

The last stop on my rounds would be a sliver of space in the front room between the end of the bar and a round window table near the entrance. The best piece of McSorley's sports history is up there, and it has nothing to do with an iconic moment or legendary athletes. It's a team picture called "The McSorley Nine," a black-and-white photograph from 1877 of a recreational baseball team sponsored by the bar and led by Peter McSorley, one of Old John's sons. The men posed, some seated and some standing, all wearing plain white uniforms with cleats and boxy, short-brimmed caps, gazing stone-faced into the camera. There isn't a smile among them—just handlebar mustaches, steely eyes, and the player in the middle with one hand on his hip and the other holding a wooden bat against the ground like a cane.

I always wondered why they looked so serious. Were they photographed after a heartbreaking loss? Were they preparing for a big game? Were men in the 1870s just like that— sturdy, cocksure, emotionless? That masculine ideal has stuck around through the ages, but I grew up around a crew of McSorley's men who knew how to play the strong, silent type but preferred the humor and camaraderie and bawdiness of bar life. There was no apparent lightheartedness among the McSorley Nine.

The greatest mystery, however, was what had happened to the last member of the McSorley Nine. Every time I walked up to inspect the photo, I'd count the players from left to right. One, two, three...seven, eight...eight. The McSorley Nine had no ninth man. And the eight guys pictured didn't seem concerned with his whereabouts. I imagined what he must have looked like. A husky first baseman—like I was back then—left-handed, adept at scooping short-hop throws from the dirt, and a line-drive hitter who always pulled the ball. Maybe he was sick that day. Maybe he didn't believe in team portraits. Maybe he was drunk at McSorley's. Maybe he was the one taking the photograph. Every week, I imagined something different, and every week it seemed as plausible as the last week's guess.

Okay, I lied. There's an even greater mystery in the McSorley Nine photo. In a way, it explains what happened to the ninth man. One of the first times I stood looking at the portrait, my father crept behind me. "Look over here," he whispered in my ear, and pointed between the player standing in the center with the bat and another player to his left. The picture was taken in a park, with lush trees and grass and clear skyline in the background. In the spot where my father directed me to look, in the negative space between the players and the tree branches behind them, I spotted the outline of another man—the final member of the McSorley Nine, or just an apparition.

"Do you see the ghost?" my father asked. It looked like a

McSorley's bartender. The empty white sky formed his dress shirt; then the branches shaped the hazy outline of an oblong head with a mustache.

"It looks like you," I said.

"That's what everyone says," my dad told me. "Now look at this." He pointed to the photograph next to "The McSorley Nine," a framed image, also from 1877, titled "McSorley Chowder Club." It was a group portrait from one of the annual McSorley picnics, when the bar's owners and employees and family and friends would head to North Brother Island for an afternoon of frolicking in the summer sun. Again, my father pointed to an area at the center-left of the image. "You see it?"

I did. It was the same apparition, the same oval head and mustache and narrow eyes formed by the white background and tree branches and leaves in front of it.

"The ghost?" I answered. It was as if my father, who hadn't set foot in McSorley's until his first night in New York City back in 1967, had been there all along.

"Yep," my dad said. Maybe ending up at the bar had always been his destiny. Maybe it was mine, too.

I'm afraid I'm making McSorley's sound like a library. The artifacts, the gravitas, the legacy—that's all part of it, but the bar's energy is often anything but contemplative. As a boy, I usually couldn't inspect the Chowder Club ghosts for more than a minute or two before a bartender or waiter would pull me aside to workshop his newest dirty joke or saloon story. Scott, who wasn't even twenty years old when he began working at McSorley's in 1986, felt like an older

THE COMPANY OF MEN

brother, and I regarded his stock wisdom on the Yankees and Rangers as if it were scripture. An ale deliveryman from Barbados named Jeffrey never missed an opportunity to recommend a product called China Brush to my dad and the other barmen — it was some kind of numbing salve that prolonged erections and made Jeffrey a world-class Casanova. Then he'd grab seven-year-old me by the shoulders and impart life lessons: *First time you get a woman, boy, you better eat the pussy good!* Due to my age, Jeffrey's love advice might have qualified as a criminal act, but inside McSorley's it was just another story. And nothing Jeffrey came up with ever came close to matching the lewd genius of Tommy Lloyd.

Lloyd was my father's sidekick on many of those Saturdays. While Bart stood behind the taps and poured ale, Lloyd would scamper up and down the length of the bar, serving customers, collecting cash, making change, and grabbing empty mugs to wash. He stood about five foot seven, with wiry, pipe-cleaner arms and a perfect bowl of straight brown hair that flopped over his forehead and stopped just short of his satellite dish ears. Lloyd had come over from Roscommon, Ireland, in the sixties. He had been bartending with my father for the better part of a decade. When he told stories and laughed, his smile seemed to take up two-thirds of his face, and around me he was always spinning those blarney-filled yarns. To a boy growing up in New York, he might as well have been an in-the-flesh leprechaun.

"Hey there, lad, your old man told me you took up an attitude with him the other night. Is that true?"

I didn't know what Lloyd was talking about. He could have been referencing any of the hundreds of times I fought with my father over sports—when I wanted to watch cartoons instead of practicing my jump shot or when I didn't feel like chasing down fly balls in the empty parking lot around the corner from our place. But it turned out that Lloyd was merely floating the attitude issue as a setup for his next joke.

Lloyd leaned forward with his elbows on the bar and patted the top of my head. "If you're causing trouble, I'll have to send you home with Omar."

My father chortled. He waved the smudged bar rag he'd been using to polish the brass busts of John McSorley's bald dome that served as the bar's tap heads. "Oh, Jim, you don't want that."

"Who's Omar?" I asked.

"Who's Omar?" Lloyd said. "Omar's gonna love you, my boy. He's gonna show you the tube steak."

"What's the tube steak?"

"You never seen the tube steak?" Lloyd said. "Here, a demonstration." He pulled open one of the lower compartments of the icebox and retrieved a two-foot log of liverwurst.

"See?" Lloyd said, holding the pink tube of plastic-wrapped meat and pretending to fellate it. I had no clue about sexuality or the specific act Lloyd was mimicking, but I had enough sense to know it was dirty, so I laughed along with the other guys and punched Lloyd's liverwurst for good measure. (I didn't know it at the time, but Omar is a regular customer whom I'd eventually serve. He's a lifelong New Yorker, and he likes to stand at the bar and chat up whoever's around. Once in a while, he meets a young man he likes and takes him home.)

"Attaboy!" they all roared. I couldn't have felt more satisfied.

*   *   *

I might as well admit that this scene—along with many, many others from my childhood—falls well outside the bounds of what's considered appropriate for young kids. Or adults, for that matter. Sarcastic jerk-off gestures, mimicked blow jobs on the liverwurst dong, the term *tube steak,* jokes at the expense of a gay customer—these aren't the best practices advised in child-rearing books. When my mother would pick me up on Saturdays and I'd brag about how Dad and Lloyd had showed me the tube steak, she'd slap me on the wrist and remind me that the things I learned at McSorley's—talk of big johnsons and bungholes and transvestites—weren't okay to talk about outside the bar. More importantly, she made sure I understood that there was more to the world than McSorley's grizzled, old-school masculinity.

But for all the faults of McSorley's male-dominated culture, the ethos of the place was egalitarian—mischief and ball-breaking for all. No creed or ethnicity or body type was spared, and while that's probably not the best way to run society, it worked in a pub. It didn't take long for me, even as a child, to understand how those old swinging doors at the front of McSorley's served as a border between the bar and the rest of the world. At work, the men of McSorley's cursed all day and tormented each other with obscene pranks, but they also knew to behave in the real world. Off the clock, they were polite members of society who said please and thank you and held doors for women and children. Inside McSorley's, they were free to clown around, and as much as I loved having access to the bar's realm of adult troublemaking, what I craved most was to grow up to be like them, and that meant more than just telling dirty jokes. It meant upholding an old-fashioned, gentlemanly code that valued honesty and chivalry and hard work. (And then telling sex jokes.)

The one McSorley's man I tried to avoid on Saturday mornings was Richie Buggy, the longtime front-room waiter whom we all called Dick. He was childhood friends with the bar's owner, Matthew Maher. They grew up together in County Kilkenny, Ireland, and then in the 1960s came to New York as young men. Matt found work at McSorley's and Dick joined the NYPD, where he worked as a decoy cop in sting operations to catch would-be muggers. In fact, just above the window table, hanging across from the McSorley Nine and the Chowder Club, was a framed full-page *Daily News* article about Dick's police work. The headline read BAIT FOR MUGGERS atop two pictures of Dick—one where he was dressed like a homeless man, pretending to be passed out on a subway platform, and another of him sitting on a park bench in an ill-fitting polka-dot dress with a tuft of hair poking out from beneath his bonnet. Dick's assignment was to wait for any of the multitude of thieves and hoodlums who gave seventies New York its fearsome reputation to take a swipe at his purse or yank the string of pearls around his neck. When they did, he pounced.

By the time Dick ended up working the front-room waiter shift at McSorley's, he had left the force. His police work was daring and heroic, but it also revealed a vigilante streak that remained with him after retirement. Every Saturday morning he'd put an arm around my shoulder and tell a different story from his days prowling the streets for

THE COMPANY OF MEN

crooks—cracking heads, the look in a perp's eyes when he's staring down the barrel of a gun, *Serpico* shit. Perhaps I was naïve and didn't understand how dangerous New York was in the decade before I was born. Yes, I had seen my mom get thrown to the sidewalk outside our building during a Christmas Eve mugging one year, and I had heard my father talk of narrowly escaping robbery attempts when he biked home late at night. But when I listened to Dick crow about violent, street-level justice in the NYPD's good old days, I could barely hide my alarm. My back stiffened, my heart beat faster, I wanted to run away.

One day, Dick, an avid hunter and fisher, led me down to the basement. It was a cold December morning, a week or two after deer season had opened, and he'd just gotten back from a trip upstate. "Take a look in the back box," he told me, pointing to the smaller of McSorley's two subterranean walk-in refrigerators. "Old St. Nick is in there, and if you've been nice this year maybe he's got a present for you." I pulled open the door and there was a freshly killed buck that Dick had shot and brought down from the Catskills. Somebody had pulled a red Santa hat over its head and threaded its front legs through the sleeves of a gray waiter's jacket. A piece of paper was taped to its chest with the words HO! HO! HO! If my parents hadn't already explained to me a year or two before this that Santa wasn't real, I might have been scarred for life.

But customers loved Dick. He had the Irish gift of gab, a way of speaking in aphorisms and witticisms and randy one-liners that delighted the bar crowd. Thankfully, whenever Dick would corner me and launch into hard-boiled cop fables, Lloyd would come to my rescue. He'd grab a liverwurst tube or the refurbished foot-long forty-millimeter antiaircraft shell that had been fired from a US battleship on D-Day (another McSorley's treasure) and start working the knob, pushing his tongue into the side of his cheek. "That's right, Jimbo!" he'd shout across the room. "Dicksie's a real American hero!"

When the clock struck 11 a.m. and the first customers rumbled in, it was my job to take the bar cat, Sawdust, downstairs to the basement. The red tabby was the same color as the wood chips that coated the McSorley's floor, hence his name, although a handful of old-timers preferred to call him Red. Several generations of bar cats before Sawdust had shared another name, Minnie, but this one's playful nature and distinctive coloring warranted a break in tradition. He had been a kitten when my father first brought me to the bar, when I was barely more than a toddler, and my earliest memory there wasn't the rich, fermented aroma of ale soaked into the bar or the sight of my father holding twenty ale-filled mugs. Instead, it was Lloyd teaching me to roll a ball of crumpled aluminum foil across the basement floor and watching Sawdust pounce on it. The cat was probably the first part of McSorley's that I fell in love with, and when my father brought me in I considered it my duty to watch over the pet.

During some of the quieter weeknight shifts, Sawdust would be allowed to roam the bar, although most of the time he'd just curl up on a chair in the pocket of warmth behind the potbelly stove. Saturdays, however, were too busy for that. By midafternoon, there wouldn't be a spare seat, and drunk customers had tried (and on occasion succeeded) to swipe previous McSorley cats when the place got too busy for the staff to notice. To get Sawdust downstairs,

I'd return to our old game of fetch, rolling a ball of foil across the floor. When the cat bolted out from his resting place to attack the silver prey, I'd scoop him up and head down to the cellar.

The basement was almost as exciting a playground for kids and kittens as the bar. Sawdust would jump into the shadows in the depths of the shelves, and I'd dangle a finger or some string at the edge of his territory, pulling the bait away just before he could snag it with his claws.

I knew I had to get back upstairs by eleven thirty, however, because that was when Larry would show up. Larry was a neighborhood bum, a lanky wraith about six foot one who always had some oversized sweatshirt or jacket dangling off a bony shoulder and bits of lint caught in his mini-twist dreadlocks. Almost every Saturday until sometime in the midnineties, Larry would show up outside the wide picture windows that frame McSorley's front door, grip the wire grates protecting the glass, and start howling: "LARRRR-RRRYYYYYY! LARRRR-RRRYYYYYY!" He barely spoke besides that, so nobody at the bar could tell if he was screaming his own name, or if he thought someone inside was named Larry, or if he was crying for some long-lost brother or friend or his childhood dog.

The guys of McSorley's loved when Larry's routine happened to catch an unsuspecting couple sitting at the window table, and they would leap from their seats and shriek in surprise. It had become tradition to give Larry a ham and cheese sandwich whenever he passed, and I would try to time my trip up from the basement to coincide with his arrival so I could be the server. As soon as I saw him lace his fingers through the wires outside the window, I'd head back to the kitchen and ask the chef for Larry's lunch. He'd slap

together a ham and cheese on rye, slather on a bit of mayon-
naise and a few slices of onion, drop it in an aluminum
to-go box, and send me on my way. Larry never said thank
you in as many words, but he'd give a nod before wandering
east down Seventh Street.

Usually, by the time Larry had come and gone, it meant
my morning at McSorley's was nearing its end. My mother
would arrive sometime in the early afternoon to scoop me
up and take me home or to a matinee movie. By then, the
bar would be halfway busy, nowhere near capacity but hectic
enough that it could be tough to keep track of a young boy
weaving through the thicket of front-room customers.

My mornings typically came to an end with a burger. I'd
sit at the tiny two-person table directly across from the taps
with my back to the wall and watch my dad work. Before sitting down, though, I'd stand at the bar and wait for him to
bring me an ale mug and a can of Diet Coke. A chef from
Chinatown named Jackie Ng (mispronounced at McSorley's
as "Noog") was the acknowledged best cook in those days.
His Noog-burger was the preferred meal for much of the
staff anytime he was in the kitchen. But Fast Eddie Swenson
made my favorite cheeseburger. He'd finish his patties off
with a dramatic plume of flame from the grease-coated
griddle, and I was a sucker for pyrotechnics.

But the charred beef and steak fries were secondary.
Lunch at McSorley's was really about watching my father
work the pumps. He'd tower in his corner of the bar, sizing
up every new group of customers as they stepped inside. His
arms never stopped moving: grabbing empty mugs off the
brass rack in front of the taps, filling them so that an inch
of foam would rise just over the lip of the glass, and turning
to make change from the cash box. He was so clearly in

charge, and I loved seeing him run this New York institution, not much differently from the way John McSorley had run it in 1854, and John's son Bill after him, and so on over the decades until Geoffrey "Bart" Bartholomew found himself pouring ale at McSorley's.

My favorite order, back then and ever since, was called two and two — two lights, two darks. As a kid, I just liked the ring of it, the symmetry of sound. But as I grew older, I came to think of two and two as the McSorley's version of yin and yang, the perfect balance of flavors. Two and two was the ideal order for a pair of lovers, for a couple of quarreling friends, or for a father and son.

CHAPTER 2

Frank's Curse

I FELL IN LOVE WITH McSorley's because I was born into it. Just days after my mother gave birth to me at New York Hospital, my father opened one of the black scrapbooks kept behind the bar for visitors to sign. He found a blank page and wrote: "April 1982: Another year, but this one brings a little Bart—my old man should have been here—crazy old place..." Between going to work with my father and listening to his bar stories as a child, McSorley's was baked into the core of my identity.

But what about the man who introduced me to McSorley's and taught me to treasure the place? How did my father fall into bar life? He certainly wasn't raised in it—he grew up in Euclid, Ohio, an eastern suburb of Cleveland. No, my father got his start at McSorley's in such an obvious way that it's hard to believe: He drank there.

My father moved to New York City in September 1967,

when he was twenty-two years old. He'd finished a bachelor's degree at Ohio's College of Wooster that spring and then spent the summer working in a steel mill in Weirton, West Virginia, just across the state line from Steubenville, where his parents had moved. When he arrived in New York, his plan was to enroll at the New School and get a master's degree in sociology. His first night in the city, he stayed at a youth hostel in the East Village, and that evening he found his way to 15 East Seventh Street and ordered mugs of light and dark.

"New York—fascinating, depressing city," he wrote in his journal shortly after arriving in Manhattan. "First few days here, spent nights in International Hostel—met three Irishmen, a Scotchman, and an Englishman. Latter were working and traveling their way around the world. Really good talks—at McSorley's Old Ale House."

It may have been coincidence that on my father's first night in New York, he drank and told stories in the very bar where he would make a career and serve ale for more than forty years. But with the role drinking had played in his family life before then, it was little surprise that my dad found his way to a place like McSorley's, and that once he got there, he never left.

Booze was my father's birthright. My dad was born July 5, 1945, the second child and first son of Frank and Louise Bartholomew. The same way I can't remember a day where McSorley's wasn't part of my life, my father can scarcely remember a day when his dad wasn't drunk.

My father's family lived in eight different two-family houses around Euclid when he was growing up—money problems and late rent meant the Bartholomews could never count on staying put for long. Yet wherever the family happened to be living, Frank would have booze stashed all over the home. He drank cheap Scotch when he could afford it and worked as an auditor for the Cleveland Pneumatic Tool Company until 1957, when he got into an argument with management and quit. After that, Frank found intermittent work as a hotel manager and in a handful of other auditing jobs, but his drinking made it hard to hold on to jobs. When he didn't have money for Scotch, Frank stuck to quart bottles of Gallo wine. Half-full and empty bottles were stuffed under pillows on the living room couch, slipped into jacket pockets, swaddled in blankets and towels in the linen closet. Frank would stash his bottles in a drunken haze and then forget he'd ever had them to begin with. Once, when my father was still in grade school, he got to class, opened his book bag, and a nearly full bottle of Scotch fell out and shattered all over the floor.

One of Frank's hiding spots was the laundry chute that connected their apartment to a washer-dryer setup in the basement. The chute had a tendency to get stopped up, and one day, after Louise tossed down a load of clothes that failed to make it to the bottom, she sent my dad downstairs with a broom to try to dislodge the blockage. He was about eight years old at the time. He went to the basement with his older sister, Lina, a few steps behind him, and they stuck their heads up the shaft to see what was obstructing it. All they saw was a dark clump, so my father took the broom and nudged the mass from below. After a few sharp pokes, the clothes came loose, along with the wine bottles that had been holding them up, which were wedged diagonally across the chute.

At least these bottles were empty, so when they tumbled down and smashed on the basement's cement floor, my dad and his sister didn't get splattered. But the crash woke Frank, who had been passed out on the couch. When he rushed downstairs to see what had caused the racket, he saw the shattered glass, had no recollection of stuffing the bottles into the laundry chute, and blamed my father for the mess. He made my dad sweep it up, and once the floor was clean Frank lifted him up and threw him against a wall.

Such abuse was a part of everyday life in my father's childhood home. Frank was nearly always drunk, and at the height of his intoxication, he'd become possessed by venomous rage. My father, the middle child, was Frank's favored target. Some shred of decency prevented Frank from laying his hands on Lina, his only daughter, or Doug, the baby of the family and younger than my father by four years. Supper was the time of day my dad dreaded most. By then, he knew his father would be plastered and on the warpath, berating Louise, calling her a "blackhearted bitch," and finding any excuse to spank and smack my father.

My grandmother was Frank's other regular victim. His violence toward her was typically less forceful than it was toward my dad, but he would often curse her, and several times his physical abuse — slapping and smacking her in the face, threatening to beat her — got severe enough that neighbors called police to the house. My grandmother never wanted to press charges against Frank, so the cops would just take him to the precinct, dry him out overnight in the drunk tank, and then send him home.

The day-to-day realities of living with an abusive alcoholic father were horrifying. It wasn't just the beatings, or Frank's habit of waking up on the couch, halfway through a bender, and stumbling over to the kitchen sink to unzip his pants and take a leak while the kids sat a few feet away, doing homework at the dinner table.

During one yearlong stretch of joblessness, Frank, with little to keep him occupied throughout the day, would lock himself in the house and drink for hours while Louise was working as a schoolteacher and the kids were in class. He would suffer from bouts of suicidal depression during those long, lonely, soused afternoons, and it wasn't uncommon for him to assemble his Remington twelve-gauge shotgun as if he planned to kill himself, then pass out before he remembered to pull the trigger. As the oldest boy, the duty fell to my father to crawl through the milk delivery hatch in the front door (because turning the doorknob might startle Frank and cause him to start shooting), then creep up on Frank to pry the firearm away without waking him. Day after day, my father saw his father unconscious with his hands wrapped around a shotgun, the barrel sometimes resting on his chest in a puddle of drool. And every time, he felt sure that if his father woke up, he would shoot him dead on the spot.

Another time, Frank went down to the basement and declared he was going to blow his brains out, and Louise asked my dad and his eight-year-old brother to go downstairs and "beg your father not to kill himself." Frank's most serious suicide attempts came about a month after that incident, when he headed out for a solo hunting trip, got drunk and totaled his car somewhere near Buffalo, New York, and had to ride a bus back to Ohio. He stopped one town short of Euclid, checked into a motel, and slashed his wrists. A maid found him, and he was taken to a hospital in time to save his life. A court ordered him to spend a year in the Ohio State Sanitarium after that. Frank came home sober but was back to drinking within a month of his release.

The years of trauma boiled over in the worst way during November 1956—the week of Thanksgiving. My dad was eleven years old. The day before the holiday, Frank decided to take him hunting on a farm near Findlay, about two hours away. Frank had a bottle of wine underneath the driver's seat in the family station wagon, and he took regular swigs from it during the drive. When they reached the bit of forest where they planned to hunt pheasant and rabbit, Frank took two shotguns from the trunk, handed the smaller one to my father, and patted down his coat pockets to make sure he had his flask. Then they marched into the woods, both armed, one drunk.

They reached a cornfield, and Frank decided this looked like just the kind of place where bunnies would hide. He told my dad to get on his hands and knees and crawl through the field to flush them out. You know what happened next: My father started rustling between the stalks, and Frank was sufficiently buzzed to mistake his movement for the animals they were hunting. Frank raised his shotgun, aimed, and let off a round. My father heard the booming crack of the weapon, dropped flat against the ground, and prayed that the buckshot would miss him.

My father was afraid to call out for his dad to stop shooting. In his mind, this wasn't some drunken mishap. He believed Frank actually wanted to kill him right there. It was a five-shot semiautomatic shotgun, and Frank fired four rounds. With buckshot whizzing over his head, my father scurried to the edge of the field. He took off the safety on his shotgun and made a decision: When he emerged from hiding, if Frank pointed his weapon at him, he was going to shoot him first.

My dad stepped out from the corn stalks. Frank kept his gun pointed at the ground. They continued hunting. Neither mentioned the shotgun rounds Frank had fired at his son.

Somehow, that near-shooting wound up being just a precursor to the horrors that awaited my father's family during that Thanksgiving holiday. When Frank and my dad returned from the hunting trip, Frank kept drinking, downing full flasks of Scotch and bottles of wine between the time he and my father got home and Thanksgiving dinner the next afternoon. My father did his best to avoid Frank that whole time, until the family had to sit down for dinner.

Frank came to the table a seething, rageful mess. He took one look at the turkey Louise had spent the entire day preparing, and snarled at her: "Bitch, why's this turkey so dry?" My dad, his siblings, and Louise ignored Frank's initial tirades, but he persisted until Louise got fed up.

"Frank, can we get through Thanksgiving without you being drunk?" she said. "Frank, what's wrong with you?" My father, Lina, and Doug ate in silence, and once they had cleaned their plates they excused themselves to find refuge in their bedrooms, or the living room, or anywhere Frank wasn't.

Minutes later, they heard Louise screaming. Not the argumentative shouts that had become the family's background noise, but fearful, life-or-death wailing. My father rushed to the kitchen and saw Frank chasing Louise in circles, three steps behind her with a butcher knife in his hand. He said he didn't care anymore—he was ready to cut her open and kill her right there. She yelled to the kids to call the police.

Lina ran to the telephone in the living room. My father ran upstairs. There's no way to know whether Frank really intended to stab his wife, with their three children watching, on Thanksgiving Day, but in that moment my father, who had experienced more of Frank's violence than anyone else in the family, didn't doubt for a second that he could do it.

So my dad ran to his room and grabbed his shotgun, the same weapon he'd been ready to turn on Frank the previous day. It fit together in three parts. He assembled it, loaded one shell, and walked halfway down the stairs. From his perch, he could see the kitchen. He pointed the barrel at his father. "Leave Mom alone and get out," he said. He told Frank that if he took another step toward Louise or approached the stairs, he was dead.

Frank squinted at my dad, his eleven-year-old son. He locked eyes with him and took cautious, deliberate steps to the bottom of the stairs. "What are you gonna do?" he sneered, drawing out the "you" in the most degrading, sarcastic way he knew how. Frank was still holding the butcher knife. My father decided at that point that if Frank took one more step toward him, he would shoot. He made up his mind, took a deep breath, and curled his finger around the trigger.

My father repeated his demand that Frank get out of the house. Frank kept staring straight into his son's eyes as he backpedaled, one slow step at a time. When he reached the front door, he went outside and waited until the police arrived. As usual, Louise declined to press charges, so he ended up spending Thanksgiving night in a holding cell and then being released the following day.

There would be more beatings in my father's adolescence, but either they were less brutal than the ones before that Thanksgiving, or they felt that way. My father had stood up to Frank and showed the old man that he was prepared to kill him if it meant protecting his mother. And even though the whippings would cease not long after my father reached high school, grew to six foot three, and became strong enough to defend himself, the psychic wounds of Frank's abuse would torment my father for years.

I don't have a clear image of Frank Bartholomew in my mind. He died September 30, 1980, a year and a half before I was born, and there were no photographs of him displayed on desks and dressers in our apartment when I was growing up. I've seen pictures of him over the years, usually when an aged three-by-five snapshot would tumble from a book my father was leafing through, or when the search for some totem from my dad's early days in New York led to a trove of family photos. But I still can't quite picture Frank, whom my dad always called "the old man" when he talked about growing up in Ohio.

Yet even though I never laid eyes on my grandfather, I've always had a visceral understanding of his cruelty and what he meant to my father.

As a kid, I was a sucker for my dad's bedtime stories. He'd usually stick with bar tales or goofball fantasies about characters named Flea Market Joe or the Dog Lady, but once in a while he'd mix in a recollection from his childhood. Every story would begin with some moment of drunken slapstick humor, like the bottles jamming up the laundry chute or a family bowling outing where Frank stumbled out too far onto a slick, oiled lane and flopped onto his back like a cartoon character who'd had a rug pulled out from under him. Despite the dark subtext of the stories, my dad would usually play them for humor, tire me out with laughter, and then leave me to sleep. One night, my dad even managed to portray his harrowing 1956 hunting trip as a madcap comedy of errors, where he just happened to end up flat on his stomach in an Ohio cornfield with buckshot from Frank's shotgun whizzing over his head.

Then, as I grew old enough to handle it, he began to reveal the pain and trauma linked to the stories. The beatings, the threats, the smashed glass, my eleven-year-old father's shattered psyche—they became parables of alcoholism and everything booze can do to destroy lives.

My father's stories painted a clearer image of Frank than any photo album could have provided. That image was rotten, although I knew from what my dad wrote in the McSorley logbook after I was born that part of him still wished he could have a loving relationship with his dad. For me, though, Frank was the bogeyman. Inside the kitchen cabinet, we had one drinking glass left over from the old house in Ohio. It had a cursive FMB inscribed on the side, for Frank Miller Bartholomew. We used it for orange juice, but it had been one of Frank's highball glasses, and it seemed to taint any liquid poured into it. Perhaps it was my imagination, but juice from Frank's cup tasted musty and spoiled, and whenever I spotted it on the shelf, surrounded by mugs and cups, the sight of Frank's initials made me cringe, and I'd reach for one of the other glasses.

*   *   *

When my father first moved to New York in 1967, he was a twenty-two-year-old eager to leave behind Ohio and his painful youth. He moved into an apartment in the East Village, on Thirteenth Street near Avenue B. His rent was $58.71 a month, and he supported himself and paid his graduate school tuition with assorted clerical jobs. He was a romantic, and he often wrote flowery journal entries about looking out at the lights of Manhattan and discussing his dreams with the women he dated. He frequently stated his desire to pass his nights in the embrace of someone with a "real, human heart." Then again, he also wrote one terse entry that read: "Drinking tea...physically shot...cock is leaking yellowish discharge...no pain yet."

He tried to befriend Bowery addicts and burnouts who crashed in the East Village flophouses and missions. Six months after he moved to New York, he took in a homeless eighteen-year-old runaway named Bruce and let him sleep on his couch. They bonded. My father wrote that he thought he could help Bruce get back on his feet and make something of his life. He wrote about the randomness of opportunity, how a couple of small differences in circumstance might be the only things separating his fate and Bruce's. Three days later, he penned another journal entry:

> Robbed. Radio, typewriter, few sweaters and other clothes, food, stamps, pennies, after shave lotion and toothpaste.... And I trusted him.... A few dollars' worth of good in exchange for trust. Such is life.

My father was staunchly opposed to the Vietnam War,

and his decision to pursue a Master's in social work at the New School was largely an attempt to avoid the draft. It took all of one semester, however, before he realized it would be impossible to work full-time and maintain his studies. He didn't have the savings or the familial support to leave work, so he dropped out of graduate school. He faced a decision: Go to war, go to prison as a draft dodger, flee to Canada and face permanent exile, or find some other way out. He had already been turned down for the Peace Corps once, but he applied again. This time, he was accepted.

In 1968, my father flew to Mexico for a month of Spanish-language training, and then to Paraguay, where he was to be stationed in a rural outpost near the town of Pedro Juan Caballero, just over the border from Brazil. He lived in the jungle, on a diet that consisted of little more than mandioca root and sugarcane rum that he'd cross over into Brazil to buy at a discount. While in Paraguay, he proposed to organize the subsistence farmers in his village into a food cooperative. They would grow carrots and lettuce and assorted other vegetables, take them to market in Pedro Juan Caballero, then split the earnings. It sounded like a reasonable plan, and my father hoped it would do something to help the people of his host community. But it never got off the ground. When formulating his plan for the co-op, my father hadn't bothered to ask the provincial government for its blessing, and even if he had, they wouldn't have given it. Local officials didn't appreciate my dad's meddling, however minor, in the economy. What did this lanky gringo with the overgrown handlebar mustache know about Paraguay after living there for all of one year?

Not long before my father ran afoul of the Paraguayan authorities, Che Guevara had been killed in neighboring

Bolivia. In those times, any foreigner with facial hair was suspicious, and the government didn't want the peasants being organized in any manner—economic or political. One morning, my father woke up to find a military vehicle parked outside the hut where he'd been living, with a roof-mounted, heavy-caliber machine gun pointed at the front door. The government had already contacted the Peace Corps to inform them that their volunteer was organizing a leftist rebellion in Pedro Juan Caballero.

It didn't matter that the allegations were insane. The government wanted him out and the Peace Corps wanted relations with Paraguay to remain simpatico, so after just one year of service, my father found himself on a jet out of Asunción, the nation's capital. When the flight attendant served him a shrimp cocktail at 36,000 feet, he burst into tears. He'd spent the past year witnessing and living in desperate rural poverty. The locals he'd been forced to leave behind had probably never seen a shrimp cocktail. He couldn't bring himself to touch the dish.

Back in New York, my father took over an apartment from a college friend who had just joined the army. A one-bedroom on the third floor of 15 East Seventh Street. That's right—he moved into a tenement upstairs from McSorley's Old Ale House, the same building where Old John had lived after opening the bar. It was 1970, two years before my dad's first shift at McSorley's, but as soon as he carried his bags up the stairs to reach his flat, my father became a fixture at the pub.

He fell in with the crew of guys—most of them a decade or more older than him—who worked at the bar or lived on the block and made up the McSorley's milieu. There was

Matthew Maher, the night bartender, who would eventually become the owner and my father's boss. Then John Smith, the barman emeritus who had been pumping ale since the mid-1940s. Smith formed the link between McSorley's past and present, and most of the bar legends I learned as a child were stories he passed on to Matty and my dad. Danny Kirwan, who managed the bar for his mother, Dorothy, the owner in those days, would stop by in the morning to check on the previous night's sales and pick up rent from tenants.

Doc Zory, my father's downstairs neighbor, was a part-time McSorley's waiter. He and his pal Johnny Purple were gypsy violinists who once upon a time had made a living as musicians on cruise ships that ferried Americans to the casinos in Batista's Havana, before the Cuban revolution, Fidel Castro's communist regime, and the ensuing US embargo. ("Gypsy" is considered offensive nowadays, but that's how Zory was known around the bar and how he identified back then.) Zory and Johnny Purple settled in New York, found jobs in places like McSorley's, and, according to my dad, subsisted almost entirely on street-corner pizza and booze. Other tenants were Bobby Bolles, a gifted sculptor and a drunk, and the Lynch brothers, who lived directly above my father and would occasionally—while soused, of course— roll out of bed while still sleeping and land hard enough to shake the ceiling in my dad's bedroom.

Down the block were Danny and Eugene Evans, a pair of excitable Ukrainian brothers whose family name apparently got butchered somewhere between Odessa and East Seventh Street. Eugene would come into McSorley's and threaten to strangle hippies. Danny worked as a bartender until he grew too heavy to maneuver comfortably behind the taps without knocking down mugs and picture frames and various other

McSorley artifacts. He got shipped back to the kitchen, a demotion he didn't appreciate and which he occasionally protested by taking his butcher knife and stabbing the pile of cardboard boxes filled with packs of saltines for McSorley's cheese plates. "GAAAHHHH! TAKE THAT, JIMMY!" Danny would scream. Back then, the kitchen was really just a small cubby in the northwest corner of McSorley's — opposite from where it's been since a 1986 renovation installed a full kitchen and a women's restroom. Danny's work space was little more than the wall stacked with saltine boxes and a counter for assembling cheddar plates and liverwurst sandwiches. And it was open to the back room, so whenever Danny blew his top, half of the bar would witness his cracker slashings.

My dad loved this shit. He loved Evans's live-wire aggression. He loved soaking up John Smith's bar wisdom when he'd go downstairs to pick up his mail, which was delivered to the bar. He loved the adrenaline rush of weekend brawls back then, donnybrooks that would flare up and die down in an instant, with no one suffering damage much worse than a busted lip or a black eye. He loved that McSorley's had a regular customer nicknamed Schlopps because at last call he'd scramble from table to table, gulping down the schlopps — abandoned ale in half-empty mugs — while waiters shouted for him to cut it out. He loved when Frank the Slob, decades before I knew him as the hunched Saturday-morning onion peeler, would reach a certain tipping point of drunkenness and rise from his seat to sing a kind of McSorley's bebop:

I want a wild, wild woman, I don't care if she stink. Give me a wild, wild woman, tell her to buy me a drink.

My father loved the nightly characters, the Ukrainian

World War II veterans who had settled in the East Village and would occasionally experience combat flashbacks at the bar. One minute they'd be sipping a dark ale, the next they'd be standing at attention, saluting an officer nobody else could see, and barking out orders.

And I don't think my father would say that he loved the drinking, but he took to it as naturally as any alcoholic's son might. He had started boozing heavily and habitually when he first moved to New York, and he found ways to keep a bottle on him most of the time he lived in Paraguay. Now, staying above the bar, he was polishing off a quart bottle of vodka from nearby Astor Wines every two days and drinking at McSorley's several nights a week. As time went on and he found himself drinking earlier and earlier in the day, chasing the hair of the dog to get over his hangovers, just to feel right for forty-five minutes before getting drunk again, he recognized what was happening to him. My dad knew the signs of alcoholism — his old man had practically beaten them into him. And he knew he was headed down the same path. He just didn't care. The men around him, the waiters and pumpmen and gypsies and barflies, all drank as much as he did. A lot of them drank more.

My father accepted his drinking problem as if it were some bleak fate, his sole inheritance from Frank, the old man's last and most enduring act of abuse. And even though my dad did most of his drinking upstairs in his apartment, McSorley's became his spiritual home. He was a drunk living above one of the most famous watering holes in the United States, a place visited by illustrious tipplers like Dylan Thomas and E. E. Cummings and frequented by workaday guzzlers with sobriquets like Schlopps and Frank the Slob.

*   *   *

My father started working at McSorley's before he earned his first official shift during business hours. For the first 126 years of the bar's existence, McSorley's was closed on Sundays. In the early 1970s, my dad joined a crew of locals, many of whom lived upstairs, who would spend Sunday afternoons doing odd jobs around the bar. The gang was led by Bobby Bolles, the sculptor who doubled as an expert carpenter. It also included a Puerto Rican body builder in his late thirties named Bobby Baez, whom I would know four decades later as McSorley's hard-of-hearing, elderly night watchman. The Baez I knew had electric eyes, dark-rimmed glasses, and a bushy white mustache, and he almost never appeared without a mammoth Saint Bernard named Bowser and a pocketful of worn Polaroids from his weight-lifting days.

The Sunday bunch would nail the legs back onto busted chairs, reset doors that had been knocked off their hinges, and oil the bar at the beginning of a new week. They were paid $3 per hour and given permission to raid the kitchen for ham and liverwurst sandwiches. Perhaps most importantly, they could drink bottles of Ballantine India Pale Ale and Carling's Red Cap Ale from the icebox behind the bar.

Throughout the bar's history, living upstairs from McSorley's has been one of the surest routes to employment. A pub that busy needs bodies. Bodies that live nearby and can work on short notice are especially useful. When a bartender drops a keg on his foot and can't stand for two weeks, or when the regular waiter is too hungover to get out of bed, you want backup to be close. My father's first shift came in 1972, and it was arranged via a fateful misunderstanding.

Late one Monday night, my father ran into Zory in the tenement stairwell. The bar had just closed and Zory was getting off his waiter shift. He was headed out to begin his night of drinking, while my father was returning home from his. My dad was in full blackout mode by the time he saw Zory, but he managed to invite Zory to a party in his apartment the following Friday. "Lots of *loobnies*," my dad promised, using the Gypsy word Zory had taught him for young, single ladies.

And that was it. Zory strutted off into the night, and my father climbed up to his room and crashed. The next morning, when Danny Kirwan showed up at McSorley's, Zory came downstairs to tell the manager he couldn't work Friday. He didn't tell Kirwan he was skipping work for a party in Bart's apartment. He just said it was personal. No problem, Kirwan said.

But there was a problem: no party. My father was barely conscious when he bumped into Zory that Monday night. There's no telling why he invited Zory to a party that he imagined on the spot and had no plans to actually host. By the time he woke up the following day, my father had forgotten every detail of the encounter — Zory, the party, those *loobnies.* Half awake, he lurched downstairs to pick up his mail from the bar, and Kirwan was still there, chatting with John Smith in a front room bustling with the day's lunch crowd.

"Bart," Kirwan said. "Can you work Friday night? Zory's taking off so we need someone to cover the kitchen and floor." Back then, the custom was for one waiter to work the entire bar until business really picked up. If and when that happened, the guy making sandwiches and cheese plates in the kitchen would step out and handle the front room.

"Sure thing," my father said. "I got no plans." He had inadvertently screwed Zory over and, in the process, booked his first shift in a career that's still going forty-five years later. (Don't worry about Zory. For a transgression that minor, forgiveness could be purchased with a fifth of Johnnie Walker Red.)

My dad's first few years at McSorley's were consumed with alcohol and his literary ambitions. He had managed to keep a journal since college, and he'd always dreamed of writing fiction and poetry. In writers like Joseph Heller, Norman Mailer, and Malcolm Lowry, he found the vocabulary to describe the manic swings and the hopelessness and the romantic but crushing belief in his own doom that were part and parcel of his drinking. He loved Lowry more than the rest, especially *Under the Volcano*. In Lowry's protagonist, Consul Geoffrey Firmin, my father recognized his own alcoholism: the cyclical logic that always led to pouring another drink and the descriptions that felt as if they could only have been written by a fellow alkie. When Lowry strung words together like this—"inconceivable anguish of horripilating hangover thunderclapping about his skull, and accompanied by a protective screen of demons gnattering in his ears"—he validated my father's despair and enabled the drinker to believe his habit could be channeled into art that was twisted and beautiful and terrible and transcendent, all at the same time.

My father wrote short stories about his upbringing—the hunting trip with Frank, the daily horror of waiting for Frank to lose his temper at the dinner table—and his work showed enough promise to get him into the MFA in litera-

ture program at the City College of New York. The faculty at
the time included Heller and the feminist poet Adrienne
Rich, and my father took seminars with Anthony Burgess
and Kurt Vonnegut, Jr. The dream of becoming an author
gave his life some purpose aside from the cycle of getting
drunk, passing out, waking up hungover, struggling through
his bar shift, and then getting pissed again. He loved the
seminars, where he could ask Burgess about inventing the
lexicon for *A Clockwork Orange* and he could hang out at
Vonnegut's Turtle Bay apartment, sipping bourbon and dis-
cussing culture and politics while going over Vonnegut's
notes on my father's latest chapter.

At night, after working at McSorley's, my dad would
head upstairs, sit at his typewriter, and crank out pages of
experimental novels fueled by boozy delusions of grandeur.
He'd stay there, smoking cigarettes and sipping Tab mixed
with brandy, and he wouldn't stop pecking at the keys till
dawn. His first manuscript was called *The Philadelphia Chromosome.* It began as a nine-hundred-page epic that attempted
to use the Argonautica myth to frame a story about a man's
quest to learn about his deceased father's career as a World
War II–era spy. My dad wanted to use Jason and the Argo-
nauts the same way James Joyce used the Odysseus myth to
frame *Ulysses.* He submitted a version of the novel as his
master's thesis, and Vonnegut encouraged him to keep
revising the work and submitting it to agents and publishers.

The Philadelphia Chromosome didn't sell, so my father put
it aside and began working on his next manuscript—a
gonzo formal experiment. He had been impressed by Lawrence Ferlinghetti's 1960 stream-of-consciousness novel *Her,*
so he decided to try something similar. The first half of the
book attempted to express the thoughts of a woman trapped

inside her head and unable to express herself after a stroke (much like what had happened to his mother, who lived the final years of her life bedridden, in a nursing home), and the second half tried to capture the same mental portrait of the woman's daughter, who suffered a stroke of her own thirty years later. But even that was apparently not enough of a literary mountain for my father to scale. In addition to depicting the inner workings of two stroke-damaged minds, my dad wrote the entire novel without punctuation. His third attempt was not as formally daring, but it certainly was imaginative — a futuristic nightmare in which New York is overrun by giant, man-eating rats. He says the manuscripts are all still in our apartment, buried in the bottom drawer of a filing cabinet in my parents' bedroom, but unlike his journals and his poetry, he's never been eager to let me peruse his novels.

He sent the books to various New York publishing houses but never heard much back from them. He suspected that it was because his fiction was too unwieldy, although he never managed to revise the manuscripts into something more coherent, perhaps due to his drinking. And because his writing was going nowhere, he wrote less and drank more. My dad's descent into severe alcoholism and depression felt like the fate of a Malcolm Lowry character.

My father hit his bottom sometime in late 1975. He had reached a point where he needed to start drinking by 10 a.m. just to get his hangovers under control enough to make it through bartending shifts. The half quart of vodka he'd been drinking each day for most of the previous five years was now a full quart. He felt like he'd been hungover, with

Lowry's demons nattering in his ears, for ten full years. Pretty much the only days he remained sober were when the flu or some other ailment rendered him too physically ill to take a drink. Even then, he often still wound up splashing brandy into his tea. There was nothing left for him but alcohol and emptiness, and yet he still wasn't ready to quit. He went on like that for another six months.

On May 8, 1976, he started drinking early—before noon. He could already feel it: *This is gonna be a shit day.* By evening, he'd finished one of those quart bottles of vodka. It wasn't too late, so he walked down to Astor Wines and bought another quart. By 5 a.m. the next day, he'd finished that, too. My father was thirty years old at the time. He got to thinking about how he had been drunk or hungover just about every day of his adult life. A third of his thirty years gone, with nothing to show for it. He had his alcohol habit and he had McSorley's.

My father opened his apartment window and climbed onto the fire escape. He'd been drinking so long that he couldn't imagine staying sober. The only way out, he told himself, was to take a header off that fire escape, and now he felt ready to do it. As he gripped the steel rail and leaned forward into the morning air, thirty-some feet above the sidewalk, he had one clear thought that saved his life (and it was delivered with classic McSorley's sarcasm): "You probably wouldn't want to do this if you hadn't polished off a half gallon of vodka in the last 24 hours."

He crawled back through the window, waited a few hours, and then went upstairs and knocked on Danny Lynch's door. Lynch's drinking put my father's to shame— he could polish off the half quart it usually took my dad a whole day to finish in one seven-hour waiter shift. My dad knew that Lynch had been in and out of alcohol treatment programs in recent years, and when Lynch answered his door, my dad asked if he had time to take him to a twelve-step meeting.

Lynch looked my father up and down. There was a hint of skepticism in the way he appraised the desperate soul on his doorstep. "You?" he asked, incredulous that my dad was ready to quit. In Lynch's eyes, my father's alcoholism had only reached the beginning stages of "full-blown." Lynch shook his head, chuckled, and in his heavy County Cork-man's brogue, said, "Whatever you say, Bart. Drinking's like an elevator. You choose when to get off, and you don't gotta ride it all the way down."

Lynch took my dad to meetings for that first week. After that, my old man kept it up. He went every day, for months, then years. Long enough to scale back to one meeting per week and not fall off the wagon. Getting sober when you live above a bar and your job is to go downstairs and sell alcohol five days a week sounds nearly impossible, but other than the time when the guys at the bar spiked my dad's ginger ale with Scotch (he spat a plume across the front room), it wasn't that bad. The career bartenders my father knew tended to be either lifelong drinkers, some of whom never developed problems and others who burned out and died young, or recovered drinkers who looked after each other. My dad joined the latter tribe. He met my mother at a meeting, and a few years later they were married and I was born.

When my dad talks about getting sober, he tends to tell the horror stories of his childhood and his own addiction in exhaustive detail, and then he glosses over what it was like to quit—all the times he must have been tempted to grab a drink, the fear and betrayal that must have shot through him when he tasted the Scotch in that ginger ale, and the willpower it must have taken to cough it up on the spot. I don't think he's hiding anything, though. That's just his truth.

I've asked him a handful of times if the job — selling the brew that poisoned the first thirty years of his life — ever felt wrong to him. Was it hard to serve customers he could spot as alcoholics? What about people he recognized from meetings? He'd done it, he said, but it didn't bother him much. He saw alcoholism in a fatalistic way — only the drinker knows when he's ready to quit for good, and nobody is going to prevent him from chasing a bottle if he hasn't reached that point.

My father took Lynch's words to heart that final morning of his drinking life. He stepped off the elevator and never looked back. His first year of sobriety, he said, was just about filling time with two or three meetings per day. *Don't even give yourself a chance to drink.* Then, once he broke the habit, he could figure out how to build a new life. He found meaning in the traditions and characters of McSorley's, jotting down lines of verse that over the years became like the oral history of the bar's last half century. Between the inspiration he drew from the pub's legacy, the camaraderie he enjoyed with coworkers, and the family he started with my mother and me, my dad finally managed to overcome Frank's doomed, drunken inheritance.

CHAPTER 3

We Were Here Before You
Were Born

WHEN I USED TO HANG around McSorley's as a kid, the waiters usually asked me to swab the tables with a damp bar
mop before we opened, but one morning, when I was about
seven years old, my father gave me more specific instruc-
tions.

"Make sure you get Joe's table," he said, pointing to the
second one in from the window. I tossed the rag on the round
tabletop, maybe four feet in diameter. I spread the mop
across the smooth, dark wood and pressed down to squeeze
the hot water and bleach out of the cloth and work it into the
table's seams. As I wiped from side to side, the table's brown
deepened from creamy chocolate to a shade as black as
coffee.

Joe's table occupied an ideal middle ground between

the small tables closer to the back room and the extra-large round table next to it. The window tables were more intimate but didn't provide the same vantage points to observe McSorley's ecosystem—the interactions between regulars and tourists, waiters and cheapskates, old-timers and barely legal college drinkers. Its seats were close enough to the potbelly stove to catch its warmth but not so close that a hot fire would roast customers. And during the afternoon, that table seemed to enjoy the longest golden hour, as the sun passed overhead and poured light through the window. The table would stay bathed in sunlight, its ketchup bottle casting a long shadow. In a timeless place, this felt like the most timeless spot.

When I finished scrubbing the table, I tossed the mop across the bar and my father snatched it out of the air with one hand, barely pausing to look up from the spiral notebook where the previous night's crew had marked down the number of kegs they'd sold.

"Hey, Dad, who's Joe?"

He flipped the notebook shut and locked eyes with me. "Joe," he said, "is Joseph Mitchell."

He told me Joe was a famous writer, and he pointed to a frame on the wall, above the McSorley Nine photo, that contained the dust jacket of a Canadian edition of Mitchell's *McSorley's Wonderful Saloon,* the writer's collection of *New Yorker* stories that begins with "The Old House at Home," Mitchell's seminal 1940 portrait of the bar.

Mitchell was one of many writers and artists, my dad explained, who had come to McSorley's and poured their creative energies into the historic watering hole. The poets Paul Blackburn and Reuel Denney and E. E. Cummings drank there. John Sloan, the Ashcan School master, painted five canvases with McSorley scenes of raucous crowds and rambunctious bar cats. Eugene O'Neill, the great Irish-American playwright, was known to meet the staff of the *American Spectator* for drinks in the front room in the years leading up to Prohibition. The folk singers Eric Andersen and Dave Van Ronk and Woody Guthrie had been customers. "They were all important," he told me. "Some were brilliant." The biggest difference with Mitchell, my dad said, was that his writing celebrated real people, working people. "Plus," he went on, "Joe never stopped coming by. And that's his table."

Mitchell was in his late seventies by then, but he'd still show up at McSorley's from time to time. It would always be in the middle of the day, and he'd only stay if he could have his table and if there weren't any other customers there. He'd nurse a pair of ales, share a few stories about the McSorley's he knew in the '30s, '40s, and '50s, and then settle his bill and walk down Seventh Street to Third Avenue, presumably on his way uptown to the *New Yorker* offices. My father always said he thought Mitchell liked to come to McSorley's because it was one of the only places that still felt like the New York Mitchell wrote about in the fifties and sixties — especially when it was just Joe at his table with two mugs of ale, a waiter serving cheese plates, and a barman at the taps, the same way it had been thirty or fifty or probably even eighty years before then.

I didn't hear much more about Mitchell until I was a bit older, when he died at age eighty-seven, a month after I turned fourteen. By then I was old enough to read his books, and my father used the passing of McSorley's best loved literary champion as an excuse to begin my formal instruction in bar lore. Until then, I'd mostly just picked up stories about the pub's artifacts and characters by listening to my dad and the rest of the staff. I knew the bar's age because it was posted, in giant block numerals, behind the bar. I knew it was a big deal because of the proclamation on the front windows—WE WERE HERE BEFORE YOU WERE BORN—stenciled in gold paint for all of Seventh Street to see. But now, in addition to learning by observation, it was time to study the bar's full history. My dad gave me his worn copy of *McSorley's Wonderful Saloon* and had me start by reading the first article. Its title, "The Old House at Home," referred to John McSorley's original name for the bar.

It didn't take long for me to grasp what made Mitchell's article so special, or how it made McSorley's feel even more significant and magical. In the first paragraph Mitchell writes:

> *There is no cash register. Coins are dropped in soup bowls—one for nickels, one for dimes, one for quarters, and one for halves—and bills are kept in a rosewood cashbox. It is a drowsy place; the bartenders never make a needless move, the customers nurse their mugs of ale, and the three clocks on the walls have not been in agreement for many years.*

I looked up from the page and asked my dad: "How old is this?" It was written in 1940, he told me, five years before he was born, and in that instant I understood McSorley's in a way I never had before. The place Mitchell was describing seemed no different from the bar I had grown up in. I had seen my dad grab handfuls of coins from those soup cups—the only difference was that now, on the rare occasions when customers paid with half dollars or Susan B. Anthony one-dollar coins, he wouldn't drop them into a separate ceramic cup, but instead change them out and bring them home for me. I had watched him count stacks of one-, five-, and ten-dollar bills into the very same rosewood cashbox Mitchell mentioned. And I recognized the still, languorous air of a quiet afternoon inside McSorley's in Mitchell's depiction of the deliberate barmen and the regulars patiently sucking down their ales. Of course McSorley's had always felt old to me—it *was* old. But when I read Mitchell, I recognized that the place was not merely old, but historic.

On page after page, I recognized the McSorley scenes I'd witnessed, along with the frames on the wall I'd smudged and the food I'd tasted. And in the fifty-plus years since Mitchell wrote the article, hardly anything seemed to have changed. The bar served a lunch of "soda crackers, raw onions, and cheese"—the same spread I'd munched on since childhood. Old John had hung a shillelagh and a sign proclaiming his original motto, BE GOOD OR BE GONE, above the entrance to the back room, and although the sign had been moved to a different spot on the wall, it still hung inside McSorley's.

Mitchell depicted the cantankerous ways of Old John's son, William "Bill" McSorley, who began running the bar when his father retired around 1890. "If a man became impatient and demanded a drink," Mitchell wrote, "Bill would look up angrily and shout obscene remarks at him in a high, nasal voice. Such treatment did not annoy customers but made them snicker; they thought he was funny." It felt like reading a description of my father reaming out a group of college kids who got out of line, and imagining the way their expressions would shift from fright to delight as they realized they could brag that they'd pissed off a McSorley's bartender.

My favorite passage described the scent that invaded my nostrils every time I stepped inside the bar and every time my father came home from work.

> *It is possible to relax in McSorley's. For one thing, it is dark and gloomy, and repose comes easy in a gloomy place. . . . Also, there is a thick, musty smell that acts as a balm to jerky nerves; it is really a rich compound of the smells of pine sawdust, tap drippings, pipe tobacco, coal smoke, and onions.*

When I read this in 1996 — before New York's restaurant smoking ban — the pipe tobacco was more likely to be cigarette or cigar smoke, and the sawdust would no longer have been made from pine, but I recognized the sweet, fermented odor that seemed to permeate every artifact inside McSorley's. It was a near-permanent ingredient in my father's musk. It was the kind of smell that made you want to sit down, order two light, two dark, and a cheddar plate, and just ripen along with the rest of the place. Or, if you were a fourteen-year-old bar rat like me, it made you want a ginger ale and a burger and an extra lifetime to sit in those shadows and become as much a fixture there as the potbelly stove.

Mitchell's "The Old House at Home" also provided me with a proper education in McSorley's first nine decades. Even though I'd heard stories about the different eras in the bar's history, they had always come as passing references to Old John's mottoes or to how the bar survived Prohibition or to Dorothy Kirwan's adherence to the ban on female customers despite being a woman herself. Mitchell took the bar legends and turned them into a timeline I could follow, from 1854 to 1940, and after that my dad would fill me in on the rest.

John McSorley came to New York from County Tyrone, Ireland, and opened the Old House at Home in 1854. He owned the structure at 15 East Seventh Street that housed the bar, and he ran McSorley's by himself, waking up each morning to throw sawdust on the hardwood floors and closing in the evenings after his crowd of drinkers had dissipated. Old John laid down the central tenets of how the bar would be run, many of which remain in effect. These days, when visitors ask my father why the floor is coated with sawdust or why the bar only serves light and dark ale, he tells them it's because the place has always been that way. In other words: Old John made it so. As Mitchell wrote: "Old John maintained that the man never lived who needed a stronger drink than a mug of ale warmed on the hob of a stove." So it was, and so it's been ever since.

John McSorley's guidelines have survived largely intact since the mid-nineteenth century. His cardinal rule, Be Good or Be Gone, is now on display in the bar's front and back rooms. When Old John opened the bar, the front made up the entire establishment. Around the turn of the twentieth century, Bill McSorley converted the private back area into public space for customers, and at some point in the ensuing years Old John's slogan was posted there, too. The sign in the back hangs inches away from an oil painting that barmen have called "the nude" for as long as anyone can remember. It's a copy of Gustave Courbet's *La Femme au*

Perroquet, which depicts an undressed, golden-skinned woman reclining on a bedsheet with a green parrot craning its neck to appraise her.

It's unclear whether the nude's placement—right beside the bar's mantra of decorum—was executed in the spirit of gentle mockery, but the edict was no joke to Old John. The motto also helps explain why McSorley's has never served wine or spirits. Old John believed that ale was a strong enough elixir, and that anything more potent would cause trouble; therefore, it had no place in his saloon. Bill McSorley, after he took over the bar, maintained his father's code of honor, and a generation after him, the barman John Smith once famously heard enough of one of Dylan Thomas's soused rants and gave him the boot. In the seventies, breaking up bar-clearing fights and rolling a group of drunks out the front door was almost a weekly ritual for my father, Zory, and the rest of the weekend crew. And nowadays all a group of customers needs to do is start slamming empty mugs on a table to get shouted down by my dad: *Try it on your head! Ship 'em! Get the fuck out! They're done!*

McSorley's other founding edict was born in part, as Mitchell noted, of Old John's affinity for onions, which he was known to eat like apples. This list of virtues contained the ingredients that Old John considered essential for a bar: Good Ale, Raw Onions, No Ladies. The formula remains two-thirds unchanged more than 160 years after McSorley's opened. Light and dark ale are still the only alcohol McSorley's serves, and the cheddar cheese plates come with a sleeve of saltine crackers and pungent slices of raw onion. Even "no ladies"—discriminatory and sexist as it is—lasted for well over a century, until, thanks to the work of feminist civil rights lawyer Faith Seidenberg, a federal court ruling compelled McSorley's to open its doors to women on August 10, 1970.

Every time the bar has changed ownership, it has been passed along with an understanding that the new owner would do everything in his or her power to maintain the bar's artifacts, traditions, and operating procedures. Mitchell wrote that Bill McSorley took the mission of preservation so seriously that in 1890, after he'd taken over his father's management duties, "it appeared to pain him physically" when some piece of McSorley's needed repairs. As bar legend has it, there was only one brief period of a few months around 1905 when Bill considered making a major change to McSorley's and started selling spirits. Old John, approaching eighty and still living upstairs, got wind of the development and nipped it in the bud. No alcohol but McSorley's ale has been sold there since. John died in 1910—he was eighty-three years old—but Bill made sure his father's visage would stay enshrined at McSorley's throughout the ages. He hung a photo of John standing outside the bar in 1903, his wide smile visible behind the white tusks of his beard. Old John's grin and lush facial hair are also on display in a small painted portrait that still hangs at the top of the wall near the center of the bar.

Bill sold McSorley's and the building that housed it in 1936, to a former policeman named Danny O'Connell, who, Mitchell wrote, had been a regular customer since the early 1900s and who retired from the force two days before buying the bar. When Danny died just three years later, he passed it on to his daughter, Dorothy O'Connell Kirwan, and she took her father's promise to preserve the bar's ways so seriously that she refused to set foot inside McSorley's during business hours. The woman who owned the famed watering hole when it turned 100 years old couldn't be served there, and that's how she wanted it.

Even in 1970, after the bar was ordered to open its doors to women, Dorothy—who still owned McSorley's but had passed the day-to-day operating duties to her son, Danny—declined to have a drink. Danny had planned to make his mother the first woman the bar officially served, but she wouldn't break the vow she'd made to her father in 1939. Instead, Danny invited Barbara Shaum, a longtime friend of McSorley's who owned a leather shop two doors down from the bar, to become the bar's first female customer. For Dorothy and the owners who came before and after her, making sure that McSorley's remained the same was about more than sentimental value and honoring tradition. It was about branding: As the bar passed the 50-, 100-, and eventually 150-year marks, McSorley's timelessness became the bar's identity, and making changes to the place could be disastrous for business.

McSorley's past sparked my interest in the history of Manhattan's East Village and Lower East Side. In Mitchell's pages, bar figures like Old John and Bill McSorley came to life. They weren't just faces on the wall, decorative miens that looked down on me and my dad and the rest of the barmen. Instead, those characters felt like family, ancestors who leaned on the same bar and shoveled coal into the same stove a hundred years before our time. Reading *McSorley's Wonderful Saloon,* I felt viscerally connected to the city's past.

Wall photographs that had never meant much to me began to take on greater significance. I was learning how the facts of McSorley's history fit together to create this landmark bar. The group photos of natty, dark-suited New York gentlemen of the 1920s gathered at McSorley's for beefsteak dinners became more than just stiff black-and-white portraits. Mitchell covered beefsteaks, which McSorley's hosted periodically before Prohibition. They were banquets— exaggerated rituals of manliness—thrown by professional associations and political parties. "The life of the party at a beefsteak," Mitchell wrote, "used to be the man who let out the most ecstatic grunts, drank the most beer, ate the most steak, and got the most grease on his ears." Attendees were encouraged to eat and drink "all you can hold" of McSorley's ale and fresh beef, and utensils were strictly prohibited. When Mitchell described the aftermath of these events—"a lot of people with goggle eyes and their mouths gapped open"—I recognized the scene as one I'd seen for myself. That look of glazed, contented, almost infantile satisfaction that appears on customers' faces when they become incapacitated with ale and burger grease has always been a part of McSorley's.

The more I read Mitchell's New York stories, the more I saw how the bar was a product of its late-nineteenth-and-early-twentieth-century environs. Old John opened his bar when downtown Manhattan, particularly the Bowery, was filled with vice, violence, booze, and the kind of chaotic humanity we associate today with developing-world shanty-towns.

McSorley's sits at the northern tip of the Bowery, where the once-notorious boulevard meets Cooper Square and transforms into Third Avenue. It's a fifteen-minute walk from the former site of the infamous Five Points slums. In "A Sporting Man," Mitchell surveyed the Bowery of 1894 and found it home to eighty-nine bars over a mile-long stretch. Along with the penny theaters, dime museums, dance halls, and card rooms that the area was known for in those days, Mitchell reports that brothels called free and easies could be found in almost every house on some Bowery side streets.

In *Low Life,* Luc Sante's landmark study of the old New York underworld, the author unearthed lurid details of life and nightlife on the Bowery during the first half century of McSorley's history. Downtown was home to bars with names like McGurk's Suicide Hall, Bismarck Hall, Gombassy's Crystal Palace, Gunther's Pavilion, Hell Gate, Chain and Locker, Milligan's Hell, and the Tombs. Many of them housed basement opium dens and rat pits, where patrons would gamble on death matches between dogs and gangs of rats. Scam artists and con men and pickpockets and prostitutes proliferated among a largely transient and often drunk population of men who lived in the Bowery's single-room occupancy hotels, Catholic missions, flophouses, and soup kitchens.

Sante's picture of the lawless Bowery milieu helps explain why women were not allowed at McSorley's. Nearly every establishment described in *Low Life* that served both sexes operated either as an out-and-out brothel or as a surreptitious rendezvous point for sex workers looking to find johns. Serving only men, as McSorley's did, was the mark of a clean establishment in late-nineteenth-century New York. Old John didn't believe that men and women and alcohol should mix in public places because in his world, just about any place that included those three elements was a cathouse. Of course, as McSorley's outlasted the other bars of its vintage and the taboo on men and women drinking together in public disappeared (a process ferried along by speakeasies and Prohibition-era nightlife), Old John's ban on the fairer sex became outdated. By the time the 1960s rolled around, a rule meant to banish crime from McSorley's turned into an affront to women's civil liberties. When women were finally allowed into McSorley's, it was long overdue.

Mitchell wrote that during Prohibition, Bill McSorley operated the bar as if nothing had changed: "He ran wide open. He did not have a peephole door, nor did he pay protection, but McSorley's was never raided." Mitchell floated the theory that McSorley's status as a favorite haunt of Tammany Hall officials and local cops exempted the bar from enforcement of the Volstead Act and from local crime syndicates that kept booze flowing throughout New York City during Prohibition.

Another version, passed on from bartender to bartender and to me from my father, says that McSorley's remained open for business during Prohibition, but that for at least part of that era Bill kept the front of the bar shuttered and led customers in through the ground-floor hallway at 15 East Seventh. Drinkers would enter the bar through an emergency exit in the back room and resume their normal saloon routines. Whichever story is true, it seems almost certain that McSorley's stayed in operation, with ale on tap, during the 1920s and '30s. New York State remained wet until repeal day on December 5, 1933—from Governor Al Smith on down to the everyday boozehounds at McSorley's.

When I read *Low Life* as a teenager, the passage that caught my fancy was Sante's depiction of typical Bowery saloons in the mid- to late 1800s:

A sawdust covered floor, a potbellied stove, a wall covered with mirrors, nudes, framed newspaper clippings, chromos of boxers and horses. In some places a stein of beer was drawn and dumped in front of you the minute you sat down. Beer was the blood.

It was as if he were writing about McSorley's, and every aspect of his description still exists in the bar today, down to the practice of serving customers two ales at a time, even when they insist on ordering a single mug.

The story of how Matthew Maher came to live in New York City, then work at and eventually own McSorley's, is itself the stuff of legend. Dorothy Kirwan was married to an Irishman she'd met in New York, Harry Kirwan. Harry came from a town called Ballyragget in County Kilkenny, and during one of his trips back home in 1964, his car broke down on a country road. The first person to pass happened to be another Kilkenny man, Matthew Maher, and he gave Harry a lift back to town. At the end of the ride, Harry told Maher that if he ever made it to New York, he'd get him a job at his wife's pub.

In a matter of months, there was Maher on East Seventh Street, fresh off the boat and hungry for work. He was looking to recoup on the debt of gratitude owed him by the Kirwans, and Dorothy and Harry lived up to their word and hired Maher as a bartender. By the time my father began working at McSorley's in 1972, Matty (the name my dad and other employees have called him by for as long as I can remember) was running the bar on weekend nights. He was a five-foot-eight spark plug with the Irish gift of gab, a belly laugh that could fill the front room, and an explosive temper when he needed it.

By 1977, a couple of years after Danny Kirwan inherited the bar from his parents, he was ready to sell the business, and Matty had saved enough to cut a deal with Danny for a down payment plus a cut of McSorley's future earnings. When Kirwan turned over the property to Matty, he passed along ownership of the entire building, which has happened every time McSorley's has changed hands. As much as any solemn oath between owners of the bar, this has been the key to making sure that McSorley's remains intact, open, and largely unchanged in its original location. McSorley's has never had to renegotiate a lease with the building's owner. It has never been threatened by skyrocketing rents and Manhattan's unforgiving real estate market. While New York has transformed over and over again, McSorley's has stayed put and stayed the same.

Matty still owns McSorley's. In fact, even though he once pumped ale alongside my father, I've only ever known him as the boss. That means in the bar's 163-year-history, only three families have owned the bar—the McSorleys, the O'Connell/Kirwans, and now the Mahers. All have been Irish, and all have agreed to make resisting change the saloon's *raison d'être*.

One of the only changes Matty has willingly instituted in his thirty-eight years as McSorley's owner came early on, in 1980. He noticed business was picking up and decided to try opening the bar on Sundays. He called my father and asked if he could handle the shift.

"Bart," he said, "what do you think of working Sunday? We'll open up for a few weeks to see if there's business."

My father agreed, Matty said "Good lad," and that trial

period has been ongoing ever since. My father has worked nearly every Sunday since then. Even now you can sidle up to the bar at McSorley's and Bart, in his early seventies, will be pulling light and dark ales and barking at his waiters to keep an eye on their tables.

When I was a teenager, Sundays became my favorite evenings to visit the bar and see my dad operate. I was old enough to explore the New York night and to witness McSorley's in its nocturnal element, yet still too young to drink or consider working there. McSorley's was rarely crowded on those nights — the mix of customers tended to be NYU kids in for cheap burgers, tourists looking for any place that wasn't empty, and a handful of lunatic regulars. That's when my father introduced me to Al, an elderly regular with spiraling wisps of white hair like cotton candy who shamelessly begged for hugs from every college-age woman who passed him at the bar.

I spoke to characters whom I recognized as frequent stars of the bar stories my father had been telling me for years. CIA Man — that's what we called him — came in every week, spinning paranoid tales about government conspiracies. He showed me the spot behind his ear where he believed the agency had implanted the tracking device, then asked me to feel it, all while my father watched from five feet away, making the jerk-off motion with his left hand while pumping ale with his right. I got to witness a famed Polish drunkard in action. He'd stand at the end of the bar, gangly in his baggy green army jacket, with gray hair dangling to his shoulders and a bulbous red nose. His order was four light ales at a time, and he'd suck the whole lot down every ten minutes, so that in the span of a couple of hours his posture would slump to the point that it looked like only his elbows, planted on the bar, were holding him upright. When his mugs were empty, the Pole would pound the bar for more, and my father would ignore him just to pace the guy's consumption. Then the Pole would summon some energy and shout, *"Kurwa! Kurwa!"* He was yelling the Polish word for whore, and my father would shoot him a quick glare to calm him down, then reward him with a pair of ales. "Four! *Kurwa!* Not two! Four!"

"*Kurwa* yourself, Jim."

There was no real heat or aggression in this exchange because both my father and his customer had been through this routine dozens of times over the years. The Pole was just a guy who liked to drink himself into a stupor and mutter *kurwa* to himself along the way. He was never done until he was passed out at the bar, still on his feet and with his head buried in his palms, everything propped up by those elbows. That's when my dad grabbed a curlicue-shaped brass horn from behind the bar and handed it to me.

"Time for the wake-up call," he said, and pointed to the Pole.

"Really?" I asked.

"Sure. It's the only way to get him out of here."

So I tiptoed down the length of the bar—who knows why I felt the need to be quiet, since customers were singing and guffawing at nearby tables and the clank of mugs was ringing throughout the room. When I reached the Pole, I held the horn behind his head, and my father shook his head. "Nope," he said. "Get up against his ear." And so I did. I took a deep breath and pushed all that air out through the horn, sending a metallic squawk through the bar, loud enough to silence everyone else.

"KURWA!"

The Pole's head shot up and he looked from side to side with wild, startled eyes, trying to figure out where he was. A few seconds passed and then it clicked. The panic vanished from his eyes, he smirked, and then he dropped a rumpled five-dollar tip on the bar before stumbling into the night. The assembled drinkers delighted in the show and gave me a round of applause.

"Give that kid a beer on me!" one customer yelled.

"Fuck off!" my dad shouted back. "That's my kid."

After I went home that night, I waited up for him to get back from work. I asked what I'd missed, what had happened after I left. "Not much," he said. "You saw all of tonight's action." Hearing that made me proud, but it was nothing compared to the next thing he said: "You know how to hold six mugs, right? Sometime when you're in on a Sunday, if it's not too busy, I'll show you how to get up to eight. That way you can fill in on the bar once you get old enough."

That was when I knew that someday I'd work at McSorley's and be part of what Old John started, what Joseph Mitchell chronicled, and what Matty and my father and all the current-day barmen kept alive.

CHAPTER 4

The Art of Storytelling

EVEN THOUGH I MADE IT over to McSorley's for a Sunday night every now and then, once I became a teenager, my weekly visits to watch my dad pump ale were over. On top of my fascination with bar life, I'd become an avid basketball player, with commitments to my high school team and a local recreation center's travel squad. Between hoops and homework, it was a challenge to find a free night to visit my dad at work. But I was still being schooled in the way of McSorley's, now primarily through my father's late-night storytelling. I trained myself to wake up in the predawn hours—usually around two in the morning—when my dad would arrive home from his Sunday-, Monday-, and Thursday-night shifts, and I'd sit across from him at the kitchen table as he unwound and got ready to sleep.

I would go to bed at a normal hour, sometime between

10 p.m. and midnight, but I developed the ability to pop out of bed the moment I heard my father's key hit the lock of our front door. The top lock opened with a high-pitched, metallic ping; then the bottom bolt followed with a thud. I had my ears primed and my circadian rhythms conditioned so that I would shoot upright as soon as he got home.

He'd rumble into the kitchen, his jeans soaked and reeking with ale and his boots tracking McSorley's sawdust behind him. A more considerate son might have taken mercy on his exhausted dad, who'd just spent seven hours on his feet and poured perhaps a cumulative ton of liquid over the course of his shift. But empathy isn't an ardent fan's strong suit, and I craved a taste of McSorley's. I wanted bar stories. I'd usually give him a few minutes to swallow a knot of ibuprofen, take a shower, and scrub off the night's grime. But once he was clean, before he'd even had a chance to pull on a pair of sweatpants, I'd be hounding him: "What happened? Any nutcases?" I wanted him to fill me in on the night's action—lovers' quarrels and fist-filled melees, tricks of the bartending trade, glimpses of the city's subcultures, McSorley legends, and the occasional bar scene that was so bizarre he'd have a hard time convincing anyone other than his adolescent son that it'd actually happened.

Nothing thrilled me like my dad's McSorley stories. That I could only hear them deep in the night, when the rest of the world was asleep, made them that much more enticing. The tales were packed with profanity and violence. They had slapstick humor, fart and piss jokes, and dark, twisted laughs. Waking up to listen to my dad meant being granted access to McSorley's in dreamlike half-hour bursts that were often more vivid than my actual dreams. But mixed with the raunchy laughs, my father also made sure to sprinkle in stories that reinforced the history of McSorley's— the most important legends, the ownership lineage, the bar's notable and ultimately wrongheaded role in the fight for women's rights. In those days, there were few greater disappointments for me than the nights when I slept through his arrival and woke up to daylight.

Before the nightly story, right after his shower and often before he'd made it out of the bathroom, I'd be waiting at the kitchen table for him to serve one last drink—a glass of chocolate milk. He always stirred Hershey's syrup into the same plastic New York Mets mug—a strategic choice, since stirring in a glass would produce a piercing clink that was more likely to rouse my mother. She wasn't crazy about our witching-hour ritual or the idea that her only son was ravenous for stories about bar fights and pukers. She never forbade me to get up to greet my father and she never told him to keep me in bed, but he and I both understood that it was better to keep our bull sessions from waking her. My father's rationalization for our behavior— *men tell stories*—came from decades at the bar, listening to customers recount bitter divorces, drunken romps, battlefield scenes from Korea to Vietnam to Iraq, and everything in between.

I loved to hear about the crazies. Early on, my father taught me the old saw, popular with bartenders, police, and anyone who works around late-night crowds, that nothing brings out lunatics like a full moon. Once, he told me about a customer who walked into McSorley's wearing a page of newsprint folded into a boat-shaped hat. The guy walked all the way up the bar to my dad, who was standing behind the taps. He ordered two light ales, paid, and drank them in silence. When nothing but suds remained, he looked up at my dad and asked for a book of matches. My dad passed one to the customer, who nodded in thanks and turned to walk out.

"So the guy starts walking out of the bar," my father told me. "And he lights one of the matches and sets the hat on fire. He lit his head on fire and walked out the door laughing." The image of a guy stepping through McSorley's swinging doors with a flaming newspaper boat hat on his head sent us into fits of breathless laughter. "But before that," my dad added, "you wouldn't have known there was anything wrong with the guy.... Well, I guess the hat sorta gave him away."

Between stories, my father would sip from a coffee mug full of milk and smear golf-ball-sized dollops of peanut butter onto a wedge of whole-wheat bread. He'd hold half a loaf in one hand like some giant turkey leg and tear off chunks with his front teeth. Even though he usually ate dinner from the McSorley's kitchen, he needed a few dense bites of Skippy-coated grain to fill his belly after a night of hustling behind the bar. The bread came from Zito's bakery, another lower-Manhattan landmark on Bleecker Street that was about half as old as McSorley's. Our family bought a loaf of Zito's whole wheat nearly every day. We ate it with meals, between meals, and, when I could get away with it, as its own meal. Whatever was left by the time my father came home from work, he'd polish off with his peanut butter.

After a few bites, my father would launch into another tale. He'd been showing me Three Stooges and Little Rascals videos for as long as I'd been able to sit still in front of a TV, and I adored slapstick humor. It primed me for bar life.

I probably heard a new vomit story every week, but they never got old. There were stories about customers who arrived at McSorley's already drunk but managed to fake their way past the doorman, then took two steps inside the bar and spewed on the floor before ordering a drink. There were stories about people who yacked in odd places — another patron's purse or the bathroom sink. Sometimes he'd bring home props, like a pair of latex gloves that a back-room waiter had supposedly snapped on to scoop chunks out of the sink. There was even one night when a McSorley's chef drank herself into a stupor and nodded out in a chair with Minnie, the bar cat, dozing in her lap. The waiters sat nearby, tippling bottles of McSorley's ale and swapping tales of Irish and New York childhoods, bad tippers, and vengeful exes. The chef had been asleep for about an hour before she stirred. Conversation stopped. Her stomach let forth a deep gurgle — some who heard it would later compare the sound to "the devil's tuba." One waiter joked that reverberations from the noise caused a ripple in his bottle. Minnie, still in the chef's lap, turned her neck and cocked a nervous, wide-eyed glance at the chef, just as the chef's jaw dropped and a deluge of beer and bile poured forth and coated the cat. They would have given Minnie a bath, but she spent the next two months hiding in the walls.

My dad saved a little something extra for his stories about projectile vomiters. In the realm of gross-out bar humor, these customers were like unicorns — less graceful, I suppose, but nearly as rare and capable of mythically icky acts. My father might see only one projectile yacker during the roughly 250 shifts he worked at McSorley's each year. When he came home after those shifts, he would be so primed to describe the night that even if I wasn't waiting for him at the kitchen table, he might creep into my room and shake my foot to wake me.

"We had a good one," he told me one night. "We could see him getting green, but there was no way to guess he would spew like that." The eruption happened in the back room, around a corner that prevented my dad from witnessing the initial carnage, but he said he guessed what was happening as soon as he saw people fleeing to the front. "Once someone starts to spew, people move fast." My father shared this wisdom with a kind of professorial gravitas worthy of an eleventh-grade physics teacher introducing Newton's laws of motion. "It was like an ack-ack gun," he continued. "He was shooting in spurts and his head seemed to swivel with each burst. People were diving under tables and using the bathroom door as a shield. By the time he finished, the whole back room had cleared out and people were lined up at the bar cursing at me, saying the bar had to cover their dry-cleaning expenses. I told 'em bring in the bills, we're good for it. Want to keep the customers happy so they can come back and get barfed on again."

These McSorley tales didn't offer much in the way of depth, but they didn't need to. Some nights, a simple laugh was all my father wanted to share and all I needed to hear. We both knew it wouldn't be long before another shift's mix of customers and circumstances would combine in other, perhaps more meaningful ways. Every night, my father introduced a new character or a new wrinkle, and I tried to catalog them all.

There was my dad's story about a slow shift when a severely intoxicated customer walked in and ordered two ales. My father said he couldn't serve him, and the man, evidently an off-duty policeman, laid his pistol on the bar and repeated himself: "Gimme two beers. I'm a cop." My dad poured two ales. "This one's on us, Officer." Always take care of the police, he taught me. Whether it's a soused off-duty detective who doesn't know when to stop or a couple of beat cops stopping in for a free sandwich and soda, stay on their good side. Besides, he'd say, the vast majority of the cops he met at McSorley's over the years were honest guys who deserved that extra display of respect.

Over the years, my dad told enough stories about Tommy Lloyd, his frequent partner on the bar, to fill a book. Lloyd was notorious for overserving customers. "Never find fault with a man until you have all his money" was a bit of Irish bar wisdom that Lloyd liked to quote, and it found a place in the canon of McSorley sayings. My father recalled a time when he caught Lloyd ordering a round for a customer who could barely keep his eyes open. My dad bitched at Lloyd to cut it out, only for Lloyd to chirp back in his singsong brogue: "Come now, Bart. God would not have made them sheep if he didn't want them sheared."

I was probably ten years old when my father shared the ultimate example of Lloyd's bartending philosophy. He had been serving a group of about eight guys, and they'd been drinking fast and steady—something like two hundred mugs of ale in less than three hours, split among the whole crew. When they stepped outside for a breath of fresh air, my father tapped Lloyd on the shoulder. "They're done, Tommy," he said. "Don't you think?" Lloyd wasn't ready to concede that these guys ought to be cut off, and right in the middle of arguing his case, Lloyd was interrupted by a loud crash out on the sidewalk. Lloyd rushed outside to see what had happened, while my dad stayed behind to watch the bar. On the sidewalk in front of McSorley's, the chef had opened the two-door metal hatch to the cellar. While he was down there grabbing a sack of fresh onions from the refrigerator, two of Lloyd's customers wound up tumbling down the six steps. By the time Lloyd got out there, they were scrambling back up the steps, brushing themselves off, and laughing. The lucky bastards were so drunk and loose that nobody was hurt in the fall. "You fuckers all right?" Lloyd said. "You ain't too drunk, are ya?"

The shook their heads, so Lloyd shrugged it off and led them back inside for one last round. Before he served them, he pointed to my father and said, "Not sure the boss will let me sell you lads any more ale after that fall." Thirty seconds later, Lloyd was walking toward the pumps, with a shit-eating grin on his face and a hundred-dollar bill balanced on top of his glasses. "Twenty light, Bart," he cackled. "And keep the change." (I'm sad to say I never got to work the bar with Tommy Lloyd, who died of cancer in 2007.)

I heard versions of all these stories when I was young, and even though I spent a lot of my childhood inside the bar, it seemed like the wildest, funniest stuff happened at night, after my bedtime. Lloyd and the upchucking chef felt more alive and exciting than the characters I watched in movies and read about in comic books. While Lloyd's ode to overserving was a way to squeeze every possible dollar out of the job, my father's midnight orations taught me a different set of words to live by: *Never find fault with a man until you've heard all his stories.*

One night, I cracked open the door to my bedroom and saw my dad bent over in his chair, his jeans heavy with ale from the knees down. He unlaced one of his boots, pried it off, and set his soaked foot down on the hardwood floor with a squish. "Motherfucker motherfucker motherfucker," he mumbled to himself in a quick, meditative patter. Profanity was the bartender's mantra, and this was how my father found his center after a heavy shift. You might think that at a moment like this, he wouldn't be in the mood to tell bedtime stories. Not true. I sensed an important lesson was coming when I saw how worked up he was. On nights like this he needed to vent; he needed to recount the night's mishaps to unwind, and I was happy to be his sponge.

"C'mon, Dad! Tell me."

"Nothing. Nothing.... Well, a couple gypsies tried to beat us for fifty dollars on the bar."

In McSorley's parlance, *gypsy* is a nonspecific term. Some are descended from the Roma people of Eastern Europe, whose families found their way to New York over the generations. Some are the Irish and English traveler families, and the native Irishmen who worked at McSorley's constantly teased each other about the amount of tinker blood in their family lines. *Gypsy* is a derogatory term, but its meaning inside the bar was neutral. It referred to a specific category of McSorley denizen. Doc Zory, the waiter who inadvertently gave my father his first shift, had gypsy roots, and he's one of the most beloved figures in recent bar history. Zory words, like *loobnies* for women and *scrog* for tips, were adopted wholesale into the McSorley's argot. The habit of calling everyone Jim, Jimmy, or Jimbo started with Zory and spread to everyone he worked with. Because of him, when I have children, I'll probably end up calling them Jimbo half the time, even if it has nothing to do with their names.

But sometimes, gypsy customers could be trouble. My

dad explained: "The ones we get are related to Eastern European gypsy clans—we think—but they're mostly born and raised here in New York or New Jersey. If you don't know how to spot them, they won't look different from any-one else on the street.

"Mustaches, leather jackets, worn jeans," he continued. "It's not much different from the construction workers and the cops you used to see on Saturdays. But there're a few signs that tell you they're gypsies.

"Gold jewelry—that's one thing. Necklaces that look like the crap they sell at Fourteenth Street pawn shops. But the biggest sign is the way they carry themselves. Loud and friendly. They take a table and clap you on the back, tell you to get a round of dark and a cheese plate. They'll pay for the first round up front and even give the waiter a good tip. Then they start asking for extras. 'Hey, pal! Why don't you bring us a little bit of liverwurst to eat with this cheese and onions? Not a liverwurst sandwich, just go back there and cut up a couple pieces of liverwurst. You can do that, right?'

"So the waiter wants them to keep tipping and he says sure. What's the big deal? We give away food sometimes: a cheese plate for a friend, burgers for on-duty police and firemen, a ham and cheese for Larry the bum. No big deal. So the waiter brings them the liverwurst. 'Perfect!' they say. 'This is great. We need another round here, and after that, we could really go for some pickles. You mind throwing five or ten pickles on a small plate for us? As many as you want. We don't want to be a pain in your ass.'

"That's their thing—they start asking for the free stuff: pickles, postcards, business cards, napkins, the plastic two-packs of saltines that come free with soup, instead of the full sleeve of crackers that you pay for with a cheese plate. Anything they know we don't have to charge them for, they'll ask for it. And they start drinking more. 'One more round, buddy! Don't worry, we'll take care of you. You're the best! I love this place—been coming here for years.'

"So the waiter is running his balls off back and forth to the kitchen, bringing the gypsies whatever they're asking for, and at the same time he's also trying to serve the rest of the front room. After the gypsy guys drink up four or five rounds, they wait for the server to return to the kitchen, and once he's out of sight—BOOM!—they bolt out the front door.

"I usually spot them on the way in and tell the waiter to keep an eye on them and make them pay as they go, but tonight was packed. I didn't notice when they sat down. Eventually, the waiter ran up to the taps—he was freaking out, looking all up and down the bar for these guys, flipping through his checkbook to see how much they owed—and he said, 'Did you see what happened to that group sitting by the stove?' By then, I knew they were gone.

"The crazy thing about these gypsies is that they aren't stealing because they need to. They make their money through fortune-telling shops, legit jobs in the trades like electrician and mechanic work, and maybe some cheap street-level scams on tourists. Hell, some probably carry a bigger wad of cash than a drug dealer. But it's like this pride thing. Or it's the culture. They can't go into a place without getting over on somebody. They're always testing the street smarts of everybody around them. If the waiter had kept his eye on them, they still would have drove him nuts asking for pickles, but they would have paid the bill. But in their world, if you're dumb enough to get taken, then you deserve it."

*   *   *

When my father would come home pissed off in the middle of the night, he tended to do housework. Extremely loud housework. The clean dishes sitting in the drying rack next to the kitchen sink? Those are getting loaded—nay, smashed—into the cabinet. The ice cube trays? What better time to crack those cubes into the bin? Sometimes he'd break out a hammer and crush ice by hand so he could funnel it through the narrow mouths of empty plastic water bottles, which I liked to refill with powdered iced tea and take to school.

On these nights, even if I somehow slept through the sound of his key in our door, the kitchen racket was a sure bet to get me out of bed. It was also a likely bet to have my mother stumble out of their bedroom with the plaintive groan, "Stop it, Geoffrey! Just stop!" For my dad, there seemed to be something cathartic about cacophony. It was as if the decades he'd spent amid clanking mugs, chanting oafs, and screeching guffaws of McSorley's had rewired his brain to be soothed by clamor and din.

On one of these nights, in 1996, I opened the door to my bedroom and sat down at the kitchen table. "What are you doing up?" my dad asked with an aggrieved snort—as if I had some other choice when he made it sound like a tornado was blowing through our kitchen.

It took four words from me to make him calm down and take a seat: "What happened at work?"

"Wander was in tonight," my dad said. Wander was Bill Wander, a historian who'd been studying McSorley's for years. "That bunghead McDermott from the Bridge Cafe got the *Times* to print an article saying we weren't open in

1854, and that we aren't the oldest bar in New York." McDermott was Richard McDermott (who died in 2015). At the time, he was a retired high school science teacher from Queens who had managed to publish letters in the *New York Times* describing his research, which asserted that the Bridge Cafe, a bar and restaurant on Water Street, near the base of the Brooklyn Bridge, was the city's oldest drinking establishment. It had only been open under that name since 1980, but McDermott argued that alcohol had always been served there, despite its having gone through numerous changes in ownership and identity.

Wander and McDermott had already traded barbs in the letters pages of the *Times,* but this latest article escalated the dispute. McDermott had convinced a reporter at the paper to publish a story detailing McDermott's research, which he believed could prove that the Bridge Cafe had opened in 1847, and—perhaps even more damaging to McSorley's reputation—that John McSorley hadn't opened the Old House at Home until 1862. McDermott's findings were based on city tax records, which didn't list John McSorley on the rolls till 1862. He also unearthed real estate records that said the lot on which McSorley's stands remained vacant until 1858. Now, here was my father, almost twenty-five years into his McSorley's career, with the bar eight years shy of its 150th anniversary, and suddenly the pub's hallowed February 17, 1854, birthday was being questioned in the paper of record.

"Wander checked it out," my father told me. "Said McDermott doesn't have the goods, but that the guy won't stop calling reporters and publishing newsletters to sell his point. Even if he's wrong, some people are gonna believe him."

Then my dad explained the case for McSorley's, based on Wander's research. "The records McDermott found that said we didn't exist till 1862 didn't go back much farther than 1860," he told me. "But Wander found other city files that showed a brick house was on that lot in 1855 and an 1857 map that shows the same brick building." These bolstered the argument that Old John opened his bar in 1854 and operated it out of the small brick structure until the building that stands today went up, sometime in the 1860s. Wander's other evidence was an 1851 shipping manifest for the *Colonist,* which listed a John McSorley as sailing from Ireland to New York. That date is backed up by Old John's naturalization date of 1856, since at the time immigrants had to wait five years before gaining US citizenship.

"Forget all the paperwork stuff," my dad continued, "we got it right there on the walls." He was referring to a framed black-and-white photograph in the front room showing a group of men seated around one of McSorley's tables and holding up mugs of ale. On the photograph, someone had written: "Feb. 17 1904—Our 50th Birthday." There were also framed newspaper clips from the early 1900s that recorded 1854 as the year in which McSorley's opened. "You think those papers were in on some hoax that nobody would have cared about back then?" my dad said. "You think those guys in 1904 were lying when they celebrated the bar's fiftieth anniversary? You think they were worried that they might need to prove McSorley's was the oldest bar almost a hundred years later? Those old humps were probably just worrying about putting food on the table like everybody else."

The Bridge Cafe, which was damaged severely in 2012

by Hurricane Sandy and has yet to reopen, was one of several historic New York bars that claim, in one way or another, to be the city's oldest. Fraunces Tavern, in the Financial District, dates back to 1762 and hosted a farewell banquet for George Washington at the end of the Revolutionary War in 1783. The Ear Inn, blocks away from where I grew up, has been open since 1817 but didn't begin serving alcohol until 1890. Neir's Tavern in Queens claims to have been up and running since 1829. The Old Town Bar and Grill just north of Union Square and Pete's Tavern over in Gramercy aren't quite as old as McSorley's, but they're arguably just as iconic.

What separates McSorley's from the pack is that it's been continuously operating in the same location since opening more than 160 years ago. Fraunces Tavern burned almost to the ground in the early 1900s, and the building that stands today was erected around what remained of the original structure. None of the bars that claim to be older than McSorley's can prove that they were open and serving alcohol during Prohibition, but McSorley's has Mitchell's account in the *New Yorker,* the E. E. Cummings poem "Snug and Warm Inside McSorley's," written in 1925, and the John Sloan painting *McSorley's Saturday Night,* dated between 1928 and 1930, which depicts the bar, open during Prohibition with nearly every customer on the canvas holding a mug of ale.

Depending on how you interpret the historical record, you can come up with an argument for any number of these bars as the oldest in New York. Our argument is that no other bar in the city has been open for business in the same spot for as long as McSorley's has, and the case to back it up is strong. (In a 2012 report, the city's Landmarks Preservation Commission affirmed Wander's research that McSorley's had opened in 1854.) My dad knew all this on that night back in 1996 when he came home so upset. He sat at the kitchen table and broke down McDermott's argument; then he ticked off all the contradictory evidence that Wander had compiled. It was enough to reassure me that McSorley's past was indeed what I'd been told it was. Yet having the stronger case didn't seem to lift my father's spirits like it did mine.

"I don't get it," I said. "If we're right, what's the problem?"

"It doesn't matter who's right," he told me. "Once it's in the paper, people will believe it. Even just because of the letters to the editor, tour guides are already bringing groups in and telling them that city records say the bar wasn't there till 1862—and of course those parasites never even stay for a drink. Just take pictures and walk out.

"What do you think we're selling in there?" he went on. "People can buy a mug of ale for cheap all over the city. They come to McSorley's because it still feels real. It's a bar that's been running the same way for almost a hundred and fifty years, with almost nothing changed. If these articles— even if they're total horseshit and we can prove it—convince people that McSorley's is phony, then the place won't ever be the same."

Maybe business would slow down if McSorley's reputation took a hit, but that's not what my father was talking about. He wasn't pulverizing ice cubes at two in the morning over a possible five percent drop in his average weekly tips; he was worried about his legacy. Ever since he'd gotten sober, he'd tethered his identity to his career at the bar. He was one of the men who ran McSorley's—the oldest in the city, the saloon whose virtues were extolled by Joe Mitchell in the freakin' *New Yorker*! That history mattered. It gave the men who worked there a thimbleful of immortality, the sense that the sweat and effort they poured into McSorley's made them part of something that would never be forgotten. Any threat to that was worth losing sleep over.

CHAPTER 5

Welcome to the Madhouse

By the time I hit my early twenties, the only thing missing from my McSorley's education was experience. But as much as my father loved the bar, he had mixed feelings about letting me work there. When I was younger, after draining, nonstop shifts, he would sometimes arrive home with scarcely enough energy to change out of his ale-drenched jeans, and when I'd ask to hear stories, he'd say, "Just promise you won't end up working there like your old man."

It meant the world to my father that he got to play a prime role in the multigenerational McSorley's story (now, at age seventy-one and with forty-five years on the job, he's on a short list of the longest-serving barmen, along with Old John himself, Bill McSorley, and John Smith). But part of him believed that bar life was plenty good for him yet not good enough for me. Like most dads, he wanted more for his son, and he was extremely proud that I was a strong student. When my parents found out I had tested into Hunter, one of New York's hypercompetitive specialized public high schools, they rushed to my elementary school in the middle of afternoon classes to share the news. My mother hugged me first, and in her embrace I sensed an enormous relief. I didn't understand this at the time, but my test score spared my parents from having to choose between paying exorbitant tuition fees to some private school (which probably would have made it impossible to support me through college) and sending me to a crowded district school with dismal graduation rates. After that hug, I turned to my dad, who beamed and squeezed the shit out of my shoulders.

"I knew it!" he said. "I knew it when you were in kindergarten. I tried telling your principal that you were really smart, and she didn't believe it. 'Oh, every parent thinks that,' she told me. And your vice-principal, she told us not to bother letting you try to get into Hunter." He seemed especially thrilled at having proved the experts wrong. For my dad, it meant that a poor working-class kid from Ohio—the abused son of a violent alcoholic—could come to New York, almost ruin his life with drink, and then turn it all around to find love, get married, and see his son rank with the city's "gifted" students. Lawyers' kids, doctors' kids, professors' kids, and me.

And according to that narrative of upward mobility, he expected me to reach a higher station in life, even if I admired his career at McSorley's more than the white-collar professions my grades could grant access to. I sometimes suspected that my dad saw me as proof that if Frank hadn't made his childhood such a nightmare, he could have achieved the professional and creative goals he thought he'd fallen short of. Of course, I don't see it that way. In his four-plus decades of sobriety, just about everyone who has gotten to know my father has been struck by his intellect and humor, his honesty and drive, and his kindness. That's pretty damn good, whether you're a bartender or you run a hedge fund.

Okay. Enough kissing the old man's ass. He had plenty of concrete reasons to steer me away from McSorley's that had nothing to do with the American Dream, the meaning of life, or whatever else we're talking about here. Like wanting his son to have a job with health insurance. Like wanting his son to have a retirement plan, and a workplace that wasn't ruled by the Darwinian logic of "you don't show up, you don't get paid." Like wanting his son to find work that wouldn't pulverize the cartilage in his knees, squeeze the disks in his spine, and break his body down to the point that it wouldn't be good for much more than getting to the bar and hustling through shifts. McSorley's is a wondrous place and it deserves to be romanticized. But it can be a punishing place to work for just one day, let alone forty-plus years.

By the time I reached my twenties, however, my father's resistance had eased. I'd found work as an entry-level editor at *Harper's Magazine,* and he saw nothing wrong with letting me fill in at McSorley's a couple of nights per week. I think he fancied the idea of me leaving *Harper's* on a Monday afternoon and hoofing it over to the bar—from the country's oldest general-interest magazine, established in 1850, to New York's oldest continuously operating bar, all in the same night. He also seemed to get a kick out of knowing that some weeks, the tips I earned from two shifts at McSorley's could eclipse my salary in a full-time publishing job.

So it happened that one Sunday morning, out of the blue, my father asked, "You want me to try and get you on the schedule this week?"

I was in.

My first several shifts at McSorley's were as the runner, a bartenders' sidekick who hustles up and down the length of the twenty-four-foot Venezuelan mahogany bar, serving customers, collecting money, and washing empty mugs for the manager, who mostly stays behind the taps. It was a childhood dream come true, yet at the same time it embarrassed me — nobody was supposed to work as a runner on the first shift. There's a pecking order, a ladder of McSorley's positions that just about everyone who works there has to climb. It starts with the busboys and doormen and chefs, then rises to the waiters and runners, and peaks with the head bartender. Here I was, starting behind the bar before I'd done anything to earn it, and I thought the rest of the McSorley's staff would look down on me for it.

I was overthinking it. McSorley's is a family business. Other than lifers like my father and Pepe, the day manager, pretty much every full-time waiter or bartender was a blood relative or de facto kinfolk to Matty, the owner. Daughters, sons-in-law, nephews from Ireland—we all owed our positions to some form of nepotism. That was damn near the only way to get hired in the first place. Besides, as soon as my first shift started and customers were shouting orders at me before I'd managed to roll up my sleeves, I realized that I'd have my hands full just learning how to keep up with the pace of service. There was no time to agonize over whether the other guys disapproved of how I got there, and the only way to prove I belonged was to work. Keep the ale going out, the cash coming in, and the empty mugs clean and racked for the head bartender to pour.

Every McSorley's shift begins with the outfit. White under-shirt, white button-down dress shirt, blue jeans, work boots. This unofficial uniform gets customized from there, depending on the job—waiters add a gray jacket from a shelf behind the bar; bartenders tuck a black garbage bag into their waistlines and tie an apron over it. But blue jeans, white shirt, and boots form the baseline of a look that's more than 160 years old. Earlier generations may have worn a vest over the shirt or incorporated a necktie, but the McSorley's aesthetic today isn't much different from what a Bowery barfly might have encountered in the 1920s, what Joseph Mitchell saw in 1940, or what the first women to drink in the bar found in 1970. And that continuity is taken seriously. If you show up without the shirt, go home—the rest of the staff can handle the shift without you.

Before my first shift, my father cut me a plastic. That's what McSorley's bartenders call the garbage bags we wear around our waists to keep our lower halves dry. (*Body con-dom* occasionally sneaks into usage when *plastic* doesn't feel fun enough.) You take an extra-large heavy-duty black gar-bage bag and cut it down the seams, so that you're left with two wide single-ply sheets of plastic. Most of the barmen are of average height, between five foot eight and five foot eleven, so when the night shift arrives to take over for the day bartenders, the guy on his way out will hand his apron and plastic directly to his counterpart on the night crew to be reused. But my dad and I are both six foot three, so the other bartenders' plastics don't quite cover our legs, and what's the point of wearing a body condom if you're going to finish work drenched from the shins down with water, dish soap, and ale suds?

The mechanics of the runner job are simple. You need to serve customers. You need to collect payment and keep track of tips. You need to wash empties and maintain the supply of clean mugs for the manager to keep pouring. When a keg blows, you have to run outside, scramble down to the walk-in fridge in the cellar, and hook up the tap line to a fresh keg. You try to keep the surface of the bar dry and clean, but the top priority is making sure the ale never stops flowing.

Taking orders at McSorley's seems like it should be the easiest part of the job. There are only two choices: light or dark. If a customer doesn't want alcohol, he or she can have a mug of tap water, a bottle of nonalcoholic beer, or a can of Coke, Diet Coke, ginger ale, or seltzer. The food menu is written on a chalkboard behind the bar. How could anyone—customer or server—fuck that up? Believe me, it happens. The bar's old-school simplicity can leave first-time patrons dumbfounded.

> *What do you mean there's no Jameson! Isn't this place Irish?*
> *Why are there two? I only asked for ONE dark beer.*
> *No credit cards? Where's your ATM? Around the corner in a pizza shop?*

More often than not, customers come around to being charmed by the menu's hard-line traditionalism—light or dark, served in pairs, the way it's been since 1854. As the runner, I had to learn how to size people up before they ordered. Were they newcomers? Did they look uptight? If so, I tried to explain the two-at-a-time policy up front, in case they would insist on single mugs. If they seemed down-to-earth, I could probably double them up without saying anything, and if they asked, I'd spit some blarney about the history of the bar and they would end up enjoying their drinks even more.

Tourists present a different set of problems. For whatever reason, "Light or dark ale?" rarely translates clearly to nonnative English speakers. This seems to be true no matter the customers' mother tongue—French, Spanish, Hebrew, Japanese. You ask if they want light or dark and there isn't a glimmer of recognition in their eyes. They look like you've asked if they want to drink with the lights on or off. So you start rattling off synonyms, hoping one of them will click: "Black beer? Blond? *Oscuro?* Amber? White? Clear?"

The runner relays the order to the head bartender by calling out the lights first, then the darks: four and four, eleven and one, four and sixteen, thirty and thirty. The manager pours the order and deposits the foaming mugs on a small chunk of bar to his left. If it's a large order, the runner better be there to move the just-poured ales out of the way of the mugs that are arriving only seconds behind them. If he doesn't, and the boss needs to stop pouring and make space in the middle of an order, then the runner is getting at least a dirty look, or, more likely, something like a sarcastic grunt that translates to "What's wrong with you, dickhead? Get over here and clear this area out!"

Once the runner collects payment, he walks back down the bar and deposits the money in John McSorley's original rosewood cashbox. The box is partitioned into three dollar-bill-sized compartments; singles go on the right, fives in the middle, and tens on the left. Twenties are stacked next to the cashbox and held in place by a brass paperweight. A fifty- or hundred-dollar bill gets slid underneath the pile of twenties, or the runner taps the manager on the shoulder and hands it to him directly. Tips get dropped into two ceramic mugs on a shelf beneath McSorley's original taps, which are now kept behind the bar.

Handling the mugs wasn't too much of a challenge for me. Guys at the bar had been showing me different techniques to grasp mugs since I was a toddler. Anyone can pick up two or four. Six isn't much more difficult—your pinkie, ring, and middle fingers slide into the handles of the first three mugs; then you cinch the remaining three with your thumb and forefinger. Eight takes some getting used to: It's pinkie and ring finger in the first three stems, middle finger in the fourth, and then pinching the remaining four with the thumb and forefinger.

When I started working as a runner, I tried to stick to handfuls of six. It was less efficient than eight and required a few extra trips down the bar, but the simpler grip reduced the risk of dropping mugs. That lasted about two shifts. Holding eight mugs in each hand just offered too many advantages to ignore. Most of the main McSorley pumpmen preferred to pour ales four at a time, and when I dropped eight freshly washed mugs onto the copper rack in front of the taps, I could drag the two outermost mugs on each side of the handful in front of the middle four to create two neat rows of ready-to-pour empties. Also, the ability to comfortably wield eight-mug handfuls was a vital distinguishing factor between the real McSorley's workers and the fill-in characters who helped out when the bar was shorthanded, and I yearned to belong with the genuine barmen.

There is no washing machine at McSorley's, only a trio of stainless steel sinks behind the bar. The machine, so to speak, is the runner, responsible for cleaning every dirty mug by hand. The sink farthest down the bar is for rags. Roughly every fifteen minutes, the runner drains it, refills it with hot water, squeezes in a shot of bleach from a plastic quart bottle, and shovels in a pile of ale-stained mops. The middle sink is the wash, kept fresh by a constant flow of near-scalding tap water and regular handfuls of powdered antibacterial dish soap. The third sink up the line is the rinse, a bath of clean, cold tap water replenished with a steady stream from the faucet. When waiters bring empties back from the tables, the runner scoops them off the bar, dunks the mugs into the wash, shakes them around in there, and then scrubs their insides with a round-headed brush. After the wash, the glasses get dunked in the rinse—in and out three to five times to remove any leftover soapy residue that might taint the ale once the mugs are refilled. Occasionally, a squeamish customer will watch the process and ask if the mugs are actually clean. The stock response: "We've been doing it this way for a hundred years and we haven't killed anybody yet."

When business is humming, there's never a problem finding space to rack the clean mugs. The manager at the pumps is often pouring ales nonstop, so as soon as the runner can get spotless empties on the rack, the boss is grabbing them and filling them. At these moments, the manager and runner work together to form what feels like a perfect circuit of effort: pour, serve, collect, return, wash, rinse, repeat. Slow nights introduce slack into this loop and force the runner to arrange and stack the mugs on a pair of stainless steel shelves underneath the bar.

None of these tasks (or the other small responsibilities that fall under the runner's purview) is difficult on its own. The challenge comes when a bachelor party's chartered bus pulls up outside McSorley's and thirty half-wasted louts tumble out, intent on going from partially to utterly slob-berknocked over the next three hours. And then some NYU seminar that just let out is right on the bachelor party's heels with two more tables' worth of thirsty college seniors. When the rush comes, the runner can't tend to his duties one at time. He has to do them all simultaneously. It's extreme multi-tasking: He's bent in half at the waist, dunking emp-ties in the wash with his left hand and wiping a wet spot on the bar with the right while peering into the crowd to take an order of four lights, six darks, and a cheddar plate from a newly arrived customer. Then he's walking toward the taps to replenish the supply of clean mugs and pick up the ten ales he's just ordered, while also swiping a few stray dollars off the bar with his free hand and flicking the bills over to the tip cups. The key to surviving the shift—and this applies to every position at McSorley's, but I first learned it as a runner—is to train your body to rush while your mind remains calm and focused on the merry-go-round to-do list that only stops at last call.

When the runner lags, the circuit breaks. The supply of ale slows down until he catches up. Customers at the bar grow frustrated, wondering why no one has taken their order. Waiters start asking what happened to the twenty lights they asked for five minutes ago. And the manager wants to know why the bartop is crowded with ale-crusted empties, yet he's down to his last dozen clean mugs. *And guess what, Jimbo? If I don't have any mugs, there's no way to pour.*

Those slowdowns cost everybody money, the animating

force behind McSorley's or any other business. Only, at a bustling, cash-only establishment like McSorley's, money feels viscerally connected to the work, especially since nowadays, in just about every other Manhattan watering hole, most customers are paying with credit or debit cards. At McSorley's, money flows through the room, from customer to waiter, from waiter to bartender, from runner to manager, like blood through our veins. And at the heart is Old John's cashbox, above which hangs an eight-by-ten-inch framed illustration that captures, in blunt, mordant McSorley's fashion, the pub's capitalist essence: The black-and-white print shows a hayseed farmer standing behind a pig with a dollar sign painted on the animal's flank. The farmer is pointing at the swine's ass, which appears as a large coin slot, as if the animal were an oversized piggy bank. The farmer's words, rendered in a comic-book-style speech bubble, could be considered the cynic's motto for McSorley's: WE TRUST HERE.

After I'd worked maybe a dozen shifts as the runner, my name and cell phone number were added to a laminated sheet kept behind the bar, and I became part of the fill-in rotation. Whenever one of the full-time guys needed to take off, I was one of the short-notice substitutes on call. And whatever guilt I'd felt over spurning tradition and working my first shifts as a full-fledged bartender was let go right then, because fill-in work usually meant taking on roles near the bottom of the pecking order. Doorman, chef, barback—all the jobs that don't get tips. It was time to pay dues.

Of all the different positions within the bar, I spent the

least time in the kitchen. On the handful of occasions I was summoned to work full shifts as the chef, it was on traditionally quiet nights like Christmas Eve or Super Bowl Sunday, when we knew there'd be hardly any business, and we'd tell the handful of stragglers who found their way to the bar that we were only serving cold sandwiches and cheese plates. If a customer hit it off with a waiter—or if the waiter thought he might be able to get a generous tip by securing special treatment from the kitchen—I'd fire up the grill and the deep fryer to cook a cheeseburger and fries. But for the most part, my chef experience at McSorley's involved little more than slicing chunks of liverwurst, slapping it onto slices of rye bread, topping it with a discus of raw onion, and dropping a pickle spear next to the sandwich.

The inside joke among the barmen, however, was that being able to cut an even slice of liverwurst made me (or anyone, for that matter) overqualified for the chef position. For as long as I can remember, the kitchen, the various cooks' culinary talents, and the overall quality of bar food have been a source of McSorley's humor. There was the scatterbrained chef whose solution, whenever he fell behind on burger orders, was to nuke them in the microwave for two minutes and then finish them on the grill. The only way to prevent him from using this foul shortcut was to remove the microwave from the kitchen. There were chefs who'd invent horrifying mutant soups called "cream-o-leek" and "spinach egg drop," the kind of fusion cuisine that comes from yesterday's soup getting stirred into today's broth. And there was the corned beef hash, scooped straight from the can and served warm—a lump of pallid gray potato cubes and pink flecks of meat, shimmering in lard and plunked onto a dinner plate beside a lake of purple cabbage juice. In fairness to the McSorley's chefs, there wasn't much they could do to save that dish, but that didn't stop waiters from relaying hash orders from their tables to the kitchen by barking and howling like rabid hounds.

That customers frequently proclaimed their love for McSorley's food only made the staff laugh harder. Some corollary to Murphy's Law seemed to be in effect, wherein the more disastrous a plate looked, the more diners complimented it. One classic tale revolved around the time a chef forgot to start a cheeseburger, so when the waiter returned five minutes later to check on the order, the chef dropped a patty into the deep fryer and then had the burger oozing grease and ready to serve in two minutes. Once the burger was served, the customer took one bite and summoned the waiter. "Holy shit!" the guy said. "This is the best burger I've ever tasted!" That story exists in dozens of slightly altered versions at McSorley's—deep-fried hash, soups garnished with cubes of liverwurst, a grilled-cheese sandwich that looked like two cold slices of cheddar between pieces of burnt toast—and it always ended with some poor sap praising McSorley's for having the best damn food on the planet. The level of satisfaction with the bar's food might be a testament to the potency of McSorley's ale more than anything else. That, plus how hard it has become to find a four-dollar ham and cheese sandwich or a decent burger and fries for less than ten bucks in Lower Manhattan.

Probably eighty percent or more of my fill-in shifts came as a barback on packed Friday and Saturday nights. Only, no one at McSorley's ever calls it a barback job; we call it the *shithouse*. The task is simple: Do all the little things out on the floor so that the waiters can focus on serving tables. Typically, it includes a lot of squeezing between customers to collect empty mugs off tables and bring them back to the bar, reminding the waiters when their food orders are up (and sometimes delivering the orders for them), bolting downstairs to change kegs, and sweeping up at the end of the night. The job gets its name, however, from the shithouse man's other primary responsibility: taking care of the bathrooms.

The story behind the name goes back to the early 1980s. Although McSorley's began serving female customers in 1970, the women's bathroom wasn't installed until a 1986 renovation in the back room that turned the old, cold-food-only kitchen into the ladies' room and installed a full kitchen in the deep northeast corner of the bar. So for about sixteen years, McSorley's only bathroom was the current-day men's room, a tight space with three full-body urinals that look like porcelain sarcophagi and date back to the turn of the twentieth century, plus one toilet stall. An informal code of conduct settled into place during the unisex years: women could cut the line to use the stall. The system must have worked without much controversy for more than a decade—until the Saturday afternoon when the shithouse job was born.

My father was working that day, and he remembers an extremely long line—maybe thirty men clogging McSorley's center aisle from the back room, where the bathroom was, all the way up to the taps. It was midafternoon on a Saturday, one of the bar's busiest times, but something seemed off. He couldn't recall ever seeing the bathroom line get that long. *Guys don't take that long to take a leak,* he thought. Meanwhile, the waiters weren't paying attention to anybody who wasn't ordering a round of ale, so they had mostly ignored the line, except to push through it when somebody stood in their way. My dad whistled at the back-room waiter. "What the hell is going on in there?" he yelled. "Make sure nobody dropped dead."

Nobody had dropped dead. Instead, when the waiter stepped inside the restroom, he found a local prostitute in the stall, charging male customers twenty dollars apiece for oral sex. She was escorted out of the bar, and from that day forward, McSorley's hired a shithouse man on busy weekend and holiday shifts. Initially, this employee's job was to guard the bathroom and make sure it wasn't used for illegal activities. Over the years, however, as the threat of being turned into an accidental bordello dwindled, the shithouse role evolved into a catchall position for someone who was expected to deal with all the unpredictable dilemmas that come up during a shift.

By the time I started working the shithouse, the primary responsibility of the job was returning empty mugs to the bar. Some guys preferred to shag empties in full-bar sweeps every twenty minutes. They'd hang out in the kitchen or sit outside on one of the green McSorley's barrels next to the front entrance, bullshitting with the doorman until it was time to make the rounds and replenish the mug supply. The problem with this system was that it meant letting the bartenders go through nearly all the available clean mugs, then flooding them with maybe 150 empties over the span of a few minutes. Too much feast or famine. I preferred to stay in more or less constant motion on the shithouse, roaming the front and back rooms, swiping three glasses off one table, four off another, until I had sixteen—two full handfuls—to return to the bar.

Besides, the shithouse job provided a rare opportunity to work the floor during McSorley's busiest shifts without feeling much pressure. Whereas the waiters had to con-stantly monitor their tables, looking for unclaimed chairs to seat ever more customers and making sure no groups of drinkers would try to run out on their tabs, the shithouse man had very little to worry about. His night's pay didn't depend on how fast he turned tables or whether he'd be able to coax a fair tip out of a crew of eight Belgian exchange students who were guaranteed to claim ignorance about American service norms. So when I was on the shithouse, it was like a semifree pass to people-watch McSorley's in full swing—a perfect storm of laughter and shouting and sing-ing, booze-addled madness, and a kind of controlled chaos that the bar had been nurturing for generations.

While doing my rounds, I had time to crack jokes about funny-looking customers with the front-room waiter:

"Brendan, how about your guy in the salmon-colored sweater in the corner?"

"You mean the fat fuck in the pink?"

I had time to watch first-time visitors' eyes bulge and tear up after they'd tried a dollop of McSorley's spicy mus-tard. And I had time to cringe at women who got drunk enough to remove their heels and traipse into the bathroom in bare feet. Of course it was better to be a waiter and make more money, but the shithouse was not without its charms.

And even though the job had expanded from its 1980s origins, minding the restrooms was still part of the shithouse shift. For starters, I had to make sure that when women went looking for the bathroom, they didn't wind up stumbling into a crowded men's room. You see, when McSorley's installed the women's room in 1986, the new addition was tucked into the far left corner of the back room, while the men's room remained at the center of the back wall. The aisle that leads all the way from McSorley's entrance to the back of the house funneled customers straight to the men's room, which was marked, as it had been since decades before women were allowed into the bar, by a sign that simply reads TOILET. The women's room, on the other hand, was behind a table that was often packed with drinkers, whose chairs usually blocked the sliver of an aisle intended to lead female customers to the bathroom. A sign at the top of the women's room door—higher than many customers would think to look—reads LADIES.

Add it all up, and it's not uncommon for female customers to mistakenly poke their heads into the men's room, where the guys lined up at the urinals typically confirm that these women have lost their way with hoots and cheers. Fortunately, I've never seen a customer react poorly to these mishaps. The women usually wheel around in a split second, embarrassed at first but then buoyed by the standing ovation from the rest of the back room, which has witnessed the whole thing. Occasionally, a guy will chase out after her and make a show of begging her to follow him back inside the men's room, and the howl of laughter and clank of toasting glasses will grow even more riotous.

Even though these mistakes tend to end well, the shithouse man is still expected to do his best to prevent female customers from entering the wrong bathroom because, well, it's all fun and games until some lout decides to whirl around from the urinal with his pecker out. Better safe than sorry. When I worked the shithouse, I felt myself developing a kind of intuition that helped identify the women most likely to wander into the men's room. There was something about the way they surveyed the room, a hesitant hitch in their gait as they headed toward the back of the bar, their eyes darting from point to point around the walls in search of a clue to point them in the right direction. That was when I'd try to dash away from whatever I happened to be doing to tap them on the shoulder and gesture toward the corner—sometimes to the disappointment of knowing back-room customers who were anticipating a laugh.

I get the feeling that I might be portraying the shithouse as a little too much fun. Sure, there were enjoyable parts of the job, but there was also an awful lot of puke. That's where the shithouse man ends up taking his lumps, and what he hopes to graduate out of whenever he gets elevated to steady waiter or bartender duty. I can't recall working a single busy weekend shithouse gig that didn't require me to clean up vomit at some point during the shift.

And when it happened, nine times out of ten, it seemed that the perpetrator had somehow made it to the bathroom and then lost control before he or she could aim for a toilet bowl. I usually knew that something was amiss once I noticed flocks of customers entering and then promptly fleeing whichever restroom had been soiled. At that point, I wouldn't even bother stepping inside to confirm what had gone wrong. I'd march straight back into the kitchen and pull on a pair of latex gloves. Among bar employees, those gloves were a dead giveaway that the shithouse man's night was headed toward a hideous five-minute detour. Certain waiters could hear the snap of the gloves around my wrists and figure out what was about to go down. "Aww, *fuck!*" Sean Buggy, another frequent shithouse man who knew my pain, would groan. "I'll make sure nobody tries to go in there while you clean it up." Cheers to the empathy of upchuck.

Since the puke rarely made it into the toilet, that meant I usually found myself cleaning it out of a urinal or the sink. Why do urinals need cleaning? Well, would you want to stand over a heap of steaming bar puke while you pee? Freshening up the urinals was pretty simple, though. I just had to reach in, remove the filter with the pink deodorizing puck, and then use a hose coiled beneath the sink to blast out the gunk. I learned the hard way that it was better to spray the filter with a gentle stream, so barf water wouldn't ricochet back into my face.

That may sound unpleasant, but it was nothing compared to when customers spewed in the sink. This disaster was typically made worse by however many customers dared use the bathroom after the puker. Almost without fail, they'd finish using the toilet or urinals, then see the clogged sink and decide that it'd still be a good idea to wash their hands. By the time I got in there to tidy things up, the sink would be just about overflowing with briny vomit juice. And the only way to deal with it was to pull my gloves as high as possible, plunge my forearms into the depths, and remove the blockage by hand. These were the cleanup jobs that had me gagging on ale, onion, and bile fumes and mumbling "fucking jerk-offs" over and over to myself.

When I'd fished out the last chunk of cheddar burger, when the water drained and the sink was clean and it felt safe to breathe again, I'd be giddy with pride. McSorley's, like any busy bar, could get pretty gross, and I was proving I could handle it.

CHAPTER 6

"Buggerized" and Barman-ized

AFTER FILLING IN ON THE shithouse for a couple of months, I started getting calls for extra waiter shifts, too. On these occasions I almost always worked the front room, the less desirable waiter position, because even if I was covering for the back-room guy, whoever was slotted to work the front would use seniority to slide to the back. A bunch of small factors combined to make the front room generally tougher to handle: You had to keep the potbelly stove glowing with coal during winter; most of the tables in front were smaller, which made it hard to seat the groups of ten or more that ran up the biggest tabs and produced the best tips; the trip to the kitchen was longer and made it easier for customers to slip out the front door without paying. But more than anything else, working the front could be a pain in the ass because as the waiter, you're competing for space with the bar, which runs nearly the entire length of the room. Every time you pick up a dozen ales to deliver to a table, you have to navigate a thicket of drunken limbs without spilling any and without attacking any of the customers standing in your way. When McSorley's is busy, it's not uncommon for the front waiter to ask the runner to carry a round of sixteen or twenty ales down to the other end of the bar, where the waiter can pick it up and serve whichever nearby table ordered it.

An hour or so before my first waiter shift, when I was pulling on my jeans and tucking in my button-down in our apartment, my dad asked, "You got your float ready?"

"My float?" I said. "What are you talking about?"

"Are you carrying enough money?" he replied.

I still didn't get it. "I got my wallet," I told him. "What else do I need? I'm just riding over to the bar."

Since I'd only worked the shithouse and the bar before that night, it had never occurred to me that at McSorley's, sometimes you have to bring money just to start your shift. I'd seen waiters pay cash to the bar for the ale they were about to serve, but I never stopped to think about whose money that was. "No, bunghead," my dad finally explained, "the float is the money you bring to start your waiter shift. You need a few hundred just to buy ale off the bar until your checks start coming in."

He was describing what I'd soon learn was the anti-quated payment scheme for McSorley's waiters, kind of like a tenant vendor relationship. Every ale that the waiters serve must first be purchased from the bar. No credit between coworkers, only cash. Up front. Like the sign above the cash-box says, WE TRUST HERE. So the only money a McSorley's waiter is guaranteed for his labor is shift pay, around forty dollars. You make the rest in tips after serving food and ale at tables in the front or back room, depending on where you've been assigned. But because McSorley's is a cash business that's been running pretty much the same way since before cash registers were invented, the payment system is rigged so that the bar is never at risk of losing money. The house gets paid first. And if by some chance the waiter forgets and walks away without paying for his ale, he can count on hearing my father, the manager, slapping his palm against the bar and grunting, "Get the money up, Jim! GET IT UP!"

When a waiter wants to serve ten lights and ten darks at one of his tables, he walks to the taps, orders from the manager, and buys the drinks on the spot from the bar, paying out of his own pocket. It's the waiter's responsibility to recoup that money (plus tips), either by keeping track of everything a group owes on a check or by charging round by round. So when you arrive for work as the front- or back-room waiter, you need a fat wad of cash—twenties, singles, maybe a few fives and tens—to buy ale off the bar until you turn a few tables and start to make your money back. If you start with a few hundred dollars, your float might dip below fifty before your wad starts to grow again. And hopefully, by the end of a shift, that couple of hundred you showed up with will have increased by a few more hundred. If you don't have money to float yourself, it's possible to borrow start-up cash off the bar, which the manager will mark down and collect at the end of the shift. But in all my years around the bar, I've never seen a regular waiter use bar money for his float. It's one of those pointless macho codes that endure in a place like McSorley's, where nobody ever says it but everyone knows that asking the bar for money to begin your waiter shift would make you look like a hapless newcomer. Maybe it's bullshit, but once my dad explained the system to me, I wasn't gonna be caught dead asking the manager for a loan.

Like pretty much every job inside McSorley's, the individual components of the waiter gig are simple. You arrive with your float, put on a gray waiter's jacket, and ask the manager for a pen and an order pad. You arrange your money and your pockets according to whatever scheme works best for you. I liked to keep my big wad in my breast pocket, twenties on the inside and singles on the outside; a smaller bunch of five- and ten-dollar bills went in the jacket's left hip pocket for when I needed to make change; my pen and pad went in the right hip pocket. Setting that routine and sticking to it often meant the difference between smoothly handling the crowd and freaking out on the floor. When you let things get mixed up, you risk mishaps like reaching for your order pad and pulling out a knot of twenties instead. Then you start to get flustered, you mix things up even more, and all of a sudden you're on panic's doorstep. Next, you number your tables: In the front, where there are seven tables, I always began with the picture windows near the entrance and counted back toward the center of the bar. In the back, I'd number tables counterclockwise, one through six, starting with a large rectangular table on the far side of the taps.

How you organize your checks is up to you. The basic setup, which I learned on my first shift, is to write the table number in the top left corner, then keep a running tally of the ales the group orders on the bottom third of the check. Food orders go in the remaining space, and when the customers are ready to leave, you add everything up, jot down the total, and hand them the bill. Not everyone does it that way, though, and the longer waiters work at McSorley's, the more willing they become to deviate from the norm.

Timmy, one of the more experienced waiters during the years I worked at the bar, jotted all his sales on the cardboard backside of his order pad, writing in a cryptic chicken-scratch shorthand that only he could understand. He often split the floor on weekend nights with Brendan, a towering, barrel-chested Irishman who's been in and out of the mix at McSorley's since the seventies, and Brendan didn't even bother writing down orders. When a table would ask to pay, he'd size up the group, replay the last hour in his head, and jot down a number on one of his checks: *Four rounds, a cheddar plate, and a chili? Let's say ninety and call it even.* That he could keep all this in his head while simultaneously serving seven tables (and the bigger tables would often be shared by two or three separate groups) was a testament to his mental acuity, for sure, but it was also a feat of sheer chutzpah. The customers wouldn't complain or contest the amount Brendan assigned them because of the authority and charm he'd handled them with all night. When he'd tell them they owed ninety bucks and offer no breakdown of the bill, they'd accept it. Of course, it helped that Brendan's math and memory were almost always right.

For me, waiting tables was the most stressful position at McSorley's. When a rush of customers hit, it felt as if you'd been standing in a puddle, and then that puddle swelled to fifteen feet of water in the blink of an eye and you were thrashing to keep your head above the surface. The primary goal of the bar's pay-first system was to protect the owner from losses, but it had ingenious side effects on the guys working the floor. Because it was their own money invested in the tables, the waiters had a strong incentive to pay close attention to the crowd and to hustle their balls off. During peak hours, it was normal for a waiter to have five hundred dollars sunk into his tables. Forgetting to mark down a round of twelve and twelve on a big group meant you were screwing yourself out of sixty-six bucks. Letting a group run out without paying wouldn't cost McSorley's a cent, but a bad beat like that could leave a waiter finishing his shift with lighter pockets than when he arrived.

This might explain the renowned surliness of McSorley's servers. Half of New York City seems to know us as "the bar where they kick you out when you stop drinking." Before I worked the floor, I'd watch the regular waiters tell a group it was time to order another round or get out, and I'd sympathize with the customers. Once I'd done a few waiter shifts and experienced firsthand the panic — my father calls it "the burning sensation," in a not-too-sly nod to diarrhea and/or venereal disease — that set in while watching three customers camp out on a table big enough to fit eight, I understood. My seated group had ordered two rounds of ale and a cheddar plate, and then sat for an hour and a half, for a check worth less than thirty-five dollars. Meanwhile, every new group of drinkers who strolled past and found seats in the back room hit me like a liver punch. I was getting reamed. Letting that group hold my table was costing me money.

Eventually, I had to follow my dad's advice. For the past hour, he'd been working the taps and grunting at me: "Ship 'em, Jimbo! Ship 'em!" I grabbed the next group of six guys who filed into the bar and sat them down with the other three, and within ten minutes of serving the new group, the lingerers had asked for their check. This was a reminder for me that even when I couldn't initially understand why things operated a certain way at McSorley's, the bar's customs had evolved over generations, and there was always some logic behind them. Telling customers things they might not like to hear—that they have to share tables, that they need to squeeze into three seats over by the stove to make space for a new group that just arrived, that it's a busy bar and if they're done drinking, it's time for the check—is just part of working the floor. You rely on whatever combination of charm and coercion works best for you, and I found that more often than not, I could ask politely and groups would comply.

The waiter's need to curate and optimize his half of the bar with as many good customers as possible makes competition between the front- and back-room waiters unavoidable. That rivalry is almost always good-natured, although a couple of times each year it boils over into one waiter shoving the other over perceived foul play, followed by an invitation to step outside and settle it. The friendly side of this dynamic is characterized by little pranks waiters will play on each other, like when the front-room waiter observes a gaggle of French-speaking tourists entering the bar and shepherds them to a big table in the back. European visitors are justly stereotyped at McSorley's for ordering very little, for squatting at tables until they're told to scram, and for conveniently ignoring the pages of their guidebooks that remind them to tip.

"Room in the back!" is a coded phrase the barmen yell out in reference to unwanted customers. It means you'd love to ship them to another part of the bar and let someone else deal with the hassle. While tending bar, I've witnessed some extraordinary back-and-forth waiter exchanges, with servers ping-ponging the same unwanted group between the front and back rooms four or five times before one waiter finally surrendered and agreed to serve the bewildered flock.

These laughs can turn to frustration and occasional conflict, however, when one waiter starts to feel "buggerized." The term comes from the verb, more common in British and Irish English, *to bugger.* Translated to McSorley's, it's the bar equivalent of getting dorked from behind, screwed over by your coworker. It also happens to create an unintentional double entendre with the last name of the Buggy clan, the Kilkenny family that has produced more McSorley waiters than any other since Matty purchased the bar in 1977. Dick's father, known around the bar as Babs, worked as a weekend doorman from 1967 till 1975, but the true Buggy patriarch at McSorley's was Dick, the former NYPD decoy cop who intimidated me as a kid, and the clan grew to include Brendan, his half brother, his nephew Richie the King and cousin Shane, and Brendan's son, Sean, who grew up around McSorley's a few years after I did. Most weeks, a day won't pass at McSorley's without at least one Buggy working a waiter shift. And sure, the Buggys could be rapacious on the floor, jamming as many customers into their tables as possible and not thinking to leave some for the waiter serving the other room. But we all did that. That's how servers have to be at McSorley's. In fact, the bar seemed to operate best when the employees all tried to outhustle each other, because that allowed the waiters and bartenders to reach a natural equilibrium where everyone got a fair share of the money available during any given shift. It was when somebody fell behind, or when some uncontrollable setback happened—like getting stiffed on a big check—that a waiter began to feel utterly and hopelessly buggerized.

Besides, whether by blood or by tradition, buggerizing each other from time to time was an act of friendly competition. It kept the McSorley workforce sharp. It kept us hungry. If we didn't serve more and more customers to earn more tips for ourselves, then the other waiters surely would, and that cycle pushed everyone to work ever harder for the bar.

So why is the front-room waiter job the most difficult? What makes it the only shift that has had me on the verge of a complete emotional meltdown, ready to rip off my waiter's jacket and stomp out of the bar once and for all?

It's everything. It's getting buggerized while couples from seven different European nations camp out at each of my tables. It's trying to navigate the crowd, holding thirty-five-pound loads of glass and ale aloft while squeezing through a human obstacle course. It's the moment of dread when muscle fatigue creeps into my forearms, starting as a harmless tingle and a tiny bit of soreness. Then it worsens on subsequent trips from the bar to the tables, and my grip starts to weaken. But now, finally, my tables are full of big groups, and they're ordering sixteen, twenty, thirty ales, every twenty minutes. I've never felt anything quite like having my arms give out on me. It has only happened once, and I'm not even sure how to describe the sensation. A quick wave of hurt coursed through my forearms, and then they went numb. Moments later, my wrists and hands turned limp and my grip disappeared. My arms were there in front of me, but I no longer had control over them, and they no longer had control over the mugs.

I made a desperate lunge for the table that had ordered the round, but it was too late. Everything from my elbows down just gave up. Humiliation came next. Half of my mugs, ale included, tumbled out of my hands and down into the sawdust. Someone shouted, "What the fuck! I didn't know they hired pussies at McSorley's!" Part of me felt fortunate that I'd managed to save half the order. Another part of me wanted to pick up the fallen mugs and smash them over the heads of everyone who was laughing at me. And another part was thinking that I'd just lost twenty-two bucks, since I now had to repurchase the eight ales I'd dropped.

I spent the final two hours of that shift in a murderous mood, telling every customer who rubbed me the wrong way to get the hell off my tables. I shouted at two guys for trying to sit in a spot I'd been saving for a larger group, only to find out that the larger group wanted to order waters and a three-dollar small cheese plate. I was buggerizing myself, but at that point it hardly mattered. My sole concern was inflicting my misery on as many other people as I could.

In the grand scheme of waiter meltdowns, however, mine was pretty tame. The most memorable one in recent history came courtesy of Timmy, who held the back-room weekend shift for much of the past decade, until he retired in July 2015. Who knows what assortment of slights and frustrations built up within him to push him to the brink that night, but the final straw became the stuff of McSorley's legend. Timmy had been serving a large group. They only ordered a few rounds, but the crew was numerous enough to run up a hundred-dollar tab. When Timmy handed a check to the customer who'd asked to pay, the guy promptly returned the bill with the exact amount owed and not a penny more. These weren't foreign tourists who could claim ignorance in the ways of tipping. Those customers, frustrating as they were, could be politely cajoled into ponying up enough spare change for a half-decent gratuity. No, what was happening with Timmy's group was intentional.

Why would these guys choose to stiff him? Well, although Timmy was beloved to many weekend regulars, you'd be hard-pressed to find a waiter who conformed less to the ideal of service taught in hotel-restaurant classes. Other waiters had rough edges, but those were smoothed out with quick-witted charm or old-school chivalry or tireless hustle. Timmy, however—he was all gruff. A solid five foot seven and built like a fire hydrant, he had been a decent amateur boxer and damn good hurler back in Ireland. Now, in his early fifties, Timmy scurried around McSorley's back room in a state of perpetual dishevelment. His frizzy shoulder-length hair had gone largely gray and looked like it might not have seen shampoo for weeks. It hung in front of his scrunched-up face, the lower third of which was obscured by a steel wool goatee. When he didn't look like a savage Celtic caveman, he resembled a burnt-out hippie. (A crew of loyal customers once showed up at McSorley's wearing T-shirts they'd made comparing Timmy to Charles Manson.) To non-Irish patrons, Timmy's brogue sounded like a growl, and he spoke to them in short, guttural bursts: *How many people you got? Sit in the corner! What're ya drinkin'?* When he served a big round of ale, he'd lunge at the table and just about throw sixteen or twenty mugs at his customers with a crash, miraculously avoiding spills and flying glass shards. Occasionally, he'd disappear into the kitchen for a snack and forget his orders. Once, while I was working the shithouse, a girl seated in the back grabbed my wrist and asked,

"Have you seen the scary waiter? We're waiting on our beer."
I slipped into the kitchen, where Timmy was hunched over a
plate, shoveling down cubes of some crunchy whitish root.

"What are you eating?" I asked.

"TURNIP!" he barked, holding out the platter of raw
tuber for me. "Want a bite?"

So yes, like raw turnip, Timmy was an acquired taste.
(Away from McSorley's, Timmy is a gifted photographer
whose humanistic documentary-style images have been
showcased at a handful of other East Village bars and art
spaces.) But that's why people come to McSorley's. They
know it's crowded, they know it's chaotic, and they know the
service is brusque. I've been chastised by patrons who felt I
was being too nice. They had come a long way to have a
McSorley's barman tell them to "drink up or fuck off," I was
told. The vast majority of customers who see a waiter hustling to serve a packed Saturday-night room appreciate how
hard that job is, and they forgive his curt manner or those
five extra minutes they spent waiting for a cheeseburger.
Which means that no matter how crazy Timmy may have
appeared the night that group stiffed him, he almost surely
did nothing to deserve it. They were the assholes, not him.

So when Timmy counted the money and saw there was
no tip, he asked what the problem was. The customer
grinned as if he'd been waiting for this confrontation and
wanted to show off for his friends. "You want a tip?" the guy
asked. He took out his wallet, riffled through his remaining
cash, removed a one-dollar bill, and tucked it into Timmy's
breast pocket. "Here."

This would make any of us blow our top. There's no
surer way to piss off a barman than to say something smart-
ass about his career. I'd seen it throughout my life—anytime

some white-collar relative or family friend let slip an accidental aside denigrating bar work, my father would turn
cold to them forever. They'd shown their true colors.
Nobody appreciates having his career and livelihood disre-
spected, and it happens a lot to bar and restaurant workers.
When it happened to Timmy that night—and in such flam-
boyant fashion—he snapped, grabbing the bill from his
pocket, crumpling it in one hand, and shoving it into the
customer's laughing mouth before the jackass even knew
what hit him.

"Keep your money and go fuck yourself," Timmy said,
and walked away while the entire back room stood to give
him a round of applause and laugh as the chastened group
of drinkers shuffled out of the bar.

Once I was part of the steady rotation, getting fill-in calls
two or three times a week, it didn't take long to feel comfortable in any position the bar tossed at me. I was a ten-minute
bike ride from McSorley's, and I would show up at a
moment's notice, so I kept getting summoned. And as a few
weeks bled into a few months bled into about five years, I
found that I was most at home working the bar. The runner
job was where I belonged.

I'd grown up watching my father work and idolizing his
position behind the pumps. The stories he delighted me
with over the years were all told from his vantage point,
looking out at the swaying, singing, chugging masses on the
floor from his nook at the far end of the bar. The best shifts
were the ones I spent working as his runner, and the second
best were when I ran up and down the bar for the other
managers. And during those nights spent pushing handfuls

of ales across McSorley's old mahogany bar, plunging empties into soapsud basins, and bolting to the basement to
switch kegs, I saw how the manager acts as the bar's nerve
center.

For starters, the job requires a kind of marvelous ambi-
dextrous coordination that can't be grasped until you've
tried to do it yourself. McSorley's tradition of serving ales in
pairs makes for massive orders. Twenty light and twenty
dark is a staple, something the managers are used to pumping out several times per shift on busy days. Even more
exotic orders — thirty-six and forty-four, fifty and twenty,
one hundred lights — don't rattle the bartenders. As long as
the bar has enough mugs to fill the order, they'll pour it.

Think about that: When a large order comes in, McSorley's bartenders can't pour four ales, close the tap, put the
mugs on the bar, and then reopen the tap to pour another
four. It would take ages to finish each order, and that would
be fatal for a business built on speed and volume. The more
ale you can serve during a fixed seven-hour shift, the more
money you make for yourself, for the waiters, and for the
owner. A bartender who can't keep up with demand hurts
everyone's bottom line. This means keeping the tap open
for pours that routinely eclipse twenty ales, filling four mugs
with your right hand while grabbing the next four with your
left, then swapping in the clean empties without losing too
much down the drain while placing the foamy, newly filled
mugs on the bar, then grabbing four more empties to keep
the process going until the order is complete.

Simply pouring a servable mug of ale can be difficult
enough to take up all of one's attention. If we grabbed a random pedestrian off Seventh Street, put him behind the bar,
and told him to pull one glass, it would end up being almost

all head, with maybe an ounce or two of ale at the bottom. Because McSorley's only serves two varieties of its own ale, kegs rarely last more than a few hours and the beer emerges frothy, fresh, and unruly. It takes a few weeks of trial and error just to learn how to let the stream of ale hit the mugs at the proper angle. If you miss it, you get the foam. And there are dozens of other factors to consider: Dark often pours heavier than light; the foam thins out for the final twenty or so pulls before a keg blows; during the last hour of a shift, when it's unlikely that you'll finish the remaining open kegs, you might need to keep track of the number of ales sold so that the next day's crew will know how much they can expect to sell from the leftovers. The times when I've worked the taps—only to give various managers a break during shifts— it took pretty much all my powers of concentration and focus to keep track of these variables. For the managers, it's second nature, earned over years and years of repetition. On top of the physical demands of pouring at McSorley's, they're keeping count in their heads of the ale that goes out and the money owed, they're flipping through a wallet-sized spiral notebook to record what time kegs run out, they're making change for the waiters, and they're constantly surveying the crowd for trouble. They're the Olympic decathletes of bar-business multitasking.

The more I worked the bar, the more I learned the different managers' tics and how to cater to them. Pepe, the weekday bartender, grew up around the corner, when the East Village was still a Ukrainian hamlet. He'd been hanging around McSorley's since his childhood and wound up working at the bar not too long after my dad started. He wore round, professorial spectacles over a pair of eyes that felt like they could cut you in half, and his slim build, tight salt-and-pepper goatee, and neatly cropped hair all reflected his fetish for order and precision. When coworkers became frustrated with him, they called him obsessive and anal, but it was hard not to respect the way he ran McSorley's. Pepe could be prickly. His name for absent-minded coworkers was "shit-for-brains," and I'd seen him heave steaming, bleach-filled rags across the front room to splatter on the heads of waiters he didn't like. Thankfully, he had an accurate arm, but every now and then we'd hear a story of some innocent customer getting caught in the crossfire. He was used to working alone behind the bar, since Monday through Thursday McSorley's wasn't busy enough between 11 a.m. and 6 p.m. to warrant hiring a runner. Pepe's fifth shift was Sunday, though, and when I worked alongside him on busy weekend afternoons I knew to stay out of his way. All he wanted was for his runner to keep the empty mugs neatly arranged and stacked on the shelf beneath the bar. Out of sight, out of mind.

Teresa, one of the owner's five daughters, is the only full-time female bartender in McSorley's 160-plus years of existence. (Matty's youngest daughter, Maeve, joined the fill-in rotation and shortly after I started, and she went on to work many runner shifts behind the bar.) When I worked alongside Teresa, she gave me the same warm, apprentice-style treatment my father had given her in the nineties. When she first convinced Matty to let her join the staff, he agreed on the condition that she work with Bart. His reasons were twofold: One, operating behind the bar would give his daughter a measure of safety in case a fight broke out on the floor, as well as some separation from potential harassment by ale-emboldened lechers; and two, Matty trusted my dad to teach her the job the way they had learned it in the seventies. There were Thursday nights in my youth when my dad would come home from work and brag about how Teresa had controlled the crowd, defusing an altercation before fists were thrown, or he would snicker about the times he'd seen her rebuff come-ons from TV news celebrities and pro basketball players. After they'd shared a Thursday-through-Monday schedule for years, my father, who was looking to switch to quieter weeknight shifts, lobbied Matty to let Teresa manage the bar on Friday and Saturday afternoons. I probably have my dad to thank for the way she handled me during my first shifts: patient but never coddling.

Michael, who shared the busiest weekend night manager job with Scott, came to New York as a fresh-faced twenty-two-year-old Irishman in the early nineties. When my dad first saw him, he thought, *That kid's not made for bar work.* About five foot eight with pink cheeks and a toothy grin, Michael seemed too innocent to survive at McSorley's. Lower Manhattan still had an edge back then. In the seventies and eighties, breaking up fights and dragging rowdy drunks out of the bar was a weekly routine for the staff, most of whom had the broad shoulders and head-to-toe bulk of rugby players. What my father hadn't foreseen when he bestowed the ironic nickname "Mad Dog" upon Michael was that Manhattan was about to embark on a decades-long transformation into a happier, friendlier, and much wealthier place. Late-twentieth-and-early-twenty-first-century McSorley's turned out to be a natural fit for Michael, even if an old-timer like my dad still thought barmen should come with a side of nasty.

In terms of demeanor, however, I noticed that my McSorley's temperament had more in common with Michael's than with my dad's. When I'd work as Michael's runner, customers would occasionally ask why our service was so courteous, and one of us would shoot back with "Would you rather we treat you like shit?"—but delivered with a smile. Still, my dad's view on what kind of person belongs working in a bar hung in my head, and I worried that I might not have the goods. When I asked him one day if I was too nice, he told me, "Nah. You're young and you've got size. You can afford to be soft."

The other regular manager besides my dad was Scott, who was nineteen when he started at the bar and wound up marrying one of Teresa's sisters four years later. I was only five or six years old back then, and even though I only saw Scott when my dad brought me to work on Saturday mornings, I worshipped him like an older brother. A couple of decades later, by the time I started working the bar with him, he'd become probably the most detail-obsessed McSorley's bartender in history. The staff lovingly called him the Ayatollah, and he treated selling ale like the director of the CIA treats keeping secrets. This trait showed most in the way he handled money. At the end of a shift, the manager fills out a sheet breaking down the bar's overall take—the number of kegs used, the amount of cash brought in from food sales, the payouts for night watchmen and shithouse helpers. But Scottie didn't just add up the earnings at the end of each night. Pretty much anytime he wasn't pouring ale during his shifts, he was huddled in the manager's corner, right beside the taps, counting whatever we'd brought in so far. Some managers liked the runner to keep tip money neatly stacked and folded in the pair of ceramic mugs behind the bar; Scottie preferred me to throw the bills anywhere on the tip shelf, so he could count the gratuities himself and enter the amounts in a notebook where he'd been recording hourly tipping data for years. Scott's fastidious counting may have been extreme, but it felt like a clear expression of his love for McSorley's and his commitment to do everything in his power to improve the business.

While getting schooled in the methods and quirks of various McSorley's bartenders, I noticed that I started to develop my own techniques and idiosyncrasies. Unless we were packed, I liked to wash mugs one hand at a time, holding the bar with the other to take the strain off my back. I'm a lefty, but I didn't want to become overreliant on my dominant hand, so I made a point of alternating: five batches of mugs with the left, then five with the right, and so on. I picked up the McSorley barman's fine-tuned sensitivity to certain sounds. In the middle of a crowd roaring with conversation and laughter, I could hear every time customers slammed empty mugs onto the front-room tables (a pet peeve I inherited from my dad, although I didn't yet have the stature to borrow his stock response — "Try it on your head!"); my ears picked up orders of soda and water from the managers; and I recognized the abnormal, extra tinny clink caused by glass cracking at the base of a mug's handle. I could look at a stack of single-dollar tips and guess when it hit twenty. I didn't even know how I knew these things, but I just *knew*. I was becoming a real creature of the bar, and that meant I was ready for McSorley's ultimate trial: working Paddy's Day as my father's runner.

CHAPTER 7

St. Patrick's Day

GROWING UP, I NEVER NEEDED a calendar to mark the end of February. The first days of March were always accompanied by daily groans from my father about "Paddy's Day." Each year he'd issue warnings to me and my mother about how this year would be the worst yet and how he expected this or that waiter to be drunk and useless by the time he showed up to work. Of course, March seventeenth was also the best day of the year—the busiest and most lucrative shift of them all. But even though my father and the men of McSorley's looked forward to the action and the money that came with St. Patrick's Day, I never heard them express much excitement over riding home with a swollen grip of cash after the holiday. The internal code of the bar frowned upon such ostentatious money-grubbing, so instead, everyone griped about what a mess the crowd would be, how many fights they'd have to clean up, how the doorman would likely earn more money selling T-shirts than the service staff would while taming the tipsy mob, and how they couldn't wait for the day to pass.

The day before St. Patrick's might have been the only time of the year when my father's bedtime was earlier than mine. As early as 8 or 8:30 p.m., when I'd still be up working on long division or watching a Knicks game, he'd be stripping down to his underwear to crawl into bed. That's because he'd have to be up around 4:30 the next morning — just enough time to suck down a few cups of coffee, shave, and eat a salad bowl full of raisin bran. McSorley's opens at 8 a.m. on St. Patrick's Day, and he had to be at the bar around 6 a.m. to set up.

By the time he'd arrive, there'd already be a line curled around the block, turning around Seventh Street onto Third Avenue and headed toward St. Mark's Place. I'd wake up before school, switch on the morning news, and without fail I'd catch a segment where some local correspondent walks up and down the line asking tipplers why they woke at the crack of dawn to guzzle McSorley's ale. They'd all be decked head-to-toe in Kelly green, with plastic beads and clovers dangling from their necks, singing "The Star Spangled Banner" before they'd even tasted a drop. I remember watching those crowds and thinking, *My dad is about to deal with* that?

The morning Paddy's Day shift ended at 5 p.m. back then — earlier than my father would come home on any other day of the year. But after nine straight hours of pouring ale, sometimes with no break to use the bathroom or even take a bite of the corned beef that all but overflows from McSorley's kitchen on the holiday, he'd always return to our apartment dragging his feet, grunting with every step, rubbing the ache out of his wrists, and trying to rearrange the wayward tufts of his thinning brown hair. His white dress shirt and jeans would be stained with brown ale blotches—he looked, more or less, like he'd been put through a washing machine that used beer instead of detergent. Most years, I remember him shuffling through the door, flicking a rubber-banded roll of the day's tips onto the kitchen table, and then proceeding directly to the shower. Five minutes later, I'd catch one more glimpse of him as he walked naked through our apartment, gnarred the words "piece of cake" to questions from me and my mother about how the day went, then tossed on a T-shirt and sweatpants before collapsing into bed.

And for some reason, every time I saw it, I thought the same thing: *I want to do that.*

And so the time came. Although I'd built up the occasion in my mind during my first year of work at the bar, there was nothing ceremonial about my first Paddy's Day. No one pulled me aside and asked if I was ready or sat me down to give pointers on handling the busiest crowd of the year. I just answered my phone one afternoon in early March and heard Michael's chirpy brogue on the other end: "Would you be able to work the bar with your father at night on Paddy's Day?...Yes? Good lad." On my end, this routine conversation felt as if I'd taken a knee and been knighted.

By the time of my first Paddy's Day, the grueling nine-hour shifts that used to pummel my father and the rest of the staff into primordial mush were a thing of the past. Sometime in the mid-2000s, Matty decided, mercifully, to begin splitting the day into three shifts: 8 a.m. to 1 p.m., 1 to 7 p.m., and then 7 till closing. I would be running the bar with my dad on the pumps for the anchor stretch of this relay.

Paddy's Day was an all-hands-on-deck affair. Each shift included two bartenders, two waiters, and two shithouse men (one for each room). McSorley's didn't have enough regular employees to cover the triple-shift schedule, which meant that just about everyone in the bar's orbit got called in for some form of duty. Rotating shithouse specialists and doormen — Coach, the aging New York Jets fanatic; an ex-cop nicknamed Marmaduke; Petey from the firehouse — who might cover a shift once a month all showed up on the same day. It was a rare departure from the bar's steady, pre-dictable schedule, and one of the only days on the calendar when employees who didn't share shifts would see each other and work together. It felt like some deranged family reunion centered around getting customers drunk to the point of blindness. On my first St. Paddy's night, our shit-house men were Sanitation Mike, a towering city garbage-man who filled out his waiter's jacket like a six-foot-six scarecrow, and Bill Wander, the bar's unofficial historian, who showed up to work with his dignified horn-rimmed glasses pushed high up the bridge of his nose.

Nighttime was considered the least desirable chunk of Paddy's Day at McSorley's. Despite the early call time, the opening shift was most coveted. At that hour, the crowd would be teeming with McSorley diehards who make plans to begin their holiday at the bar year after year. They arrive sober — which means their drinking won't slow down until ten or eleven (noon, if you're lucky). They put in giant orders of forty light and forty dark or a hundred light. And they're regulars, so they tip well when it's time to go.

The first hour and a half after opening on Paddy's Day are probably the most physically demanding ninety minutes of the year at McSorley's. When the clock strikes 8 a.m. the number of customers jumps from zero to 157—all the bar can legally hold—and all of them want service, pronto. Nobody nurses their first drink on St. Patrick's Day—they pound them in three or four gulps and call for another round. The bartender pumping ale will pour between fifteen hundred and two thousand mugs in that initial sprint, breaking only to make change for the waiters and to mark down when kegs blow. By 10 a.m., the crowd usually settles into a steadier, but still heavy, drinking pace. If the pump-man's forearms didn't already look like something from a Popeye cartoon, they will by the end of that opening rush.

Serving the Paddy's Day morning crowd—"taming" them, we sometimes say, since a quart of ale and a few slabs of cheddar tend to plunge customers into a rosy-cheeked, stuporous bliss—has become a mark of McSorley's prestige. It's like being called up from minor-league baseball to the Big Show, and even though it's a punishing gig, it's a shift that bartenders and waiters take pride in working.

The middle shift, 1 to 7 p.m., is valued for different reasons. It's the closest McSorley's comes to being quiet on Paddy's Day. By *quiet*, I mean that the bar will still be as busy as it is during peak weekend hours, but on St. Patrick's Day you take whatever small victories you can claim. Working the afternoon, you don't have to wake up early and you don't have to deal with the 8 a.m. deluge. The customers are lubed up and happy. You can just stroll in, serve as much ale and corned beef and cabbage as six hours will permit, and then walk away with the hard-earned spoils. The money might not equal the morning or night shifts, but you don't have to break your back to make it.

Then there's the night shift, also known as the total shit-show, which would be my first Paddy's Day experience. My father told me what to expect earlier that afternoon, while we sat around our kitchen table, lacing up our boots and inhaling pasta before hopping on our bikes to ride over to McSorley's:

"We might make money; we might not. You can't count on a good cup tonight." Translation: The "cup" meant tips, in reference to the pair of ceramic mugs where the bartenders stuffed the dollar bills customers left behind.

He continued: "By the time we get them at seven or nine or eleven, they're going to be so zooted that they either have no money left to tip or they'll empty their pockets for us and let us keep half of whatever they're holding. Honestly, we'll probably get more of the no-tippers. The regulars are all gone by night on Paddy's Day. We're just going to get drunk kids and wandering skels."

Translation: *Zooted* is a word for *drunk* or *high* that I knew from the underground rap I listened to as a teenager, but someone must have used it in the bar because my father took a liking to it. *Skel* is a bit of dated NYPD slang used to describe the city's low-life element. In McSorley's it became a catchall for scuzzy customers and creepy solo drinkers. The skels rarely caused trouble, but they portended it and they set the staff on edge. They were also notoriously cheap, a distinction they shared with fresh-faced twenty-one-year-old college drinkers. My dad expected those two groups to make up much of the crowd for my first Paddy's Day, and he wasn't particularly eager to serve either of them.

And finally: "It's going to be packed, and almost everyone inside the bar tonight is going to be so sloppy we might not even serve them on other days. But if you refuse to serve drunks on Paddy's Day then you're refusing to serve the whole city. Just make sure you get the money off them before you hand over the ales, because half the time they're so plastered that they'll order twenty ales before they realize they spent all their cash. Hopefully the waiters will be able to turn them over pretty fast at the tables. The already-drunks will come in, order a round, then pass out and become impossible to get rid of. What a shitshow. And remember, if you see a fight, it's not worth getting in the middle of it. The bar will get sued if we put hands on anyone, and you don't want to get a mug broken over your head. Just yell at them, tell Dick and Big Kevin on the door, and threaten to call the cops."

It was 6:15. Time to pedal over to McSorley's. My dad had one last note of advice for the bike ride: "Don't ride across Bleecker. The drunks at Red Lion and Wicked Willy's will be spilling out into the street and one of them might stumble into you and knock you into traffic. Take Houston and then go up Lafayette. Or try going across West Fourth. Fuck it, there's gonna be skels everywhere. Just go slow and keep your eyes open."

It was time to work.

The bicycle ride from our apartment in the southwest corner of Greenwich Village over to the bar took about fifteen minutes, like usual. My father brought his ride into the first-floor hallway of the tenement building that houses McSorley's, locked the back wheel to the frame, and leaned it behind the stairwell. I went to chain mine to the metal post of a parking sign outside the front door on Seventh Street. This is where I always locked my bike, but this time, Big Kevin waved me off.

"Bad idea," the doorman said in his high-pitched Brooklyn whine. "We already had about six mooks puke right there." I looked down the long, wobbly line of glassy-eyed customers who were still waiting to get inside and *begin* drinking, then thanked Kevin and walked the bike across the street to find a safer signpost.

We had a solid twenty minutes before the shift change, so I stopped to catch up with Kevin before heading inside. When I was a kid, Kevin had been a regular weekend doorman at McSorley's. He used to come to Mets games with me and my father in the late eighties. I'd skip out on school after lunch and we'd ride the 7 train out to Shea Stadium. During the game, I'd keep my eyes on the field and hope for a chance to catch a foul ball, but my ears would be locked in on my dad's conversations with Kevin — stories about working as a bouncer at McSorley's and the Brooklyn nightclubs where Kevin pulled doorman duty during the middle of the week.

Kevin's constant refrain was that the McSorley's crowd was as meek as a kindergarten class compared to the hotheaded Italian crowds in Bensonhurst and Gravesend. Kevin knew what he was talking about. He'd lift the side of his shirt to show me and my dad the jagged scar beneath his ribs where an irate customer had stabbed him after Kevin tossed him from a club. Kevin stood a hulking six foot four and 240 pounds, with a chest as broad as the grill on a Mack truck and a crew cut of the most perfectly erect brown hair I'd ever seen, and the knife wound only made him seem more invincible.

As I grew older, Kevin became a rare sight around McSorley's. He found steady employment with the city, which meant health care, a pension, and no reason to hang around drinking holes in the East Village and South Brooklyn, corralling loonies and dodging box-cutter blades. Only on occasions like Paddy's Day, when Kevin knew he could make a nice, quick payday, did he still work at McSorley's. And on that soused holiday, Matty liked to hire Kevin as extra muscle to keep order inside the madhouse and to back up sixty-something retired waiter Dick Buggy, who switched onto the door on Paddy's Day to sell McSorley's T-shirts. If trouble broke out and it was too much for Dick or the regular employees to handle, Kevin was the equalizer.

When I arrived that night, Kevin was sitting on a green McSorley's barrel just outside the entrance, his knees splayed in front of him. Whenever Dick decided to let people in from the front of the line, Kevin would pull the door open for them. We shook hands and I asked where he was working these days.

"Now? I'm working for the MTA. They got me inspecting city buses. It's pretty easy. All I do is walk through the empty buses in the yard and check for roaches."

Roaches?

"Yeah, it's bullshit, though, like everything else in this city. I'm not supposed to look too hard. Don't go flipping over the handicap seats or shining my flashlight in the corners. The roaches never come out in the open anyway. If you wanna find roaches, all you do is pop the panel off the back wall behind the seats. They're crawling all over each other back there like some goddamn hive. It's near the engine—they like the heat."

I asked him how Paddy's Day had gone so far. Any crazies? "You kidding? This is the best day of the year for me. I don't do nothing but sit here and open the door, and by the end of the night, I make as much money as you do sweating your balls off on the inside."

He was referring to Dick's world-class salesmanship along the customer line. Every Paddy's Day, Dick would show up with a truck stuffed with hundreds of commemorative T-shirts he had made for the occasion, and he'd spend the entire day, from 8 a.m. until one the next morning, hawking shirts to people as they waited to get inside McSorley's. To the staff working on the inside, it seemed like Dick managed to convince every customer who stepped inside to buy a shirt. This had been his St. Patrick's Day hustle for the past decade. Even drinkers who arrived at McSorley's wearing T-shirts they'd bought from Dick in previous years often wound up being persuaded to buy new ones.

Kevin's job was to handle the traditional doorman duties of looking tough and maintaining order, while occasionally running down the block to haul a fresh box of shirts from Dick's truck. The employees inside never heard from Dick how much money he raked in on Paddy's Day, but since he stayed on the door from opening to closing—eighteen straight hours with customers lined up to get inside the bar—it had to be a damn good day's wages. And he always gave Kevin a healthy cut of the action.

Five minutes before our shift began, I pushed my way through the entrance, smiling when I heard someone on line griping behind me: "What the fuck? How come that guy didn't have to wait?" It took Big Kevin all of two seconds to snipe back: "Calm down, jerk-off, he works here."

Once I got through the swinging doors and into the front room, I started shimmying to the bar, turning sideways to squeeze through the thicket of limbs and using a swimming motion to reach up, over, and then through the bodies in front of me. Each stroke created a sliver of space to step into and wedge myself a step closer to the bar. As I inched forward, I could feel customers' damp, hot breath against my cheek, and I inhaled pungent whiffs of raw onion and brown ale.

When I arrived at the hatch that allows employees to get behind the bar, my dad was there waiting for me. He'd made his approach from the opposite side, through the slightly less congested back room, where he'd stopped in the kitchen to slurp a couple of bowls of lentil soup before work.

"Lentils, Jim," he said, flashing a grin. "Gonna be blowing gas in case I need to thin out the crowd."

"What about me?" I asked.

"Better hold your breath," he said. "Once you're on the other side of that bar, you ain't coming out till one a.m. Hope you took a big piss before you came through that door."

I flipped the hatch up and held it open for him to pass through first; then I pivoted around it and followed him behind the bar. McNamara, another member of the younger McSorley's generation, had been working the runner job during the day shift. He nodded at me, then untied his apron and untucked the garbage bag skirt from his belt. He handed me the plastic and the apron, and as I wrapped both around my waist and double-knotted the apron's string, McNamara slipped through the hatch and out into the morass. "Have fun!" he chirped on his way out. "Watch out for the maggots!"

In times of barroom stress, McSorley's servers sometimes referred to customers who annoyed them as maggots. It was a love tap of a slur, shared privately between employees and aimed at mostly harmless customers who take too long to order or sip Diet Cokes for hours on end. On a day as hectic as St. Patrick's, every patron can seem like a maggot, and taking time to deal with a customer's complaints about mugs that have too much head and not enough ale can give a bartender a panic attack.

Can't you see the empties all over the bar? We got a job to do, pal.

But at the beginning of my first Paddy's Day I was too excited to be mad at anyone, even when the first order I took — six lights for a lanky guy with glasses — turned into a minor fiasco because the customer disappeared into the crowd and never returned for his drinks. Luckily, with maybe a hundred drinkers packed into the front room, finding another taker wasn't going to be a challenge. I simply walked down to the end of the bar, where I recognized a couple of guys my dad had already told me about, Paddy's Day regulars who buy rounds of ale by the hundred and hand them out to everyone who walks past.

"You fellas need six more?" I asked, holding up the freshly poured light ales.

"We'll take 'em," they yelled back, "then bring another forty-four light and fifty dark on your way back."

I headed back toward the taps and told my dad to pour ninety-four ales. He glanced down the bar to make sure the guys placing the huge order looked like they'd be good for it. He locked eyes with one of them for a split second, gave a quick nod, and shouted, "Okay, mamacita!" While he pumped the ale he strung together a handful of his timeworn non sequitur catchphrases to get the night going. "Blow it out the hole, tonight, Jimbo! We're humming!"

When I woke up earlier that day, I expected to remember every moment of my shift, as if my first St. Patrick's Day would be a milestone on par with high school or college graduation. When the moment actually arrived, however, those six hours passed in a blur. There wasn't a spare moment to run to the bathroom or pour myself a mug of water from the tap, let alone take in the scene. I was too busy collecting empties, swiveling them around to line up the stems, sliding my fingers through the handles, grasping sixteen mugs at a time, and dunking them in the wash and rinse. When I wasn't cleaning mugs, I was taking orders, serving ales, taking cash and making change, trying to convince this one meathead not to sucker-punch a drunk European who was leaning on him, wiping glass off the bar when mugs got chipped, and reminding our waiters to serve plates of corned beef to customers at the bar.

Besides the work, I barely absorbed a single detail. I remembered seeing Mohawk wigs, cowboy hats, bowler hats, and leprechaun-style top hats—all in Kelly green. I remembered everyone in the bar singing "Happy Birthday to You" twice, "Take Me Out to the Ball Game" once, "God Bless America" twice, and "The Star Spangled Banner" once. I remembered a forties-ish blond who could barely keep her eyes open, sighing deeply and telling me she wished she could be twenty-five again. I remembered my ears latching on to the stupidest conversation I ever heard—three college dudes debating whether it was possible to "strengthen your cock muscles." (Two out of three believed it was.) I remembered a dwarf, dressed as a leprechaun, standing at the bar for about five minutes. I didn't remember much else, and I wonder if I really did remember that last part. All the memories felt gauzy, like I'd sped past them in a car and I could only piece together fragments of what I'd seen.

By 12:55 a.m., when I rang the wall-mounted chow bell behind the bar and my father bellowed, "All right, scummers! Last call!" my jeans were drenched from the knees down, my socks were squishing inside my work boots, and the dye from a beaded plastic necklace someone had put on me had mixed with sweat and drawn a green noose around my neck. I was toast.

The memory that most stuck with me from Paddy's Day was seeing my father run McSorley's at its wildest, like watching a character in the movies ride and tame a dragon, or some fanciful crap along those lines. That shift gave me a full understanding of how his decades of experience made my dad one of McSorley's legendary pumpmen, and why his reputation among the staff could be so fearsome. He would flash his temper every so often behind the bar, but that's not what made working beside him daunting. He was among the most laid-back managers when it came to how he expected the runner to line up empties and stack them underneath the bar. His hand-eye coordination and lifelong knowledge of the space around the taps meant he could grab however many mugs he needed, with either hand, pretty much anytime he wanted. His most noticeable bartending hangup was his need for a steady supply of freshly bleached rags, which he demanded I keep pristine, at the expense of seemingly more important tasks, even during the heaviest Paddy's Day rushes.

The thing that made working with my father so intimidating was his relentless, almost oppressive proficiency. He never slowed down, never lost focus, never put off a task for later when it could be done sooner. And as he ground along in perpetual excellence, he forced everyone around him to keep pace. If you didn't, he might not say anything, but he'd notice, and you'd notice him notice. When he looked down the bar and assessed your work and it wasn't good, your sense of self-worth was like an empty soda can getting flattened under tank treads.

My dad has always believed his way of doing things stems from his alcoholic past. To quit drinking, he needed to develop ironclad vigilance. He could never allow himself to take a break, to share just one round of ale with the lads and then hop back on the wagon the next morning. Absolutism was the only way to keep addiction from ruining him, and after more than thirty years of sobriety, of consistently stomping down any kernel of temptation, of never allowing an exception or a cheat day, that ethic spread into almost everything he did. I can't recall ever seeing him put off a household chore to watch a boxing match or a Mets game on TV. When he cooks, he washes the pots and pans before he sits down to eat his meal. Even though folding laundry has officially been "Rafe's chore" since I was about eight years old, once a load of clothing comes out of the dryer, my father gives me a grace period of about two minutes before he jumps in and starts folding. It's not because he's mad that I haven't started yet, it's just that he can't leave things undone.

Now imagine someone with that kind of obsessive streak and give him more than forty years of know-how and muscle memory at McSorley's, and you've got the recipe for tyrannical competence. No matter how hard you try to match my father's effort and attention to detail, you end up wilting before it. That's because you, like most people and like most everyone who works at McSorley's with my dad, allow yourself an occasional break. My father doesn't; that's the only way he knows how to survive.

That said, a lifetime spent with the man prepared me well to keep him satisfied behind the bar. I learned in my adolescence—when I would try to skip going to the local recreation center to work on my jump shot, and he'd tell me to "quit dicking around"—that making an effort was enough to keep the old man off my back. I probably also developed a hardier resistance to his three-word broadsides— *What the fuck?...Did you finish?...Are you kidding?*—than the rest of the McSorley's staff, who didn't grow up hearing them. Some of the younger waiters told me that stepping to the bar and ordering their first set of sixteen ales with my father staring down at them with his dismissive little squint was among the scariest moments of their lives. And, of course, since I'm his son, I have a safety net like no one else at the bar—no matter how much I piss him off, I know he still adores me, and I know he tends to go easier on me.

That first Paddy's Day, we moved faster behind the bar than I'd ever moved. And even when I felt as if keeping up with him was impossible—even when I sensed the exasperation start to creep in behind his eyeglasses after I forgot to bring the seltzer he asked for on two consecutive trips down the bar—taming the holiday crowd with my dad was a dream come true. Working next to him on my first Paddy's Day was like passing my McSorley's final exam.

Many of the bar's employees had amateur athletic back-grounds. The Irishmen played soccer and rugby and hurl-ing; my father and I each had strong high school basketball careers followed by piddling college ones. And while I'd stop a few hundred miles short of comparing the physical side of our work to what professional athletes do—there's a reason they make millions and we're worth minimum wage plus tips—I loved the teamlike mentality that set in during the busiest times at McSorley's. It felt like we were all work-ing in sync, limbs of the same organism that existed to wash mugs and pump ale and haul beer to the tables. On Paddy's Day, when the bar was packed and we were all hustling as fast as we could, when there was no time for wasted move-ment or a trip to the pisser or even a bite of hamburger, I felt the kind of euphoria that comes when you're part of a team and everything you do on the field or the court is turn-ing out right.

Never was that feeling more perfect than when I worked with my dad on Paddy's Day. If team chemistry is a product of familiarity and trust, it's hard to imagine any situation more familiar than toiling beside the man who raised me, in the bar where he brought me as a child, and doing the job I'd always watched him perform. The way each of us sensed where the other was, what the other needed, and when we needed it—that was innate. He didn't need to yell down the bar and say he needed empties for a big order that Timmy had just put in. He could start pumping, and before he poured eight mugs I'd have sixteen new ones, washed and gleaming, right in front of him. Thirty seconds later, I'd have sixteen more right behind them, and so on and so on until the order was filled. When he would turn around to make change in the cashbox, I'd lean over the rack to move two sets of four mugs over to his right-hand side and create space on his left for my next delivery of clean empties. When he hovered over the pumps to pour, that's when I'd slip behind him to make change for the customers on the bar. The give-and-take, the balance between manager and runner, felt perfect.

That feeling of connectedness, of real interdependence, is something I've never felt while working in an office, but it's a part of just about any pursuit that involves teamwork. Working at McSorley's with my father reminded me — strangely enough — of a description of early-twentieth-century lumberjacking that I read as a teenager. My father went through a heavy-duty fly-fishing phase around the time I was thirteen years old and the movie *A River Runs Through It* was released on video. It only led to one real-life fly-fishing trip for him and his brother, but he bought dozens of instructional books and literature about the sport. He even got me reading the author Norman Maclean's books about Montana, and the writer's description of sawing in a story called "Logging and Pimping and 'Your Pal, Jim'" always stuck with me:

As to the big thing, sawing, it is something beautiful when you are working rhythmically together — at times, you forget what you are doing and get lost in abstractions of motion and power. But when sawing isn't rhythmical, even for a short time, it becomes a kind of mental illness — maybe

ST. PATRICK'S DAY

*even something more deeply disturbing than that. It is as if
your heart isn't working right.*

Working with my dad on my first St. Patrick's Day, feeling our movements interlock behind the bar and getting
lost in the physical side of bar labor—call it McSorley's nir-
vana, call it just simply serving beers.

143

CHAPTER 8

Super Bowl Sunday

No one goes to a bar on Super Bowl Sunday. Chances are, even if you don't care about sports, you still end up at a friend's house to watch the game, dragging corn chips through seven-layer dip and straining to come up with a clever comment about the commercials. Hell, even if recent studies on long-term brain damage in National Football League players has convinced you never to watch another NFL broadcast, you probably don't end up choosing to boycott the event at a bar.

Super Bowl Sunday, a de facto national holiday that's arguably just as much about guzzling beer as it is about deciding the NFL championship, is one of the quietest shifts of the year in bars all over the country. And nowhere does business feel more dead that night than at McSorley's, where Super Bowl Sunday and Mother's Day share the honor of being traditionally the slowest workdays on the calendar.

This makes sense: Where's the last place you'd take your mom to make her feel loved on that special day? Probably a bar that touts its 116 years of banning women as a mark of historical authenticity; a place where female customers had to share a single men's room stall for sixteen years *after* they were allowed to start drinking there; a drinking hole that's likely to imbue Mom's new blouse with the rank, sweet odor of fresh ale; and an establishment whose most celebrated menu item—the cheddar plate—is almost certain to leave the heat of raw onion on her breath deep into the following afternoon. And if I'm wrong and the scene I've described is exactly how to make your mother's heart melt on the second Sunday in May, then it sounds like you have one hardcore mom. (Also, why haven't we seen you in McSorley's?)

A separate litany of factors makes McSorley's possibly the last bar on earth where most people would choose to spend their Super Bowl Sunday. More than 100 million Americans watch the event nowadays, and most of them tune in at home or at someone else's house party. But in a city as massive as New York, of course there are exceptions—foreign visitors who want to see why America cares so much about this game, business travelers whose Super Bowl house parties are back in Minneapolis or Omaha or Albuquerque, or just stragglers and loners who decide to get out of their apartments during the game. Among the grab bag of customers seeking a bar to watch the game, however, few are likely to find themselves in McSorley's, a place where until just a couple of years ago, the lone TV was an antique tube model with a twenty-four-inch screen and no high-definition picture. Many days, the staff at the bar didn't even bother turning it on, and when we did, it was always left on mute. By choosing to watch the Super Bowl at McSorley's, an NFL fan would be signing up for a version of the game that he can't hear and, by modern standards, he can barely see. Why accept these viewing conditions when there are dozens of sports bars within a few minutes' walk or cab ride? Even the unknowing customers who wander in on Super Bowl Sunday usually turn around and head for the door once they see the empty tables and the small, outdated television. Whoever's working that night will be lucky if these folks stick around for a five-minute courtesy drink.

Super Bowl Sunday was a different sort of rite of passage at McSorley's—the opposite of St. Patrick's Day. Okay, you can handle the busiest day of the year, but can you survive the doldrums of a dead bar, in the dead of winter, on the slowest night of the year?

I got summoned for my first Super Bowl shift late on the Thursday before the game. My father called me from the bar to let me know. "You planning to watch the game anywhere Sunday?" he asked. "Michael and Shane wanted to switch off so they can go to a party with the guys from Swift's." Swift Hibernian Lounge, a few blocks south of McSorley's, is an after-hours haunt for the McSorley's staff and also run by a mostly Irish crew. My dad expected business to be so slow that we could run McSorley's with half the manpower—my dad holding down the bar while I covered the front and back rooms as waiter. No chef. If anybody showed up they could have cold cuts, cheese plates, and maybe a burger if I got bored and felt like turning on the stove.

"Sure, I'll do Sunday." Even though I'd played and been a fan of sports for nearly my entire life, I never got into football growing up in Manhattan. The local ball field for youth soccer and baseball had no grass, just dirt. Neither my elementary school nor my high school had a football team or even a field to practice on. It didn't help that my father couldn't stand televised football. If I happened across an NFL game while channel-surfing on a Sunday afternoon, his ire seemed to compound itself with each passing minute of bloviating sports talk and Budweiser ads. By the time I hit high school, basketball became the focus of my athletic passion, and I didn't really have a reason to think much about football until I got to college in the Midwest. By then, it was too late: I checked out a few Big Ten games, mostly out of half-assed anthropological curiosity over what motivated my peers to wake up before six on a Saturday morning to partake of rituals like kegs and eggs (a surer recipe for vomit there may never have been), followed by five hours of standing in below-freezing temperatures. I never came up with the answers for my faux–social science investigation, but it didn't take long for me to decide that I didn't care enough about football to spend half of my Saturday freezing my nuts off.

Flash forward a few years, and it didn't feel like much of a sacrifice for me to skip a Super Bowl party to work at McSorley's. I told my dad this the Friday morning after he called to offer me the shift, and he cocked an eyebrow at me. "Why? It's gonna be dead. I was going to tell you to find something else to do." I sat across our kitchen table from him and tried to explain that there was something neat about having the bar to ourselves: just us and the photographs and portraits and newspaper tear sheets on the wall. Just us and the McSorley's ghosts, the two Bartholomews living inside a time capsule, paying little or no attention to the football game that was captivating the world around us.

"What have you been smoking?" my dad said. He was well acquainted with the romantic side of working at McSorley's, but by this point in his career he'd seen hundreds of dead nights. "Let me share a trade secret, Jimbo. You can appreciate the bar and make a buck at the same time."

I wasn't there yet. I hadn't seen everything McSorley's had to offer, and I still felt like I was collecting experiences: every different permutation, working different roles during different shifts on different holidays, during different seasons, and with different coworkers. I'd slogged through quiet nights on the bar during the dog days of August, but how was that different from working the floor in late January for Super Bowl Sunday? I told my father this and he shook his head in disbelief: "I'll tell you how the two shifts will be the same. You'll be on your feet all night and you'll go home with zilch."

Friday mornings were probably the worst time of the week to engage him in this kind of discussion. For most of his career, he began his workweek with a double shift from Thursday night to Friday day. That meant getting home around two on Friday morning, needing an hour to unwind before falling asleep, then waking up five hours later with sore knees and a tight back to rush over to McSorley's for seven more hours behind the bar. During that harried forty-five-minute stretch on Friday morning, when he sucked down coffee and combed his wispy brown hair before leaving for work, the chances of getting a pleasant reaction out of him, for any reason, were slim. Back in high school, I could have shown him a straight-A report card on a Friday morning, and he'd probably have glanced at it and asked which teachers' asses I had to kiss to get those grades. (Don't get me wrong. My father has always been an involved and supportive presence in my life. But if I bugged him in the middle of that double shift, he was gonna break my balls and then make up for it after work by bringing home chicken and ribs or comic books or a black plastic bag filled with *Penthouse* magazines. I'd always cringe and curse his dirty ass for bringing the latter, then wait an hour before locking myself in the bathroom to check it out.)

That particular Friday morning, once my dad saw there was no point in trying to talk me out of my excitement over working Super Bowl Sunday with him, he finished his bowl of raisin bran, double-knotted his bootlaces, and left to complete his double. I stayed at the kitchen table by myself for a few extra minutes, envisioning how I was about to pass another benchmark in this McSorley's apprenticeship, a milestone that existed only in my head and which none of the other bar employees gave a damn about, but which nonetheless meant the world to me.

When Sunday came around, at a few minutes past 5:30 p.m., I hopped on my bike to ride over to McSorley's. An icy cold had swept into the city over the weekend, and I pulled on two pairs of gloves and wrapped an extra scarf around my face to keep it from getting stung by the wind. When I got to the bar, I stashed my winter coat and accoutrements in the basement and headed inside to start my shift. It was a few minutes before six, but I figured I might as well get started, so I asked Pepe, who was finishing up at the bar, to toss me a waiter's jacket and a check pad. Out of the corner of my eye, I spotted my father standing in the doorway to the kitchen, tearing into a turkey sandwich. He noticed me and quickly put down the sandwich to grab his crotch with one hand and flip me off with the other. There was no reason for it, nor did he need one. I pretended to scratch my neck with my middle finger. If no customers showed up all night, we'd be entertaining ourselves with these dumb pranks till closing.

Pepe returned with the jacket. "You sure you need the book?" he asked, his voice dripping with sarcasm. "Tonight you'll be able to keep the tabs straight in your head." But right then, about a half hour before kickoff, business looked decent. A handful of drinkers stood at the bar and most of the tables were occupied. The crowd looked middle-aged, and I spotted enough Fodor's guides to assume that a majority of the customers weren't local, but at least we had bodies. As a waiter, when you work the entire floor instead of just the front or back room, even a slow night serving the stingiest customers can produce a respectable haul. I started to think maybe I'd luck out and get to work the Super Bowl and earn some money at the same time.

At the beginning of an evening waiter shift, the incoming server huddles with whoever's been working until then to settle the remaining balance on the day waiter's tabs. If the waiter who's about to clock out has open checks worth more than twenty dollars, he'll probably choose to go cash out with those groups, but smaller amounts usually get passed along to the replacement. Before I started hustling my tables on Super Bowl Sunday, I found Michael, who'd worked the floor that day, and asked how much I owed him. He surveyed the room, eyes darting from table to table while he added up the orders.

"Four ales and a small cheddar for the couple at the stove," he said. "Two ales for the guy in the corner; a round of six and a large fries for the kids back by the ladies' room.

Sooooo..." He paused to do the math in his head. "Forty even. The rest are taken care of."

I peeled two twenties off my roll of bills and passed them to Michael. "Good lad," he said, then wished me goodbye with a tap on the shoulder before dashing out the door to join Shane at the Swift's Super Bowl party. I wrote new checks for the three tables I'd bought from Michael, then circled the room to see if I could convince any of the groups who had already finished to order one more round of ale. At each stop, I heard a different rendition of *Thanks so much, but we're leaving to watch the game.*

So I killed ten minutes fixing the fire inside the potbelly stove. Between mid-October and April, there's an unspoken rule in McSorley's that the waiters must never let the fire burn out during business hours. If I got a good blaze going early in the night, I'd be able to ignore the stove until late in the shift, then build it up once more before closing. I wrapped a bar mop around a handle at the bottom of the stove, grasped the piece of hot metal, and shook back and forth to expel the ash that had accumulated underneath the fire. Then I placed about six pieces of dry scrap wood on top of the red-hot coals and closed the stove's hatch. Five minutes later, I pulled it open and flames shot out. This meant it was time to dump in two shovelfuls of coal, close the hatch once more, and let that sucker heat up. After that, I popped into the men's room to scrub the soot off my hands and was ready to do another sweep around the tables.

By then, the bar was empty except for the three tables I'd inherited from Michael and a lurker nursing two dark ales at the bar. At the first two tables I approached—the couple with the cheese plate and the trio with the fries—both groups requested their checks before I could ask if they'd like another round. They were headed to friends' nearby apartments to watch the game. When I walked toward the single customer seated at the front room's corner table — my last customer — my steps became wary, as if tiptoeing over to the guy might make him more likely to stay.

When I arrived in front of him, he didn't immediately ask for his bill. That felt reassuring. "Can I get you another round?" I asked. He uttered a long, unmistakably French "euuuhhhhh" in response. "Wa-teur?" he continued. "Is it possible to have *un verre d'eau*? I'm sorry, my English." A glass of water. I was fucked. I filled a mug and brought it over, and five minutes later he asked for *l'addition*, left a quarter tip, and was out the door.

We had the TV tuned in to the Super Bowl pregame show, and by the time some glitter-cheeked pop star was belting out "The Star Spangled Banner," the bar was empty except for me and my dad. I'd gotten my wish — six and a half hours to kill and no work to do at McSorley's on a Sunday night.

Bar work at McSorley's bends time. When the place is packed and the line outside extends halfway down to Third Avenue, seven hours can pass in what feels like fifteen minutes. On a desolate Super Bowl Sunday night, the hours warp and elongate. Between seven and eight, I must have glanced at the big wall clock above the bar a dozen times. That's once every five minutes. And every time I looked up, I thought, *A half hour must have passed by now,* and the clock confirmed that my sure-shot thirty minutes had in fact been seven. My most ridiculous misjudgment came at 7:39. I

My father outside McSorley's
in the 1980s.

My dad serving ales down the
bar in the early '80s.

One of the first shifts we worked
together, back in 2006.

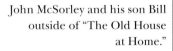

John McSorley and his son Bill
outside of "The Old House
at Home."

'Tis the season for vulgar holiday decorations.

Pepe and my father wearing green bow ties for Paddy's Day.

A bust of President John F. Kennedy sits above a print of Nat Fein's Pulitzer-winning photo of Babe Ruth.

McSorley's owner Matthew Maher working the taps a few years before he bought the bar in 1977.

My dad and Richie the King before opening the bar on a weekend morning.

A medieval-style mace hangs high above McSorley's bar, next to a pair of Civil War–era shackles from the Andersonville prison camp, and not far from a "Be Good or Be Gone" sign.

My father behind the bar with Brendan Buggy.

Bart's perch.

The McSorley Nine portrait, where only eight players are pictured.

The McSorley Chowder Club photograph that I would stare at as a child.

Before a shift during the holiday season in the late 2000s.

My father with a handful of freshly poured mugs.

A taxidermied fluke affixed to the wall behind the bar.

The bartending duo I most loved watching on Saturday mornings: Tommy Lloyd and my dad.

My dad and Teresa pose during a shift.

A pair of aged coconuts hanging from the ceiling. Bartenders occasionally try to convince customers that they are shrunken heads.

Me, working a runner shift circa 2011.

Bart lays down the law on Paddy's Day.

Catnapping with one of the many "Minnies" who've prowled McSorley's throughout history.

My father serving McSorley's ale from the Stanley Cup on the day of the NY Rangers 1994 NHL championship parade. (Tim Whelan)

My dad shoots the breeze with Teresa's husband, Gregory De La Haba.

What bar would be complete without the mythical jackalope?

My dad signing a
copy of *The McSorley
Poems.*

Standing in the back room to introduce my father during the release
party of *The McSorley Poems Volume II.*

A pair of handcuffs that once
belonged to Harry Houdini.

Posing with Teresa during one of my
afternoon waiter shifts.

Michael and Scott, the managers
who've run weekend nights at McSorley's for much of the past twenty years.

A pair of shoes dangles from th[e] back room ceiling. There's no proof, but my father guessed th[at] they belonged to George McSo[rley,] one of Old John's sons who die[d in] a 1906 diving accident.

Me, pumping soap into the sink and almost certainly laughing at a dirty joke.

Taking a load off at the window table after closing down McSorley's on New Year's Eve, 2013.

The WWI wishbones, before they were dusted in 2011.

checked the time, went to the kitchen to grab a handful of saltines, then jumped behind the bar to help myself to a Diet Coke. Ate a couple of crackers, washed them down with a swig. *That felt like five minutes* ran through my head. So I looked at the clock. It read 7:41.

I looked at my father. He had come out from behind the bar—no need to stand there and keep up appearances on a night like this—and he was sitting in the back room, near the TV, looking at nothing in particular. He'd turned up the sound on the game, and he must have been lending half an ear to its progress, since he'd shift his attention to the screen for important third downs and touchdown replays. But mostly he just seemed zonked, like the wax statue of a McSorley's bartender.

Over his years at the bar, he'd developed a mental on/off switch that I didn't yet possess. During slow shifts, a restless mind was torture. I tried to occupy myself by studying the walls. I reread old favorites: my dad's twenty-year certificate; the framed British broadsheet from 1815 that reported the beginning of Napoleon's Waterloo campaign; a 1970 newspaper column called "The Inquiring Fotographer," which featured headshots of regular New Yorkers answering the week's question, "Has the atmosphere in McSorley's Ale House changed since women gained admittance?" At the bottom of the column was the face of Frank "the Slob" Slovensky, much younger than the gruff onion peeler I'd known as a child, whose response was characteristically cranky (he even gave the reporter a slightly fake name, "O'Slovensky," as a sly nod to his adoption into an old Irish pub, despite his Polish-Ukrainian roots): "I'd say the atmosphere we had before women were admitted has pretty much returned. At first, they came in numbers and there was some unpleasantness. Once the barrier came down, the women's libbers lost interest. That's women for you."

I returned to drawings and photographs I'd examined dozens of times over the years, hoping to spot a new detail. I counted the eight players in the McSorley Nine. I looked at the panoramic group photos of McSorley's friends-and-family outings from the 1940s and spotted the bald, cigar-chomping prankster who sat on one side of the group at the beginning of the film's exposure, then ran to the other side before the camera had captured the entire image, so that he'd appear in two places at the same time. I looked at the picture of a young Charlie Sheen outside the bar with his arms around Brendan and Richie the King, and it made me remember how badly I wished to have met the *Major League* star back then, when my father told me Sheen had been to the bar.

It was a lovely trip down memory lane, but it took all of fifteen minutes. Meanwhile, my father had barely moved. He's the kind of man who would have scoffed and cracked a joke about "boogah boogah vegetarians" if someone suggested meditation to him, but whether or not he'd ever admit it, he knew how to find his zen at McSorley's. "Just zone out, Jim," he told me when he noticed me pacing up and down the front room. "We got a long way to go."

So I sat down in the back, one table away from my dad, and tried to clear my mind. I failed, so I wound up doing the one thing I'd planned to avoid by coming to work that evening. I watched the Super Bowl.

For the first time in my life, I saw two hours pass without a single customer stepping inside McSorley's. My father and I just sat in the back room, with him drifting blissfully about in his fugue state and me struggling to care about the Super Bowl. During the first half of the game, the closest we got to seeing any action came at the end of the first and second quarters, when half a dozen employees and regulars called the phone behind the bar to ask if their box in the gambling pool had paid off. My dad broke into consciousness to laugh each time the phone rang. "Just watch, Jim," he told me. "It's always some skel who wins. Murphy's Law."

He paid attention for the first time during the halftime show, when it was time to deliver a patented *get off my lawn* old man rant about how the pop stars performing represented everything that's vapid and wrong about America. No matter who appeared on screen—whether the performer was Beyoncé, U2, or Madonna—my dad would pretend not to know the artists' names. I'm pretty sure he knew who they were, but he took pride in not recognizing celebrities. To him, they were just good-looking people who got rich by making lowest-common-denominator music or movies or TV programs, and no matter how famous they happened to be, they hadn't created something worth being recognized by name. I'm almost certain he knew exactly who Bono was, but the time the U2 frontman appeared in McSorley's, my father looked at the Irish rock royalty and said, "Boner who?"

Midway through the halftime show, the circus arrived. No, it wasn't a sudden influx of customers. Instead, in the span of about five minutes, two of the great McSorley's hangers-on of the past twenty years showed up and took over the night: Johnny Wadd and Katz.

It's hard to call them employees, but these characters definitely perform a job at the bar, and their kind has been part of the McSorley's ecosystem for generations. They are the night watchmen and local gofers, guys who are retired, living off pensions, sometimes collecting disability, who hang around McSorley's and do the little things that nobody on staff wants to do. They tend to be either lifelong East Village residents or former regulars who spent so much time at the bar that as they reached old age and slowed down their drinking, they kept showing up and got absorbed into the running of the place. They picked up odd jobs, tasks like fetching coffee and kaiser rolls for the morning crew; or keeping the doorman company on Friday and Saturday nights and checking IDs when he ran inside to take a leak; or showing up at closing time to sweep the day's sawdust and crumpled napkins and fallen french fries, to give the weary waiters a break. Each of these acts was worth a tip, somewhere between five and twenty bucks, and even though a waiter or doorman had the right to turn down help, most of the staff honored the unspoken ethic that if the guy showed up to do the work, it was wrong to deny him a chance to earn ten dollars here and there. Plus, even though the staff might not always *need* help from the hangers-on, it was useful to have them around. You could almost call them the glue that held McSorley's together.

These guys also split the overnight job, a position that entails sitting in the dark inside McSorley's between the hours of 2 and 8 a.m., until Pepe and the morning waiter arrive to open the bar. Overnight shifts paid about fifty dollars and required the watchman to fill a few ketchup bottles, keep an eye on the stove so the place wouldn't burn down, and hopefully make it to a phone to call the police if someone tried to break in. Mostly, though, the overnight man would just lie back on a row of chairs, close his eyes, and try not to imagine what spirits might be drifting around a 160-year-old tavern.

The hanger-on I saw the most of growing up was Frank the Slob, who didn't work the overnight but peeled his way through a fifty-pound sack of onions each morning, and whose McSorley's renown was linked to Tourette's-fueled rants that Frank would holler from the bathroom stall anytime he had to take a crap. The other members of Frank's generation of overnight guys showed up at closing, way too late for preadolescent me to see them often, but I knew them through my father's stories. Cyclops was a movie stuntman with one glass eye and an under-control taste for illicit substances. When the movie *Titanic* came out at the end of 1996, he told everyone at the bar that he had an unforgettable role in the scene where the ship finally sinks. His was the body dangling from the stern that fell and ricocheted off the propeller, he said. Who knows if it was true—there's no way to see the poor schmuck's face before he takes that swan dive into the Atlantic Ocean. After Cyclops, there was Mychek, a wraithlike recovered heroin addict whom my dad called the skinniest living person he'd ever seen.

A generation before Cyclops, Mychek, and Frank the Slob, my father remembered an overnight character named Spuds from the seventies. Spuds was an older distant relative of some clan connected to the bar, and he had a surgically installed shunt in his side, from which he needed to periodically turn a valve to release waste from his cirrhotic liver. Spuds could barely drag himself up and down the cellar stairs, yet the staff still made him lug fifty-pound sacks of onions and potatoes up to the kitchen whenever he worked. It could be cruel and unforgiving, but McSorley's still operated according to an old-world pecking order, and the hangers-on were at the bottom—even when they might be kin. *You want to be around the bar? Well, this is what you gotta do.*

At the same time, for the down-and-out types who tended to become overnight men, picking up McSorley's scutwork was an easy and consistent way to supplement their fixed incomes, and for men who'd outlived their loved ones or didn't have many people left in their lives, the bar became a surrogate family. It's a family that might appear cold and demented to folks on the outside, but the bonds were real, and guys like Spuds, Mychek, and Frank the Slob could count on McSorley's barmen to look after them when they got sick and injured, to make sure that if they were laid up in the hospital, someone would visit, and to help these life-long misfits and loners feel like they weren't quite so alone.

The overnight characters usually didn't spend much time inside McSorley's during business hours. They'd pass through and say hello on the way back to the kitchen for a sandwich or a cup of tea, but they mostly lingered out front, lounging on the antique wooden ale barrels that frame the entrance. They know better than to take up space inside McSorley's while the place is busy, so they usually hang outside until a few minutes before last call.

The night my father and I covered the Super Bowl, however, Johnny Wadd and Katz knew that business would be dead, so around 9 p.m., as the third quarter started, they shuffled into the bar one after the other. There was no reason to shoo them out—we weren't serving any customers, so I brought Katz his customary two cans of Diet Coke and pulled out a chair for Johnny. Johnny reached down and cradled his wad, a football-sized hernia, and collapsed into the seat. "Thanks, Rafe, you're a sweetheart," he said with the kind of gravelly New York accent that was becoming hard to find in the city's younger generation. "I swear to God I'm dying," Johnny added, panting. "I can barely make it up and down the stairs."

"Johnny, you mook," my father answered, "we're gonna have to bury your ass if you don't get that thing fixed, and then we're gonna need two separate plots—one for your body and one for your wad." The hernia was a grave hazard to Johnny's health. He had suffered the injury almost twenty years earlier, but thanks to a paralyzing fear of hospitals, Johnny had never gotten the simple surgery to repair his abdominal wall. Over the intervening years, his intestine had poked out from the muscle tear and had gradually grown to its current grotesque size. If the intestine ruptured or became strangulated, Johnny could develop severe gangrene or a possibly fatal blood infection. But since he was already in his early fifties and hadn't had a checkup since he was a young man—and because the hernia still hadn't killed him—Johnny seemed to believe he could carry that blimp of stray intestine around in his pants indefinitely. He even used his hernia for prop comedy, letting people pose for pictures next to it and boasting to naïve customers that his nickname was Johnny Wadd because his bulge was bigger than seventies porn star John Holmes's thirteen-inch penis.

My father had known Johnny, who was born and raised two doors down from McSorley's, since my dad moved in above the bar and Johnny was in high school. Johnny's uncle, Tony "Fats" Milone (because he weighed five hundred pounds), had been a McSorley's chef and was photographed in the bar for a *Playboy* spread in 1969. Johnny was a fixture of East Seventh Street, as much a part of the block over the past forty years as St. George Ukrainian Catholic

Church or McSorley's itself. He inherited the rent-controlled apartment he grew up in and never left. By the time I got to know him, Johnny was splitting time between working as a McSorley's overnight man and helping out at the Peter Jarema Funeral Home two blocks east of the bar.

Johnny walked with a hunchback shuffle, he was mostly bald, and he'd lost several teeth on account of fearing dentists as much as he dreaded doctors, which gave him the hollow cheeks and pursed mouth of a rodent. But Johnny knew how to work his woeful appearance, and he could charm customers in a dozen different ways. Sometimes he was the cuddly East Village grandpa women cooed over, sometimes he was the sharp-tongued, seen-it-all New Yorker who could get away with mouthing off to anyone, and sometimes he morphed into this gonzo mélange of impulse and humor that seemed like it could only exist inside McSorley's. When I was in high school, he convinced a visiting Japanese TV crew to film a segment celebrating him as the quintessential New York neighborhood character. Good-natured, irascible, folksy—they called him Johnny San, and the name stuck around McSorley's for a few years, until Johnny's wad outgrew his fifteen minutes of Far Eastern fame.

If you ask anybody who works at the bar—or anybody who's spent substantial time around East Seventh Street, for that matter—every one of them will have a list of personal favorite Johnny stories. Here are mine: Once, while I was working the shithouse on a Friday night, I stepped outside to get some air and found Johnny planted on a barrel. While we exchanged bar gossip, three hip kids in their midtwenties passed us on the sidewalk, and Johnny and I both managed to overhear the same morsel of conversation. One of them reached out in front of the group, demonstrating the way he'd stimulate an imaginary lover, and he said, "I just wanted to slide my finger in her ass like this!" Johnny, not missing a beat, yelled to them, "YEAH! Give it a good sniff!" The startled trio scrambled down the block as fast as they could, while Johnny had coined a catchphrase that remained in heavy rotation among the bar staff for years: *Oh yeah, Jimbo! Give it a good sniff!*

Johnny's other all-timer came inside the bar, on a rowdy Saturday night when he wound up defusing what might have become a full-bar brawl. Two tables had gotten into a YAN-KEES SUCK! BOS-TON SUCKS! call-and-response battle that escalated into something more serious. One guy (on the Yankees side of the dispute) was about six foot five and 230 pounds, with the expansive shoulders and vein-popping biceps of a body builder. It's unclear whether something specific set him off or he was just drunk and full of 'roid rage, but in the blink of an eye this customer sprang out of his seat to tower over the group who'd been taunting Yankee fans. He tore his shirt off with a single, one-handed swipe and pounded his chest. "Come on, you bastards! Right now! RIGHT NOW!" The group of guys he was challenging exchanged incredulous looks, but as soon as they realized the provocation wasn't all in good fun, they stiffened up and the smiles dropped from their faces: *We're not backing down.*

By now, everyone inside the bar had caught wind of the brewing disaster. The crowd that had been roaring thirty seconds earlier was now hushed. That's when Johnny leapt into the fray and started hugging the enraged muscleman. "It's okay, big guy," he said, now rubbing the customer's bare chest, tracing the lines of the guy's tribal tattoos with his fingertips. "You're okay," Johnny added. "You're okay. You're a beefcake. Now relax. Everything's fine. We all know you're a beefcake." At first, nobody knew what to do. Johnny's intervention made no sense. But he kept rubbing the guy's pecs and murmuring the word *beefcake* until everyone inside the bar burst out laughing, including the shirtless instigator, who shared a deep, hysterical hug with Johnny Wadd and then exchanged high fives with the customers he had planned to tear limb from limb. When he returned to his seat, the entire back room gave up the YAN-KEES SUCK! chant for "BEEF-CAKE! BEEF-CAKE! BEEF-CAKE!" By the time the bar had returned to normalcy, Johnny Wadd had already shuffled back outside to plop himself down on the barrel.

When Johnny and Katz were around each other, as they were that Super Bowl evening, they bickered like an old married couple. Katz might have been the only character in the bar's milieu who could make Johnny seem normal by comparison. Short, squat, and built like a three-hundred-pound blueberry, Katz had tousled white hair and eyeglass frames big enough to be windshields. Before McSorley's, Katz had been a collection agent, but with his squeaky whine, it was hard to imagine him convincing many people to settle their debts.

Katz was beyond eccentric. He was soft-spoken and generally sweet to the bartenders and waiters—probably thanks to familiarity and because he needed to stay in our good graces to keep his night watchman gig. He was like a walking encyclopedia of Major League Baseball facts and statistics, but unlike many know-it-all sports fans, Katz almost never volunteered evidence of his mastery of the game's minutiae. It would only come up when someone asked him.

I remember being amazed the first time my father coaxed a demonstration out of him. He told me to ask Katz any question about baseball, and I came up with a pretty run-of-the-mill piece of trivia about Mets pitcher Bobby Ojeda nearly slicing his finger off with a pair of hedge clippers. Katz nailed it, but just about any New Yorker who was alive in 1988 would remember that snafu.

"No way," my dad said. "That was too easy. All right, Katz, which batter made the last out for the Cleveland Indians when they lost the 1954 World Series to the Giants?"

It was a fact my father recalled from his Ohio youth, and Katz talked himself to the answer: "Well, that's the series where Willie Mays made the famous catch over his head. But that was game one. Johnny Antonelli started and won game two for the Giants, and I remember him coming in for the save to clinch game four—it was a sweep. The last out was a pop fly, and I think it was a pinch hitter... Dale Mitchell!"

"Holy shit, Katz," my dad replied. "You don't have to pull the trash tonight, you just earned your tip." My father handed over the five-dollar bill he usually left behind the bar for Katz, who earned it by dragging the two trash bags from behind the bar out to the sidewalk for pickup so we wouldn't have to. Then my dad looked down the bar to me: "I told you, Jimbo. Katz knows his stuff. You pull the trash tonight."

What made Katz a genuine bar curiosity, however, was the manner in which he occasionally harassed customers. You'd think Matty would have avoided hiring a night watchman who freaked out the patrons, but Katz knew not to set foot inside McSorley's until a few minutes before last call, so he couldn't do much to hurt the business. Sometimes it actually helped to have Katz around, when his presence helped goose lingering tipplers out the door and allowed the staff to clean up and go home.

Katz, you see, had a couple of unsettling habits. For starters, he meowed. Often, and without warning or explanation. This had to stem from some measure of identification with his last name, but he didn't adopt any other feline affectations—no licking his pretend paws, no nuzzling into people's laps. (Perhaps we should be thankful for this.) All he would do was find a table, sit down, and between sips of Diet Coke, he would meow. It was a realistic meow, not too loud, and not directed at anyone in particular, and that's what made it so disturbing. He could unnerve people without trying. My father and I would just about fall down laughing at the way customers' expressions would shift from amused to baffled to disturbed to *We're gonna die if we don't get out of this bar* with each successive meow.

That was the effect Katz had on bystanders when he wasn't trying to menace them. Every once in a while, though, he'd decide he didn't like the cut of somebody's jib, and things would get even weirder. The customers he targeted tended to be suits—Wall Street guys, lawyers getting off work late, consultants visiting from Texas—and their over-dressed dates. He wouldn't meow or even say a word to them, but eventually someone in the group would notice Katz staring at them from a nearby table—short, shaped like an overgrown guinea pig, and pointing at them with his fist, his pinkie and thumb extended like horns. It was Katz's hex, and he kept it trained on whoever rubbed him the wrong way until they either left or complained to a waiter or bartender. If the group had tipped well and treated the servers right, we'd tell Katz to knock it off and sit somewhere else. If the customers had been pricks, however, the hex might stay on them till they decided to drink up and go home.

On Super Bowl Sunday, we witnessed Katz's crazy reach a new level. He walked in that night with one hand wrapped in a soft cast and clutching a small plush dolphin with the other. The injury was news to me and my father, and Katz explained that he'd had an accident while crossing the street. While he was walking, he said, a bus tried to make a wide turn around him, cut it too close, and brushed him. It could have been worse, but the impact knocked Katz to the ground and he suffered a fractured wrist. Despite the close call, Katz was in high spirits. He planned to sue the city and receive a meaty settlement.

By this point in the story, he'd already sat down, placed the stuffed dolphin on the table, and rested his injured hand atop it. "That's why the doctor gave me Mel Gibson," Katz said. "He said I need to rest my wrist." I looked at my dad and he looked back with the same quizzical eyes. We both turned to Johnny Wadd, seated a table away from Katz, as if to say, "Did you also hear that?"

"What the fuck are you going on about?" Johnny asked. "Mel Gibson?"

"Yeah, Mel Gibson the dolphin," Katz answered. "Ain't that right, Mel? They made you come with me because I'm a Jew and they had to punish you for being an anti-Semite."

As if this weren't already absurd enough, Katz raised his voice an octave and responded as Mel Gibson: "Go to hell, you goddamned Jew! Get me outta here. I'm an Oscar-winner!"

More looks of concern were exchanged among me,

Johnny, and my dad. Some giggles, too—how is anyone supposed to keep a straight face through stuff like this? Katz's
ventriloquist act continued as we sat and watched the rest of
the Super Bowl, and not once did he break character to
acknowledge that Mel Gibson was an inanimate stuffed
marine mammal, about ten inches from nose to tail. Katz
and Mel argued over calls in the game, whether to drink
Diet Coke or dark ale, who was the best quarterback in the
NFL, and whether the Holocaust was real. Katz asked me to
check the Super Bowl pool to see if Mel Gibson had a
chance to win the three-hundred-dollar pot at the end of
the third quarter. Johnny Wadd tried to coax Katz back
toward reality, but his nagging calls for Katz to snap out of it
were only met with more invective from the dolphin.

"You think I don't know you're a Jew, too, Johnny? You
go to hell with the rest of them!"

Eventually, Johnny gave up. "Whatever you say, Katz," he
said. "You're turning into a real fuckin' fruit loop. A talking
dolphin—and they bust my balls about this hernia!" He
grabbed his wad and shook his crotch: "If that stuffed animal is Mel Gibson then who the hell is this? Tom fuckin'
Cruise? Give me a break."

And that was pretty much how the night went. My dad
and I watching in disbelief as Johnny Wadd, Katz, and Mel
Gibson the dolphin went round and round, insulting each
other like characters in a vaudeville act. Every half hour or
so a customer would walk in to check the Super Bowl score,
but if any of these patrons had planned to stay and order a
round of ale, they probably changed their minds within seconds of seeing our two night watchmen quibbling over lotto
numbers and the true word of God.

When we shut down the bar that night, with Johnny

sprawled on a bank of chairs, Katz locking the front door behind me, and no light inside McSorley's but the glow of 2 a.m. infomercials emanating from the back room, my father met me on the sidewalk before we hopped on our bikes and rode west.

"Well, Jimbo, we didn't make any money," he said. "But you were right about one thing. I'm glad we got to work tonight, because we might not see anything that crazy for another twenty years."

CHAPTER 9

The McSorley Poet

Between worn arms, near the dark stove,
Orange ears twitching, weaving cat dreams;
Sawdust-tailed beggar, warm friend to all,
To be again graced, the scarred seat waits
— "RED," BY GENE HALL, 1995

MCSORLEY'S HAS ALWAYS ATTRACTED POETS, but my favorite verse about the bar wasn't written by any of the heralded bards who drank there over the years. Not the E. E. Cummings one that begins "*I was sitting in mcsorley's. / Outside it was New York and beautifully snowing. / Inside snug and evil.*" Not Reuel Denney's "McSorley's Bar," which contains a couplet whose beauty never fails to leave me gobsmacked: "*The grey-haired men considered from their chairs / How time is emptied like a single ale.*" Nothing by Dylan Thomas, who never published a poem about the bar but who drank there often enough to get eighty-sixed by John Smith once upon a time. Not Woody Guthrie, a poet of sorts, who visited McSorley's in 1943, when *LIFE* magazine photographed him strumming his guitar for a group of workingmen huddled over mugs of ale in the front room. And not Joseph Mitchell, whose *New Yorker* prose about the bar carried the simple beauty of poetry and perhaps best captured the essence of McSorley's.

The poem that has always sent me reeling with joy and heartbreak and nostalgia wasn't published anywhere, and it was written by Gene Hall, a McSorley character best known for fixing anything that broke inside the bar with gaffer's tape. Clocks, chairs, typewriters—it didn't matter. Tape was the answer. Gene was a retired member of the merchant marine who lived in one of the apartments above McSorley's. During the couple of decades he spent at 15 East Seventh Street, Gene functioned as a quick-fix handyman who could be called downstairs at a moment's notice to patch up minor malfunctions around the bar. Perhaps as a testament to the practical skills he picked up during years at sea, or maybe because it took a full-blown catastrophe to get anyone at McSorley's to call a professional plumber or electrician, Gene's short-term solutions often became semipermanent. Gene was quiet—it's easy for me to recall his black mustache and dark bottle-cap glasses, but I can't remember speaking to him once during my childhood. But my father and Michael and Scott and all the other guys I looked up to talked about Gene with a measure of reverence that made it clear he wasn't just another local screwball who hung around the bar to pick up odd jobs. And even if Gene and I never shared a face-to-face connection, I felt like he was whispering in my ear every time I read the poem he wrote in memory of Sawdust, the McSorley's cat I grew up playing with on Saturday mornings.

"Red" is a four-line poem about a bar cat named both Sawdust and Red. I called him Sawdust. He was an orange tabby, and the last great cat to spend his entire life—1985 to 1995—at the bar. I grew up dangling strips of cold-cut ham and turkey for him to claw out of the air, then sitting beside him and petting him in his favorite spot, a chair behind the potbelly stove. He was fearless and outgoing— my father could set a mug of water on the bar and Sawdust would leap up and start lapping it up between amazed customers. He was daring—my dad loved to tell the story of the time Sawdust sprang from a hidden, dark corner of the bar to sink his claws into a banker's thigh, right in the spot where a roach had passed moments before. Mischievous and tender and ever ready for some new friend to scratch behind his ears, Sawdust was adored by pretty much every person who met him, and he died too soon.

When my father returned from work one Friday evening in 1995 and told me that Sawdust had developed some form of feline cancer and had to be put to sleep, I remember thinking it was impossible. He was only ten. At home, my family's neurotic house cat Bismarck (obtained through a McSorley's cat litter and distant cousins with Sawdust) was ancient, nasty, and showed no signs of slowing down. Why'd we have to lose Sawdust?

Gene must have felt the same way, because he typed four timeless lines about Sawdust (though he called him Red), which were then framed and hung on the wall behind the stove, just above the chair where Sawdust loved to sleep. The final image in Gene's poem, of the empty seat, marked by Sawdust's scratches and awaiting an impossible return, brings the image of the cat coiled in slumber straight to the front of my mind, as if I'm seeing it in real life. And at the same time, it reminds me how forevermore I'll see Sawdust only in my memories.

I love this poem because it connects me to a specific time in my bar upbringing. If not for that overpowering bit of nostalgia, I'd choose any of my father's poems as the most vital bits of McSorley's verse ever put down on paper.

Back in 1976, shortly after my father got sober, he traveled to Vancouver, British Columbia, to visit Cates Park, where Malcolm Lowry wrote much of *Under the Volcano*. It was an alcoholic's final pilgrimage, my dad's chance to pay his last respects to this patron saint of drunkards. When my father was drinking, Lowry had provided him with a fatalistic ideal of how addiction, even at its most destructive, could produce something transcendent. Sure, Lowry drank himself to death. And by most accounts, he sank into abject misery as his alcoholism progressed and gradually overwhelmed his literary talent. But along the way, he wrote *Under the Volcano*. Was that not worth it?

When my father was depressed and drinking, the answer to that question—fucking A it's worth it!—seemed clear. When he saw no way out, when he assumed he'd just keep boozing till he died—the dead alcoholic son of a dead alcoholic father—that inevitability could even feel inspiring: *I know I'm screwed. Frank fucked me up as a kid and I've only fucked myself up worse. But while I'm around, maybe I can create something that matters.*

So when my father stood along a path named Malcolm Lowry Walk on a raw and gray Pacific Northwest afternoon and looked out on Vancouver Harbour, not only was he saying goodbye to the vodka-infused self-hatred that he'd carried throughout his adult life, but he was also walking away from the writerly ambition that had been his sense of purpose in those years. That creative impulse had kept him from being just another Bowery wino, but the practice of writing had become too tangled with the habit of drinking for my father to give up one and continue the other. To have a shot at a better life, he had to quit both.

So he wrapped rubber bands around his manuscripts, shoved them inside leather portfolios, and shoved those inside shoe boxes: the Argonautica novel; the punctuation-less screed about bedridden stroke victims trapped in their own minds; the sci-fi tale of New York terrorized by two-hundred-pound rats. He locked them away in file cabinets and put his energy toward staying clean, working at McSorley's, and devoting himself to family life. Besides love notes to my mother and birthday poems for me, my father gave up creative writing for the better part of two decades.

But he never let go of the written word. When I was young, the first thing my friends would say upon visiting our apartment was always "You have a lot of books." My mother, who'd left the hotel and corporate kitchens she had cooked in before I was born to teach hospitality management and culinary arts at a City University of New York campus in downtown Brooklyn, had a wall of cookbooks opposite our front door. Each room in our place had its own mammoth bookcase — a shelf for my father's accumulated dictionaries, musty Modern Library editions of *Crime and Punishment* and *Moby-Dick* with their onionskin-thin pages, a corner filled with novels and essays and letters by Lowry, Kurt Vonnegut, Jr., Norman Mailer, and other practitioners of the virtuosic, manly prose my father admired in the seventies. Even the TV "entertainment center" in our living room was more bookcase than anything else. The floor-to-ceiling complex of shelves and cabinets was entirely stuffed with books, except for a small, square space in the middle to house a television set.

Although I don't remember seeing my father sit down at a typewriter when I was a kid, I understood that he'd been a writer, saw his creative writing MFA diploma hanging on our wall, and heard about his unpublished novels. He tried to build the foundation of a literary sensibility in me, insisting that we spend Sunday mornings reading *Huckleberry Finn* aloud to each other as soon as I got far enough in school to speak full sentences. It didn't work. Twain time might as well have been Sunday school to me, and until my midteens I pretty much always chose going to the movies with my mom or playing pickup basketball over cracking open a book.

At times, I could even be contemptuous of my father's passion for reading and writing. I have no clue what motivated this occasional nastiness, other than the wanton tantrums of adolescence and the impulse to lash out at one's parents. It was during one of these moments when I committed what I now think of as the most shameful act of my youth.

I was nine or ten years old. It was a Sunday afternoon and my parents took me to a diner a few blocks north of our apartment for lunch. I can't remember what, if anything, made me angry that day. Probably, my dad had called me out for getting outhustled on a rebound during a rec-league basketball game that morning. Late in the meal, as I picked over my remaining french fries and avoided a mayonnaise-oozing cup of coleslaw, my mother asked me about a recent playdate with a friend from elementary school, inadvertently hitting a nerve with my father.

After the playdate, when my dad had come to pick me up from the other family's apartment, my friend's mom gushed to him about friends of theirs whose son would soon publish his first book. The kid was the same age as me, and his forthcoming book was some cutesy how-to gimmick about growing up in New York from the point of view of a real third grader. The notion drove my dad crazy. The child author's family was wealthy and connected: address on Park Avenue, Dad in finance, Mom a high-powered media somebody, attending the prestigious and completely unaffordable Dalton School. He was the kind of kid whose parents dress him up in Brooks Brothers suits—and who actually likes it. He was the type of character guaranteed to rankle my father's working-class sensibility. And because this kid's family knew everybody who was anybody, this nine-year-old was getting a chance to achieve a dream that had eluded my father.

"Next time Rafe goes over there you better pick him up," he told my mom. "I don't think I can take that again."

"Why?" she asked. "What happened?"

"Well, I walked up there and the girl's mom wouldn't stop jabbering about some other kid they know who's so brilliant and who's going to publish a book. Give me a break. It's just some rich kid whose parents pulled strings for him."

Even at that young age, I felt aligned with my father's sense of class conflict. I'd never met this boy, but I didn't like him, either. But I was still stewing over our basketball argument, so I decided to say something I knew would hurt my father: "You're just mad because he has a book and you don't."

As soon as the words jumped off my tongue, I knew I'd crossed a line. My chest tightened, and I felt like a fist had risen up from my belly and lodged itself in my throat. I stared down at the paper place mat in front of me, filled with little square ads for neighborhood dry cleaners and bakeries. I couldn't look up at my dad, who didn't even respond. He didn't show anger or sadness or disappointment, and that made me curse myself even harder. Why the hell did I say that? Why would I call my father, whom I loved and just about worshipped, a failure? I didn't even believe what I'd said, but I said it because I wanted to stick it to him. He probably doesn't even remember that moment, but now, almost twenty-five years later, I feel sick thinking about the silence around that table and the look on his face when I finally raised my eyes from the place mat. His face was empty—just numb. As if his only thought were *How could my son do this to me?*

My jeers that day were especially hurtful because during those years my father had begun to consider changing careers. He was a little more than twenty years into his tenure at McSorley's, and many of the guys he'd worked with and grown close to in the eighties had left the bar for more fulfilling lines of work. Noone gave up his front-room waiter shifts to become a college math professor; another waiter, Fuller, got hired as a manager at the flagship Barnes & Noble bookstore in Union Square; Farnan, one of my dad's partners behind the bar, married a surgeon and moved to

Connecticut; and there was Bart, my father, staying put behind the taps and wondering if he should also try something else before it was too late.

He got close. For two years, he rode the train up to Hunter College on his off days to take graduate courses in education. He earned the necessary credits for a degree, wrote his master's thesis, and gave serious thought to becoming a high school English teacher. But he couldn't complete the program and receive his certification without a half year of student teaching experience, and that would require him to quit McSorley's and spend six months working for free. He could have made it work—my mother's City College job was secure, and because she and my father had already paid off the remainder of the mortgage she and her previous husband had taken out on our West Village apartment, my parents were carrying hardly any debt.

But the prospect of not earning for half a year made my father question how badly he wanted to run a high school English class. On one hand, he was eager to try something different and he believed he could develop into a great teacher. With his passion for the written word, his ability to read people and treat them with appropriate levels of compassion or toughness, and his bar-honed street smarts and sense of humor, he knew he had it in him. But was it worth everything he'd be forced to give up? It would take years before his teacher's salary caught up with the money he was already taking home from McSorley's. He'd no longer be able to work nights—a schedule that allowed him to spend time with me in the afternoon and attend nearly all my basketball games. And what if he got stuck in one of the city's underserved and overwhelmed public high schools, forced to spend his class time maintaining order among forty or fifty rowdy, hormonal teenagers instead of teaching the work of the novelists and poets and journalists he loved?

In the end, it took two years of course work and arriving right at the edge of a decision to leave McSorley's for my father to realize he wanted to stay at the bar. He didn't need to change careers to find satisfaction. He just had to find a way to inject the bartender's life with a greater sense of purpose. The solution was obvious: He had to write again.

My dad likes to say that the novels he wrote in his twenties never got published because he wasn't sober and clearheaded enough to complete a fully realized work of fiction. That theory is as good as any, but here's another: Those books were all some form of imitation. They didn't really spring from my father's experience and imagination. The reimagining of the Argonautica myth was a nod to James Joyce and *Ulysses*. The stroke novel was a stab at Lawrence Ferlinghetti's avant-garde formal experiments. The attack of the giant rats book is tougher to trace, but its blend of sci-fi absurdism and sense of impending doom could have been influenced by my father's graduate school instructors, Kurt Vonnegut, Jr., and Anthony Burgess. My father had spent a decade working on three books, but not one of them was truly *his*.

It took those unrealized novels, plus a couple of decades at McSorley's and an aborted attempt at changing careers, for my dad to finally settle into his voice — that of a wizened, slightly weary everyman bar poet. After he decided to junk the plot to become an English teacher, my father began work on *The McSorley Poems*.

During my last few years of high school, he was nocturnal. On Sunday, Monday, and Thursday nights, he'd arrive home from McSorley's around 2 a.m., take a shower, and then park in front of our family's massive desktop computer. His workstation was set up in a corner on the other side of my bedroom, and I got used to waking up in the middle of the night and seeing the glow from his monitor creeping toward me through the crack at the bottom of my door. I'd fall back asleep to the staccato clack of his fingers on the keyboard.

He went on like this—stealing hours on the graveyard shift, writing and revising and refining between two and six in the morning—until one day I woke up before school and found a binder on the kitchen table, right where I usually sat down to eat my cereal. I flipped it open and found an early manuscript of *The McSorley Poems,* by Geoffrey Bartholomew.

I don't really like poetry. I blame myself, not the poets or the form. Maybe I'm too impatient, maybe I've got the wrong temperament, or maybe I'm just too simpleminded, but I've always been the kind of reader who prefers plain, straightforward writing about a subject that interests me. There may be beauty and mystery in some poetry's broken syntax and delicate metaphors, but often, by the time I've decoded a line's meaning—*if* I've decoded its meaning—my first response hews toward "Why bother?"

But *The McSorley Poems* spoke to me. Feel free to chalk that up to filial piety—I was going to find a way to like the book even if my father had decided to write the entire collection in nineteenth-century Gaelic. But from the first pages of the manuscript, I found myself genuinely and deeply engaged. In every line of every poem I recognized the artifacts and characters I'd grown up around and felt them come alive with language.

The first third of the binder described various McSorley's

artifacts—the World War I wishbones; the stuffed jackalope behind the bar; Harry Houdini's handcuffs dangling from the ceiling as if the great escape artist had been hanging there with them, freed himself, and left behind a souvenir. The middle section consisted of poems devoted to "Unsorted Regulars, Misfits, Liars, Heroes & Psychos." The language was raw, peppered with black humor and full of tragedy—a reminder that for all the laughter and communal goodwill I associated with McSorley's, the men and women who are drawn into the bar's orbit typically arrive with some scars. These were my father's people, the alcoholics and loners and deviants he made his life with, and even at their darkest, the poems shined a light on his characters' humanity. The first stanza of his poem for Doc Zory made me feel as if I'd finally met the waiter who spread the McSorley's plague of calling everybody Jim, Jimmy, and Jimbo, a figure who existed in my head as some kind of long-lost uncle:

Big Z was my old man
first Gypsy violinist
 to play Carnegie Hall
Ma died young on us
so he taught me the axe
honing an edge to call shadows
until beauty was airborne
I'd hear him at wolf's hour
 that moan of catgut
 barely touching
then madly bowing
wrenching their love
when he died
I joined the Navy

The plainspoken lines were a step and a half removed from prose poetry, and my father was telling the stories of a career's worth of bar denizens. The manuscript was a history as much as it was a collection of verse, with the third and final section reaching back to portray Old John McSorley and the bar's founding family through a blend of archival research and my father's imagining of the emotional lives of the Irish clan that came to the United States in the 1850s and opened the Old House at Home.

He put the finishing touches on the manuscript in 2000, my senior year of high school, and gave the book a title: *The McSorley Poems: Voices from New York City's Oldest Pub.* Twenty-five years after he'd earned his master's in creative writing, my father found his voice, and it happened to be in the bar where he drank on his first night in Manhattan, back in 1967. McSorley's cast of sad sacks and strivers was a perfect fit for my father's storytelling poetics, filled with the pathos and hope and explosions of humor that made pub life so rich.

My mother reached out to the handful of friends she'd made over the years who worked in publishing. Regulars at the bar offered to pitch *The McSorley Poems* to their cousins and nieces who worked for the *Times* and public radio. Fuller, the former waiter who'd left to work at Barnes & Noble, vowed to give *The McSorley Poems* choice placement near the front of the store whenever the final product was released. Despite the best efforts of the McSorley's extended family, however, my dad's poetry never found a publisher.

My mother and I ended up feeling more disappointed when publishers shunned *The McSorley Poems* than my dad did. He approached the project with a practical understanding of how difficult it was to publish *any* book of poetry, let alone a collection written by a fifty-five-year-old first-time author who hadn't been part of the literary or academic poetry scene since the late seventies. While my mom and I licked our wounds and snuffed out our fantasies about Clint Eastwood growing a mustache to play my father with tight-lipped dignity in a Hollywood adaptation of my dad's life and career, my father was researching how to self-publish the book. He found a printer who specialized in small press runs and had experience with other poetry collections. He registered *The McSorley Poems* with the Library of Congress and applied for an ISBN number. He even lined up a deal with a local book distributor to have the book sold in New York bookstores, including the Barnes & Noble where Fuller worked.

He printed up the first batch—a run of two thousand books—near the end of 2001, and the following February held a launch party at McSorley's. That night, he stood on a table in the back room and read "Minnie the Cat" and other selections for a giddy crowd of regulars, coworkers past and present, and unassuming drinkers who just happened to pick the evening of a book launch to grab a pair of ales. Over the next few months he was written up in community newspapers and did readings and interviews for a handful of talk radio shows.

My father planned to sell the book at the bar, on a *McSorley Poems* website, and at bookstores for as long as they'd keep it on shelves. Hopefully, he'd manage to sell out the entire first print run. Well, *The McSorley Poems* is now in its fifth printing. A reporter from the *Los Angeles Times* stopped by the bar in 2010 and wound up profiling Bart the bartender poet almost ten years after the book came out. After the first run, my dad has sold the book mostly in person, at McSorley's, at a rate of about thirty copies each month. When he reaches the end of the current batch he'll have hit six thousand sold. Unless you're the poet laureate, those are damn good numbers, better than what some nationally recognized poets sell.

Over the years, as he sold and signed copy after copy of *The McSorley Poems* while working his shift, the rest of the staff noticed an unfortunate pattern. Whenever would-be buyers asked to peruse the book, it had an uncanny knack of opening to page fifty. While that's not the exact middle of the book—the page count is 112—it seemed that some physical characteristic of the binding made page fifty the most likely to open first. We inspected the main bar copy for dog-ears, strategic bends, or some other kind of manipulation meant to increase the odds of the book opening there: nothing. The paperback showed no signs of tampering, and besides, the pattern held true over multiple copies of *The McSorley Poems*. Somehow, with mysterious frequency, when customers first picked up the book, the first poem they saw was right there on page fifty. Its title: "Rectum Lips."

There are probably a dozen poems in the book that are darker and more graphic, but none with such a smutty title. It's a short, three-stanza story written in the voice of a meek gay customer who gets caught peeping in the men's room. It ends tenderly, with the character criticizing the bartenders' nickname for him—Rectum Lips. It isn't apt, the character says, because "I just like to watch."

It's unclear how many sales my father has lost to "Rectum Lips" over the years. The other barmen have taken the book's stubborn insistence on opening at page fifty as further proof that there is no governing superstition at McSorley's more powerful than Murphy's Law: If anything can go wrong, it will. More often than not, however, *The McSorley Poems* overcomes its first impression, and the customers flipping through the book absorb the language and decide whether or not it sings to them.

The McSorley Poems never led to a Clint Eastwood movie, but it marked a far more meaningful achievement for my father. He'd turned his creative energy into a work of art that deepened the bond thousands of readers already felt with McSorley's, and he made the leap from being a guy who always dreamed of writing a book to being an author.

I wasn't able to attend the book launch of *The McSorley Poems* in 2002. I was in Illinois, a second-year journalism student at Northwestern University. I thought I'd skip a couple of days of class to fly home and see my father's first public reading at the bar, but just before I had planned to book my ticket, I bombed a statistics midterm. It was the first time I'd screwed up on a test I had studied for, and I panicked. I called home, asked for advice about what to do, and talked myself into staying at school to focus on pulling up my grade. I got an A in the course, but looking back on that winter, the only thing I can remember is sitting through stats class the Tuesday morning before my father's reading and hating myself for missing his moment.

Fortunately, I got a second chance. In October 2012, my father released *The McSorley Poems Volume II: Light or Dark*. He'd spent much of the previous five years pecking away at a second volume, which he planned to sell from behind the bar alongside the first book. Volume two begins with a miniature epic—a fourteen-page, 160-couplet poem depicting historical events in and around the bar from 1854 to 2011. From there, the collection features a familiar mix of verse devoted to McSorley characters and antiquities. The book is dedicated to me, and my father asked me to introduce him at the launch, another back-room Tuesday-evening affair at the bar.

That night, I stood on a bank of seats in the corner near the kitchen and told a crowd full of McSorley's regulars who'd known me since I was a toddler how proud I was of my father's work. Then he stood up and read "Fathers and Sons," which now trails only Gene Hall's "Red" as my favorite McSorley poem:

> *When I turned twenty-one*
> *my Dad took me here*
> *we got a good buzz on*
> *we actually talked, too*
> *I don't know about what*
> *women, a job, the future*
> *the big hazy things that*
> *you don't listen to your*
> *old man about anyway*
>
> *Well, ten years later*
> *I got the call to meet him*
> *he said to get the same*
> *table, if possible, and I did*
> *the one by the coal stove*
> *it was early November*
> *a gray quilt on the city*

I got cancer, he said
it'll kill me but not yet

You pick a special place
to tell your son you're
dying, it's that simple
he knew I could go back
and back again, though
it's not much to hold onto
sit down with a couple ales
and wonder at how fast
all this shit disappears

It's probably not a perfect poem. But damn if it ain't true to life. Every McSorley's barman and woman has a story like this: the time a customer brought his ailing brother for what might be their last drink together, and the front-room waiter shipped an entire table's worth of customers so they could have some peace and quiet. McSorley's is a place for rabble-rousing, a place where you can get kicked out for not drinking to excess, but it's also a place where people come to share some of the most intimate moments of their lives. I don't want to think of the day when my dad and I have to have a talk like the one in "Fathers and Sons," but if it comes, I know where it will happen, and I know how much the time we spent working behind the bar together will have meant to us.

CHAPTER 10

Mom

So far, my mother—Patricia S. Bartholomew—has barely been a part of this story. That's not because I wasn't close to her during my childhood, it's just that my life in and around McSorley's centered around my dad. He took me there when I was young, he told me bar stories when I woke up in the middle of the night, and he taught me to treasure the pub's history. My mother let us have that bond. Throughout my youth, her role, when it came to McSorley's, was limited to picking me up from the bar on Saturday afternoons and reminding me not to repeat the dirty words I learned there when I was at school.

But my mom was everything else. When my father worked nights, it would be just me and her at our apartment. She'd cook us dinner—it could be anything from frozen chicken nuggets to the delicate bouillabaisse she had prepared in her previous career as a fish chef at the Waldorf

Astoria Hotel—and then we'd sink into the couch and watch rented VHS movies. (The day she decided to let me watch *Robocop* probably ranks among the top-five happiest of my life.) My taste in film and books comes from her— nonfiction, true crime, genre escapism—more than from my father, with all his MFA creative writing erudition.

Whatever toughness I possess, I think it came from my mother. By the time she and my father met, she'd been married and divorced twice and had spent years in and out of rehab. Alcoholism had already ruined her life twice, and once she emerged from the darkness of addiction, she had little time or tolerance for nonsense or self-pity. She had started college at a small Catholic university in western Pennsylvania, but ditched the place after one year and moved to the city in the midsixties. She did a two-year culinary arts program at City College and spent the next several years working in hotel and corporate kitchens. In 1984, two years after I was born, she returned to City College to finish a bachelor's degree, then began putting herself through NYU graduate courses in food studies, one class at a time while taking care of me and teaching hospitality management for the same program she'd attended decades before. She just kept going, credit by credit, until she earned a PhD in 1994, with a dissertation about pioneering female head chefs in New York fine-dining establishments.

At five foot ten, slender and blond, with a tendency to dress all in black, she cut an intimidating figure. When I would complain about homework or being exhausted or just feeling blue, she would remind me of a simple philosophy: *So what?* Feel however you want to feel, she'd say, but "feelings aren't facts." Don't let it stop you from doing what you need to do. When her life was a mess—when she was squeezing the alcohol out of Sterno cans she glommed from catering jobs—she always had an excuse. It wasn't till she stopped making excuses and just started acting that she recovered. The message might have been harsh, but pretty much every time it was right: *Suck it up.* When I got over myself and just did something I'd been avoiding—schoolwork, chores, exercise—I felt better afterward.

So that was my mom: one tough lady, a true New Yorker (she earned it, even if she was born in Jersey), and maybe the only PhD in the state who drank Sterno once upon a time. She and my dad were equal, indispensable forces in my life. She just never had much involvement with my McSorley's upbringing. My mom and the bar remained separate influences on me until the mid-2000s, when tragedy brought them together. She was dying of cancer then, and the bar helped fill the hole left in our lives after she died. The bar couldn't replace that emptiness—nothing could. But at that point in time, it was all my father and I had, besides each other.

I was five in the autumn of 1987, when doctors first found cancer in my mother's neck. She'd been a smoker for the previous twenty-five years, and even though the cancerous cells were discovered near her throat, doctors believed that the disease had spread from elsewhere—most likely her lungs. Further tests failed to detect the primary site of the disease, so doctors came up with a plan to treat what they could find: surgery to remove the tumors and an aggressive course of radiation that they hoped would blast whatever dangerous cells might be hiding elsewhere in her head and neck.

I know this now. At the time, I was in kindergarten with no hope of understanding my mother's diagnosis, treatment, or chances of survival. I remember wondering why my mom suddenly disappeared for six weeks and why my dad stopped taking me to McSorley's for a few months. My grandmother flew in from Phoenix and stayed in our apartment to watch me, and my father spent nearly all his time away from work in the hospital, at my mom's bedside. I don't think my parents tried especially hard to shelter me from her illness. I remember being told that she was sick and had to go away to get better. At five, I couldn't grasp much more than that.

The handful of times when I did sense the gravity of my mom's condition came via the way others treated me. I was attending a small Episcopal school on Hudson Street back then, and when the priest mentioned my name in chapel one morning and asked the congregation to pray for my mother's recovery, instinct told me to hang my head and avoid eye contact while my insides churned in murderous somersaults. I sniffed overcompensating sympathy in the wan smiles of my classmates' parents. When my friends all stopped teasing me at once, the only conceivable explanation was that their moms and dads had warned them not to be mean to the boy with the dying mother. But even though I understood that something bad was happening to my family, I don't remember confronting the likelihood—at the time—that my mother would die.

There was no way for me to realize how sick my mom had been until she returned from treatment, when she'd already survived the worst of it. When she came home, it looked like the right half of her neck was gone. In its place was a swath of irritated, strawberried skin dotted with radiation tattoos.

It looked necrotic. I was afraid to touch it—because her neck looked so fragile and because it just scared me. A couple of months later, when my father felt comfortable enough to take me back to McSorley's with him on a Saturday morning, the looks of relief on the faces of Scott and Michael and Tommy Lloyd and Richie and Dick Buggy made it clear to me how bad things had been while my mother was in the hospital—both with her illness and my father's stress-induced short temper at work.

My mother's treatment had been successful, and my childhood flipped back to its precancer routine—friends who weren't afraid to joke around with me, afternoons at the recreation center, Saturdays at McSorley's. But what my parents didn't tell me at the time was that my mother's doctors expected her cancer to come back. They'd wiped out everything they could find, they said, but they weren't confident that they had found and treated the spot where her disease had originated. When my mother was released from the hospital, doctors told her she had five years to live. (This reveals another reason why my father decided not to follow through with his plan to become a teacher: Only four years after my mother had fallen ill, he was afraid that if her cancer came back, he wouldn't be able to raise me on a teacher's salary.)

I never knew. I just thought my mother had been sick and then she'd gotten better, the way my parents had said it would happen. But years passed and my mom only got stronger. There were no recurrences, no further complications, and no reasons to explain her original prognosis to me. She went back to work, completed her dissertation, and eventually became chairwoman of her college's hospitality management department. Around my eighteenth birthday, when I was preparing to leave for college in suburban Chicago, my parents finally explained to me that, once upon a time, doctors had told her she wouldn't live to see me finish elementary school. The revelation was scary, but it was a far-off warning that my mother had overcome ten years earlier. She continued to have regular checkups, and her doctors were puzzled by her complete and long-lasting recovery. Even though they'd never found the patch of cancerous tissue they believed had made her sick to begin with, after five years in remission they declared her cancer-free.

In October 2002, only eight months after my family had rejoiced over the publication of *The McSorley Poems*, my mother noticed a tickle in her throat. It felt like a cold, but it persisted for weeks, and then the tickle became a scratch became a lump, and my mom knew she had to tell my father and see a doctor. I wasn't even in the country when it happened. It was my junior year at college, and just weeks before my mother sensed that itch, I had flown to Paris to spend four months studying abroad.

It was my first extended trip outside the United States — my first time seeing much of a city outside of New York or Chicago — and long before her diagnosis, my mom had planned to visit me in France. When she arrived for a week in mid-November, though, her trip had become about much more than sightseeing. By then, my parents had consulted with several surgeons and oncologists. CAT scans and MRIs had been done, and the results confirmed their worst fear. They knew what was coming, and now she was flying to Paris to break the news to me, explain the treatment she'd chosen, and try to enjoy one last week of normalcy—or as close as she could get to that—with her son.

Not long after she touched down in Paris, my mom summoned me to her hotel room. When I got there, we hugged, and her embrace felt as strong as ever. She seemed tired, but transcontinental flights and jet lag can do that to anyone. Still, her demeanor seemed more solemn than it needed to be. I could tell something was wrong. At the end of summer, when she was planning the trip, she'd told me repeatedly that Paris was her favorite city and that, as a culinary arts professor and former professional chef, she couldn't wait to show me the simple beauty of French food. But now, instead of immediately heading out into the city to find our first taste bud–exploding meal, she asked me up to her room, and there, as she sat on the edge of her bed, cuisine seemed far from the front of her mind.

"Sit down with me," she said, patting the bed. "I need to tell you, Rafe, that after you left we found out that I have cancer again. It's in my neck." There was no preamble, no detailed setup. She made it quick, then waited while I buried my head in her lap to muffle a sob. "How?" I asked. "Why?" Even though her previous bout with cancer made her statistically more likely to get sick again, she had been healthy for as long as I had been aware of my surroundings. I knew what had happened when I was five, but my memories were so blurry that it didn't feel real.

There was no way to know where this cancer came from, she told me. Maybe the long-dormant payload her doctors had warned her about in the mideighties had finally awakened. Maybe it was related to the treatment she'd undergone previously. Back then, she wasn't expected to live another five years, so blanketing her with radiation that might not prove harmful for another two decades was a reasonable trade-off. It didn't matter, she said. No explanation was going to make sense, and even if one did, that wouldn't make her any more likely to live or die.

The good news: The disease hadn't spread. The bad: The tumor was aggressive and needed to be removed before its growth could squeeze her windpipe or constrict the artery that carried blood to her brain. She was scheduled for surgery in two weeks, and the procedure doctors had planned sounded like something out of a horror film: To get to the tumor, her head-and-neck surgeon would have to split the bone at the point of her chin, slice a straight line down to her clavicle, and then open up her neck like a butterfly's wings. He'd remove the tumor, the cancerous tissue around the tumor, and the potentially cancerous margins around that. All this would leave a hole the size of a silver-dollar pancake in my mother's pharynx, which the surgeon planned to replace with a skin graft borrowed from my mom's left wrist (with skin from her inner thigh used to patch the wrist).

The procedure would take fifteen hours. It was risky, but it also represented her best chance at survival. Without it, she might have only a few months to live. The part that really scared her—the part that had her muffling sobs into my chest—was that if the surgery was successful, she might never be able to eat again. The tissue in the back of her throat that needed to be removed was full of nerves that triggered her swallowing reflex. It was going to be replaced with ordinary skin from her wrist.

"They said my throat should heal fine," she told me. "But my chances of being able to swallow afterward are bad. They'll conduct tests, to see if there are enough nerves left, but they told me I'll probably be tube-feeding for the rest of my life."

There could be no crueler outcome for my mom. Ever since she got sober in 1978, outside of family, food had been her prime mover. She loved cooking at home. She loved taking my father and me out to the gourmet restaurants where she'd conducted her doctoral research and explaining how the kitchens worked and what made a simple hanger steak and *frites* plate so delicious. She was fiercely proud of her research and her City College hospitality management students who went on to open restaurants and run Fifth Avenue hotels. She had never contemplated a life without the experience of food, and she admitted that when she'd first heard that she'd probably never swallow again, she'd considered nixing the surgery and letting herself expire.

But the operation meant a chance to add years to her life, and she was willing to fight for more time with my father and me. Survive first, then figure out the rest. After she explained all that she and my father had learned about her illness and treatment, she let me hold her and whimper for another five minutes, and then she shook me off and stood up. "I have one week to eat in Paris," she said. "We can cry when I see you in New York. Take me out to dinner."

It became a week of epic, purposeful gluttony. *Pain au chocolat* at every breakfast. Warm baguettes between meals. Soft French butter spread on anything we could eat it with. We scarfed tender, garlicky falafel sandwiches under framed snapshots of Lenny Kravitz in an Israeli café. Crispy buckwheat *galette* crêpes folded over slabs of country ham and Gruyère cheese, all bonded together by the runny yolk of a fried egg. Profiteroles and crème brûlée and chocolate mousse every night. If my mother wouldn't be able to eat normally after her surgery, we made sure that she went into that operating room with three years' worth of new taste memories.

My parents insisted I not fly home for the surgery, which was scheduled for the day after Thanksgiving 2002. My study abroad program would be over by the second week of December—right when my mom was due to be released from the hospital—and it just made sense for me to return to New York then. It was the first decision in what would become a pattern in the way my parents handled me during my mother's cancer treatment: They refused to let her disease derail my "normal" life. This meant there was never any discussion of me taking a break from college to help care for my mom. Of course, to me, nothing felt normal about writing a fifteen-page analysis of *ESPN The Magazine* for an editing class or binge-reading Guatemalan novelist Miguel Ángel Asturias for a Latin American literature seminar, then calling home to hear the hellish gurgle of the suction machine my mother needed to remove phlegm and saliva from her throat between sentences.

I was aching for some way to be a direct help to my parents, but allowing her cancer to pull me away from school would only have added to my mom's burden. By letting them shield me from some measure of the horror she was facing, I was giving her a reason to stay alive. I understood this, but

I still yearned to be at every doctor's appointment and follow-up procedure with her and my dad. And I just couldn't.

I wanted to do what I saw my father doing, which was plainly heroic. I'm not convinced he slept during the six months after my mom's first surgery. He kept working five shifts a week at McSorley's, and, as it had the first time my mom had cancer, his temperament at work turned vile, according to the other barmen. In those days, a routine mistake like bleaching the rags less than twice per hour or forgetting to serve a cheddar plate at the bar could bring a coworker face-to-face with Bart's white-hot rage. He took my mother to visits with ever more surgeons, oncologists, radiologists, physical therapists, and infectious disease specialists. While she slept at home, he'd sneak off to the computer to read everything he could find about squamous cell cancer, pain management, chemotherapy side effects, proper dosages of prescription meds, and what to ask her doctors. He wrote me letters, confessional dirges shot through with fear that would bend into giddy bursts of McSorley storytelling and then conclude by urging me to stay the course, keep my grades up, and only come home when I had time.

I flew back to New York whenever I could: a weekend every other month, holiday breaks, summers. And at every homecoming, my mom seemed a little stronger. Her neck healed, her tracheotomy hole closed, and her voice returned. Doctors conducted test after test to see if she might gradually regain her ability to swallow, but it never returned. For as long as she lived, "eating" would mean attaching a plastic funnel to a tube implanted in her stomach, then pouring down a can of milky nutrients. Despite this grim reality, I helped her cheat this physical limitation with occasional spoonfuls of hot chocolate or rich beef stock. She couldn't swallow, but she could swish the liquids around, coat her tongue with the taste, and then rinse out her mouth.

Her cancer remained aggressive, so after her first, major surgery, her doctor scheduled regular operations in which he used a laser to zap out trouble spots whenever scans showed the appearance of new cancerous tissue. The procedures were quick and relatively noninvasive and seemed to be working. She went on like this for more than a year, and her overall health kept improving. Even so, one summer afternoon, I lay down next to her while she was napping, and when she woke up a half hour later and saw me beside her, tears welled at the bottom of her eyes. "I know you think we can go on like this," she told me, as if she sensed my hope creeping ahead of reality. "But someday, I'm going to die from this." She didn't mean she was giving up, but instead that there was only so much that could be done to keep her disease under control.

Not long after that afternoon, the setbacks started to hit. While my mom was in the hospital to recover from one of her laser surgeries, a severe, drug-resistant bacteria crept inside her and festered around her vertebrae. It took weeks of trial and error for doctors to find an antibiotic cocktail that could keep the infection in check: a mix of Cipro, Zosyn, and clindamycin strong enough to treat anthrax. And even this antibiotic carpet-bombing wouldn't fully wipe out the infection. She'd have to stay on Cipro for the rest of her life to contain it. The risk of further infection made it impossible for her to continue her laser treatments, which meant she had to give up the most effective means of corralling her cancer.

Chemotherapy was her treatment of last resort. The weekend I was to graduate from college, she took her first doses. My aunt visited from Massachusetts to take care of my mom while my father drove to Illinois to attend my commencement ceremony. As I crossed the stage to shake hands with the journalism school dean, my dad held his cell phone aloft so my mother could hear my name being called. After collecting my diploma, I rushed with my dad back to the room I'd been renting and packed my belongings, and we started driving back to New York.

Chemo took its dehumanizing toll. Hair loss, of course. But one of the drugs my mom was on also caused extreme chapping and cracking of the skin on her hands and feet. She wound up spending what little energy the treatment didn't sap from her on the Sisyphean task of moisturizing her pale, withered, and bruised hands. She tried Vaseline, specialty salves, French moisturizers, rubber gloves and socks to keep the squishy coating around her digits and prevent them from splitting. Meanwhile, the tumors in her neck returned, their advance slowed but not stopped by chemo. Her surgeon called: My mom's latest scan showed that her cancer was beginning to press against her windpipe; she'd need a permanent tracheotomy to open her airway beneath the point where the tumor was closing it. Afterward, she'd need to stick a finger in her neck anytime she wanted to talk. Months more of chemo. More scans. Another call: Now it was time to insert an eight-inch stent in her carotid artery. The tumor looked poised to grow right through the artery, which would sever it and lead to massive internal bleeding and death within minutes.

Thanks to my mom's battery of treatments, the cancer's march had been slow. She'd been diagnosed in fall 2002, and almost three years later, despite her declining quality of life, I could still take her to movies, still smuggle her tasty liquids, still laugh with her. And even if my accomplishments during those years had been less selfless than my father's and less courageous than my mom's, I had held up my end of the bargain by graduating from college and snatching a journalism master's less than a year after finishing undergrad. Then, midway through 2005, I learned that I'd received a Fulbright grant from the US State Department to move to Manila and study the role of basketball in Philippine society.

Once again, what felt like an impossible choice—to spend nine months living eight thousand miles away from home—was not even up for debate with my parents. It was the most adamant I'd seen my mother since she got sick. Even if she couldn't raise her voice anymore, she narrowed her eyes and spoke in a low, resolute tone: "You're taking that grant." A couple of months before my departure in November 2005, she switched to a new chemotherapy treatment, one that succeeded in shrinking her tumors back to less threatening dimensions. The scans looked good, she told me. I had to go.

"I'll visit."

I whispered these words into my mother's ear while hugging her from the opposite side of an airport security rope. She'd stayed next to me, on the other side of the flimsy barrier, all the way from the back of the line until now, a step away from the X-ray checkpoint. Here we had to say goodbye. She repeated that I was doing the right thing. I told her I'd fly home for a week in January. "Only if you need to," she said. Before I let go to pass through security, she squeezed with more force than I'd felt from her in years. Her words had been fearless, but I felt in her grip what I already knew—I might never see her again.

My first two months in Manila were smooth. I wrote emails and called home just about every day, earning easy laughs from my mom with common expat stories of learning to live in a tropical megacity: how crowds in packed public squares could lift me off my feet when they got moving in one direction; the way people would see me, a six-foot-three American walking down the street in basketball shorts, and demand that I go to the nearby court and try to put down a dunk (the results were almost as disappointing for me as they were for the folks in the street); how quickly I learned to love drinking soda that was served in a plastic bag with a straw. Much of the mail my father attempted to send to the address I was living at never arrived, so it felt like the best kind of omen when a card from my mother arrived a few days before my first Christmas spent anywhere besides New York. It was dated December 15:

> *My dearest Rafe,*
>
> *I will miss you more than I can say this Christmas. But feel somewhat better knowing I'll see you soon thereafter and that my current treatment is effective and I'll see you many times after that as well. I love you very much.*
>
> *Mom*

I did end up spending a week in New York in early January, and things seemed about the same as they had been when I'd left. On the nineteen-hour flight over the North Pole and back down into Asia, for the first time since November, I felt something other than dread about being so far away, for so long, while my mom was so sick. That hope ended up being short-lived. At the beginning of February 2006, my dad sent an email telling me it was time to come home. Since they'd seen me in January, my mom's health had deteriorated rapidly. Her cancer had stopped responding to chemotherapy. Doctors said they'd exhausted the reasonable options and suggested my parents consider palliative care. My mom decided she wanted to spend whatever time she had left at home, rather than in a hospital, and my father was telling me to get back to New York as soon as possible, so we could be together at the end.

I flew home on Valentine's Day. Before I left, my father warned me how sick my mom had become. As the disease spread through her body, she was losing the ability to perform basic functions that people in good health take for granted. She could still stand up and walk, he said, but she was weak and needed someone nearby to catch her if she fell. She wasn't talking much anymore, and her eyesight was fuzzy. She needed assistance with eating, bathing, and going to the bathroom. He told me she was communicating by writing on a small dry-erase board, but she might not be able to write legibly for much longer.

It was a devastating scene to imagine coming home to — my mother, minus half the qualities that made her who she was. The reality turned out to be more wrenching than anything I'd envisioned on the flight back to New York. When I stepped into our apartment, my father opened the door and hugged me. My mother was lying back in a recliner chair in our living room, with her mom and one of her sisters standing behind her. They'd set up a chair next to her, waiting for me.

"Pat, someone is here to see you." I didn't understand why they were talking to her like my coming home was a surprise visit from the Easter Bunny, and neither did my mom. She looked back at her mother and sister and rolled her eyes, lifting her palms in a "what the fuck?" shrug. Then I sat next to her and took her hand. It felt bony, frail. "Mom, it's me," I said, and at first she just gazed blankly at my face from six inches away, like she didn't know whether to believe her ears. Her hand traced a path up my arm to my shoulder, then my neck, and finally my face. When she palmed my nose, she seemed to finally find the confirmation she needed, and she clapped her palm around the back of my neck and pulled my forehead in so it was flat against hers. The relief that she was still there overpowered those ten seconds of heartbreak when I knew she wasn't sure who I was.

Finally, my parents made me a full partner in our family nightmare. There was no longer any reason to shield me from the ugliest details or to use whatever future achievements might be waiting for me as motivation to keep pushing back against cancer's advances. Nobody ever said this to me, but I understood that all we had left was a little bit of time for the three of us to share our love.

The way we expressed that bond was by sharing the work of taking care of my mother. Insurance paid to have a hospital bed and an IV stand installed in our living room, and my dad and I took turns feeding her, administering pain medication, turning over the tape on the cassette Walkman she used to play audiobooks. We helped her change in and out of sweats, until eventually that became too difficult and she began wearing a hospital gown.

I saw my mom in ways that when I was younger, I would have assumed no son would ever want to see. Squirting liquid morphine into the funnel that connected to her feeding tube, washing it down with water, holding the tube up and watching the liquid drain through a port in her belly. Feeling the bones in her back and rib cage jut out more and more as her weight plummeted below a hundred pounds. Watching her stand up from her bed, angrily wave my dad and me away when we moved to help her, then crash to the floor after two steps. (It was her first such fall, a sure sign that she was getting weaker, and we made sure to be at her side for every step she took after that.) One night, while my dad was working at McSorley's, my mother woke up and realized she had soiled her bed. I was asleep in the chair next to her, and she pawed at my cheek to rouse me. She could neither talk nor write by then, so she pointed between her legs and looked at me with the most sadness I'd ever seen in her pale blue eyes. I knew why: It was the indignity of having to ask her son to carry her to the bathroom and wipe her ass. "So what?" I told her, the same way she'd told me all the times I had let far more trivial insecurities get the best of me. I held her trembling, naked body upright with one arm and cleaned her off with the other. We dealt with it.

Those horrific scenes are among the proudest times of my life. Maybe that sounds insane, but it meant so much to me to be the one watching over my mom, to be sharing this duty with my father. It felt like something sacred among the three of us—a bond we held together during the most punishing trial we would ever face. Every lucid moment my mom had in her final weeks—every time the spark of recognition or humor or affection returned to her eyes—either I was there to catch it, or my father was. Cancer pushed a tidal wave of suffering into our lives, and we stood in front of it and never fucking budged.

*   *   *

The other indelible moments from that winter came when some unexpected occurrence would lead us all into wild, hysterical fits of laugher. These respites were easily recognizable as McSorley's humor—cynical and a bit wicked, as if dredged from the dark side of bar life.

There was a long-scheduled window-washer appointment we'd forgotten to cancel, so that a worker arrived one day to dangle outside our third-story apartment and rinse a few years' worth of grime off our windows. He was exceedingly polite and made a great show of not reacting to the hospice center set up in our living room. After he'd finished half the job, he swung back into the living room through an open window to take a bathroom break. On his way back through the kitchen, I offered him a soda and some lunch— "Just water, thanks" was his reply—but before he could return to the job my mom flung her arm out and stopped him. She pointed to her dry-erase board, where she'd scrawled: "This must be fucked up! Thank you!" By then, her laughter was pretty quiet, but it lifted our hearts to see her flash a withered smile and rock forward while the window washer broke out in an apologetic giggle.

We developed a recurring gag about the massive amounts of painkillers the doctors had prescribed for my mother. Vicodin and Percocet pills piled high in our medicine cabinet, while the cheese drawer in our fridge was wholly taken over with liquid morphine bottles, their accompanying eyedroppers, and fentanyl patches. We kept a running commentary about everything we could buy if we cashed in this mother lode of opiates on the black market: a new truck for my dad, a year of rent-free living anywhere in the world for me, a formal indulgence from the Pope for my mom (a lapsed Catholic). "Go straight to heaven, do not pass go!" was the line that took the cake. My dad began devising increasingly elaborate plots to apply fentanyl patches on my cousin's yippy little terrier. The dollar-bill-sized adhesive strips provided a time-released dosage of potent, narcotic painkillers, the application of which to the fifteen-pound pet would mean a quick, hazy trip to the doggie afterlife. *Here, Monty, let me slap this on your head...*

After a couple of weeks, we noticed my mom was starting to sleep more and interact with us less. A full day might pass without her doing anything to indicate that she was still conscious and aware of her surroundings. Then, for brief, joyous moments, she'd snap out of it and come back to us. On one of these days, my dad was next to her while she lay in the hospital bed. He was caressing her forehead and talking to her, unsure what, if anything, she was hearing. He was being sweet, reading the newspaper aloud to her and promising to take good care of her, but somehow his doting tone stirred my mom's fierce independent streak. Patricia Bartholomew was never one to be babied. She opened her eyes, smiled, and pulled one of her hands out from beneath the covers. Still grinning, she pointed down — a symbol for my dad to remove her blanket. He started pulling the sheets back from underneath her chin, and when he got past her shoulders, her other hand peeked out. She was giving him the finger.

Besides splitting the caretaker duties during that winter, I also started picking up half of my father's McSorley's shifts. He'd never asked me to work for him before, but now it made sense for me to cover some days to give him extra time with my mom. It ended up being my first extended stretch of bar work, and it was when I started to realize how much I loved the mechanics of the job. The interconnected labor of runner and bartender, moving in sync to carry out the McSorley's process of converting mugs of ale into piles of cash, reminded me of the joy and camaraderie of team sports. I also understood the role McSorley's had played in helping my father endure the previous three years of misery. It was so easy to get lost in the hard, repetitive work behind the bar. You'd be focused on the visual and audible cues that tell you when to serve a round of ale, when to wash a handful of mugs, and when to prepare a fresh batch of bleached bar mops, and your mind could ignore everything but the task in front of you. If he ever managed to escape from the despair, worry, and helplessness that tortured him in those years, it would have happened at McSorley's. And after a heavy shift, it often won't matter what issues are weighing on your mind—you can't help but pass out and get a decent night's sleep.

That pretty much describes my day on Thursday, March 9, 2006. Madison Square Garden was hosting the Big East conference college basketball tournament—a traditional McSorley's mob scene day, when crowds of alumni dressed in Syracuse orange, St. John's red, and Villanova navy blue cycle back and forth between the bar and the arena. I worked the day shift—it was the busiest day I'd seen so far, and I didn't commit any major fuckups. I rode my bike home on a high, with a few hundred bucks in my pocket and the phone number of some Syracuse girls I had served who invited me to meet them uptown after the Orangemen game. I told them I had family stuff to do, but maybe I could step out later. Once I got home, I locked up my bike in the stairwell, kicked off my boots and peeled off my wet socks, and changed into basketball shorts. I kissed my mom on the forehead, then crawled under the covers in my parents' bed, turned on the remaining tournament games, and passed out before I'd seen either team score a basket.

My dad woke me up around midnight. "Jimbo, time to trade," he said. He had spent the evening beside my mother, and now he was claiming his bed for the night. I settled into the recliner next to my mom, popped open my laptop, and hummed along to an album of acoustic Filipino ballads I'd been using to help learn Tagalog. The band was called MYMP—an abbreviation for Make Your Momma Proud, which would have been horribly corny under any other circumstances than mine. After the last song, I gave her another peck on the forehead, rested my cheek on her chest for a few seconds, and squeezed her hand goodnight before wandering off to bed.

I woke up around 3 a.m., and my first thought was to go to my mother. My dad and I had both been getting up every couple of hours for the past several nights, always aware that when we checked for her breaths, there might not be any. That predawn Friday, once I got a step or two away from her, I had a feeling that this was it. Even though she'd barely moved for the last few days, she seemed more still than before. When I touched her arm, there was no give. I felt for her breath and it was gone. I touched her face and it was cold. Her eyes were closed. I hugged her, took a huge breath, and went to wake my dad. He gave a start when I squeezed his bicep. "Huh?" he said. "What?"

"It's over," I answered. "I think it's over."

"What do you mean?"

"Mom," I told him. "I'm pretty sure."

He rushed out to the living room, felt her hand, and

made a sound like fifty breaths got knocked out of him all at once. He blanketed my mom in a hug, kissing all over her forehead and repeating "I love you" in a tender, desperate whisper. Then he stood up, faced me, and pulled me into a hug that must have lasted ten minutes, with each of us taking turns to hold the other up. Eventually, he let go and said we should call the funeral home where we'd arranged to have her taken.

The receptionist on duty offered condolences and said a team was on its way to collect my mother's body. While we waited, we gave each other five minutes alone with her to say goodbye. I went first, and while my dad disappeared into the bathroom, I just stood over my mom, telling her I loved her and wondering what else to do. When I finished, I knocked on the bathroom door and gave my dad his time to say goodbye.

The funeral home employees arrived around four in the morning. They were a pair of men in their fifties, short and frumpy and dressed in worn suits that looked three sizes too baggy. They were pushing a metal-frame gurney. One guy had one of the biggest noses we'd ever seen, like a butternut squash had grown out from the middle of his face. The other wore a black fedora atop his vaguely serpentine head, which was shaped like an upside-down triangle. "We're very sorry for your loss," the man in the hat said with a heavy Bronx accent. "Why don't you guys take a few minutes to pay your respects and then let us know when you're ready?" My dad and I walked over to her one last time, felt her hands and caressed her cheeks once more, and whispered final pledges of love into her ears. Then we walked back to the front door, nodded at the men, and headed to the bath-

room to wait while they zipped her into a body bag and
wheeled her out of the apartment.

Inside the bathroom, at perhaps the most unlikely
moment, we were struck by another jolt of McSorley's
humor. "You notice anything funny about those two?" my
dad asked me.

"Besides them looking like rejects from the circus?" I
said.

"Well, I was thinking that it makes a lot more sense now
that Johnny Wadd has that other job at the funeral home."

The comparison was spot-on and hilarious. These guys
were cut from the same cloth as Johnny Wadd, Katz, Cyclops,
and the whole ignominious lineage of McSorley's overnight
men. "I guess there's only a handful of options out there for
these guys," I said. "You could work for the funeral home or
you could be a night watchman at the bar."

"Or you could do both," my dad added, and we laughed
long and hard before a knock on the bathroom door broke
the spell: "Okay, we're done."

We walked outside, thanked the men, and watched them
push the gurney out our front door, into the lobby, and then
into the elevator.

Nine days later, at my mother's memorial service, I read the
poem "Funeral Blues," by W. H. Auden, in front of a couple
of hundred assembled friends, family members, and
well-wishers. Before she died, she'd asked that I read it
there. I made it through the last line — "For nothing now
can ever come to any good" — without bursting into tears,
and then when I took a breath and looked into the crowd, I

noticed that the McSorley's attendees outnumbered almost every other group inside the chapel. After the service, the line of barmen and McSorley's characters who stopped to shake my hand and say a kind word about my mom felt like it included half the people I'd ever met: Matty, the owner; his daughters; Michael and Scott and Brendan and Timmy; retired waiters like Fuller and Noone; bartenders who'd worked with my dad decades ago, like Farnan and Tommy Lloyd; Mary the chef; Alan, the Scotsman who rented an apartment above the bar and worked as a waiter two nights a week; people who'd known me since I was a toddler. They were another sort of family to me and my dad. Not like the family we lost when my mom died, but a looser tribe related to McSorley's that would band together to support their own in times of need.

My mother officially died in the early hours of March tenth. Exactly one week later, my father woke up early to work the taps on St. Patrick's Day. It was his first day back. Later that week, I joined him for a couple of shifts behind the bar, and we did what we knew how to do in the only place that felt right to do it: serve ales, crack wise, and be part of McSorley's.

CHAPTER 11

Working Pains

THE PADDY'S DAY AFTER MY mom died, part of me was dumbfounded, struggling to understand how my father managed to show up for work only one week after her death. Those days, I often felt as if we were lucky just to make it to sundown with our sanity intact. How was he able to get through the most hectic shift of the year at McSorley's while I still wasn't sure how to hold myself together on a five-minute walk to the deli?

Pumping ale at McSorley's had helped my father keep his head straight during my mom's more than three years of treatment, so even in this gut-wrenching moment, he was eager to return to the safety of his notch behind the taps. But my dad's speedy return may have had less to do with the mourning process than with sheer force of habit. He'd worked through all manner of physical discomfort over the course of his career, from flus and stomach viruses to broken bones to herniated disks in his back to the chronic pain of two severely arthritic knees. Now, with a broken heart or a ruptured soul or whatever cliché you want to throw at it, why wouldn't he show up for his shift, like he always did?

My dad's most dramatic feat of on-the-job physical endurance came four years after my mom's death, on the Friday leading into Labor Day weekend 2010. That morning, as my father sat at the kitchen table and touched up the waterproofing on his boots, he mentioned a dull ache in his stomach. His appetite also wasn't up to par — he'd worked the previous night, and he'd usually polish off a big morning-after bowl of yogurt and granola before heading out to complete the double shift. This time, however, he could only manage a couple of noncommittal nibbles before flinging the remainder into the trash. "Something weird," he grumbled, half to me, half to himself. "Like a warm lump in my abdomen."

I probably should have showed concern, but a line like that was too good a setup. "Do me a favor," I said, "save that warm lump for the toilet at work."

"You said it, Jimbo," he replied. "Once I blow one out the hole, I'll feel fine." He grabbed his bike helmet and left for work like any other Friday.

The chance to "blow it out the hole" never came. Instead, he barely budged during his seven-hour shift. When he wasn't pouring ale or making change for the waiters' payments, he would step back into the corner and rest against the wall beside the cashbox. Michael was filling in as the front-room waiter that day, and he noticed my father moving slowly and looking gray in the face.

"You all right, Bart?"

"Yeah, I think my guts are just stopped up," my dad said. "Feels like a large piece of lumber is sitting sideways, and it's moving *really* slowly. Gonna ask Rafe to pick up some laxatives tonight. Lube up the insides, big-time."

It probably eased Michael's concern to hear that my father's sense of verbose, scatological humor was intact. The afternoon passed like any other Friday at McSorley's—quiet until about 4 p.m., then a two-hour rush from the after-work crowd before Scott and the cavalry arrived for the 6 p.m. shift change. By the time my dad had counted up the day's earnings, split the tips with the runner, and emerged from behind the bar, his face had turned ashen, with a few strands of his hair plastered across his clammy forehead. Throughout the day, his bellyache had been growing. The pain was never sharp, but with each passing hour it seemed to pulse outward through more of his body. His insides felt hot, his appetite still hadn't returned, and he hadn't been able to clean out whatever was ailing him.

"You're looking rough, Bart," Scott said as my dad walked toward the hatch to get out from behind the bar. "Don't come in tomorrow if you need to take it easy."

Dad left McSorley's, climbed on his bike, and pedaled home. By the time he pushed open the front door to our apartment, he was bent over, cradling his sore midsection with one hand, and ready to collapse into his chair at the kitchen table. "Something ain't right," he said, taking a deep breath. "Let me check it out online, but just in case take a walk to the drugstore and get me a bottle of saline laxative. I think I'm just constipated real bad."

"Oh, man," I told him. "When you finish on the computer, do us both a favor and lay out a tarp in the bathroom."

He bent his grimace into a grin. "Yup, it's gonna look like Gallagher rolled into town," he said, referring to the eighties-era prop comic famous for splattering his audience with sledgehammered watermelons. Like Michael earlier, I figured my dad couldn't be too sick to his stomach if he was still sick in the head.

Fifteen minutes later, I returned with a bottle of lime-flavored laxative and found my dad still sitting at the kitchen table, about to hang up on a phone call with his brother, Doug. He'd looked up his symptoms online, he said, and based on what he'd read he might have appendicitis. He doubted it, though, because the condition usually occurred in adolescents and young adults, not sixty-six-year-old men. He'd already called Anne, a nurse from New Jersey he'd been dating for a few months and the first woman I'd seen him find any kind of romantic connection with since my mother died. Anne told him that if he had an inflamed and infected appendix, he probably wouldn't have any questions about it. The pain, she said, would be overwhelming. Then he called his younger brother, who had had his appendix removed several years earlier. Echoing Anne's advice, my uncle said he recalled a pervasive, nauseous flu feeling throughout his body.

My dad didn't feel that, so when he saw me walk in with the laxative, he held out his hand. "Pass it here, mofo," he said. "Let's see what this stuff does." He poured half a bottle into his coffee mug and started sipping, and I wandered over to the living room to watch whatever basketball I could find on TV. Ten minutes later, he poured the rest of the solution into his mug. "How's it feel?" I yelled across the apartment.

"I'll let you know in about fifteen minutes," he grunted back, wiping sweat from his forehead with a McSorley's bar mop.

Not long after he'd consumed the entire bottle, he stood up from his chair. "Damn," he grunted, "something's happening." From the corner of my eye it looked like he was headed to the bathroom. As encouragement, I yelled one of his McSorley's catchphrases—the random lines he'd shout in the middle of shifts just to entertain himself: "Blow it out the hole tonight, mamacita!"

He took one step away from the table, moaned, and then keeled over on his side. "Fuck!" he sputtered. "Call an ambulance!"

"You serious?" I could see he was in pain, but I'd been watching him brush off all manner of agony for my entire life. Throughout the day, from his morning stomachache until the appendicitis discussion and after, I had never worried that something serious might actually be wrong. My dad was getting up there in age, but he was also made of granite.

"Yeah, I'm fuckin' serious!" he blurted out. Then he let out a booming, guttural "*GUYNNNHHHH,*" perhaps for emphasis. That convinced me. I called 911, told them my father had collapsed and we thought he might have appendicitis, and an ambulance was on the way. When the paramedics helped him up, got him downstairs, and loaded him into the vehicle, one of them asked him to rate his pain from one to ten.

"Eight," he told the paramedics, then took a couple of deep breaths in an effort to remain calm. "Ten was the kidney stone," he added. "But this, I could work through it if I had to."

*   *   *

At the emergency room, it took a physician all of five minutes to diagnose my father with appendicitis. A couple of
questions about the pain, a gentle poke in his right side, and
they were ready to order a CT scan to determine whether
his appendix had ruptured. While he lay in the ER, curled
in the fetal position and clutching the rail of his hospital
bed in white-knuckled agony, a nurse came in to gather
more information. Her first question: "What time did you
first feel the symptoms?"

"Probably around eight this morning," he answered.

"So over twelve hours ago," the nurse continued. "What
did you do between that time and when you came to the
emergency room?"

"I went to work," he told her.

She raised an eyebrow. "Huh. And were you experienc-
ing this pain while you were at work?"

"Yeah, a little bit."

"Mr. Bartholomew, do you mind if I ask what you do for
a living?" she asked.

"I'm a bartender at McSorley's, on Seventh Street."

The nurse continued through the rest of her questions,
but for a split second, after he'd told her he worked at
McSorley's, she couldn't hide the disbelief in her eyes: *This
guy stood around serving drinks all day while his appendix was
about to pop?*

My dad defied the doctors' expectations again with
regard to whether or not his appendix had already ruptured. At one point, while he was waiting for the CT scan
results, I tracked down his surgeon and asked why it wouldn't

be better to operate sooner rather than later. "If his appendix burst, isn't he at risk of a really dangerous infection?"

The surgeon smiled at my naïveté. "You know that episode of *The Simpsons* where Homer has appendicitis, and after Dr. Hibbert removes it, he throws it like a live grenade and watches it explode?" he asked. The *Simpsons* reference struck me as an odd choice, but I knew exactly the episode he was talking about. "Well, the real thing isn't like that," he continued. "If your dad started feeling pain this morning, then statistically it's unlikely that his appendix would rupture by now, and most patients who do experience a rupture are in such acute pain that they can barely answer questions once it happens." Conducting the test first, the doctor explained, would help him decide on the appropriate surgical approach: If the appendix hadn't ruptured, they would operate laparoscopically, using a thin, lighted tube to locate the organ and cut it out in a relatively noninvasive manner; if it had ruptured, they might need to open up my father's abdomen to clean out pus and prevent infection.

This made good enough sense, but I knew my dad. This was a man who had walked around with severe arthritis in both knees for more than a decade, and the closest he'd come to acknowledging the grinding, bone-on-bone torment were a couple of stray mumbles of "motherfucker motherfucker." Profanity was his dogged survival mantra. Forty-five minutes later, the doctor returned with two nurses, who immediately began helping my father onto a gurney to transfer him to an operating room. "The MRI showed that he did have a rupture," the doctor said. (My dad and I later guessed that the bottle of laxative he downed after work had caused his appendix to blow.) "We're taking him to surgery."

As he was being wheeled out of sight, my dad yelled back to me: "Call the bar. Tell them I'm probably out for tomorrow."

When I reached Scott at McSorley's, he could hardly believe that my dad had finished work earlier in the day. "He didn't look *that* bad," Scott said. "Tough old bastard, ain't he?" Ten minutes later he called back and asked if I was available to work as the doorman the following night, since the guy covering for my dad had been penciled in as Saturday's bouncer.

My dad got out of surgery a few minutes after four in the morning, and once he was settled in the intensive care unit, the nurses let me sneak in for a visit. As soon as I saw him, I started breaking his balls: "Which idea was worse: working with an about-to-explode appendix or coming home and chugging the laxative?"

"Fresh stitches," he said, wincing. "Don't make me laugh." The slightest chuckle from him would hurt like hell. In addition to the soreness associated with any operation, the doctors had flushed out his abdominal cavity with saline solution—basically hosing down his innards to sterilize them and make sure none of the toxic gunk from his appendix remained inside him. I told him the guys at the bar were astounded that he'd managed to stand through a whole shift just hours before getting rushed to the ER. "Sounds pretty good, huh?" he said. "But it wasn't that bad until I got home. I've worked through worse."

Sure, he was downplaying the feat. According to the McSorley's code of macho humility, that was the only appropriate response. But there was also some truth to his claim. Appendicitis may have been the only affliction that required him to undergo surgery right after work, but the dull, persistent stomachache he'd felt that day probably did pale in comparison to some of the pain he'd brushed off in the past. Over the years, he must have gashed his hands and forearms on broken mugs a few dozen times. (He or another bartender would manage to spot nine out of ten of those jagged glasses, but every now and then a broken mug eludes detection and cuts someone.) The remedy, no matter how deep the resulting wound, was to throw a Band-Aid or some gauze on it, then slip the bloody hand into a latex glove and keep working. About halfway through one of the first ten-keg nights I ever worked (double digits being the mark of an extremely busy shift), he went downstairs to tap fresh kegs and dropped a full one—about 160 pounds—on his foot. When he got back behind the bar, I noticed his limp and asked what had happened. "I probably broke my toe," he said. "Gonna try to stand in one place and finish the night." That's exactly what he did, and later, around two in the morning when we were home and it was time to peel off his socks, his right big toe could have passed for a prizewinning beet at the Pennsylvania State Fair.

Fortunately, he had the next couple of days off, so he kept the toe submerged in ice water and made an appointment with a podiatrist, who prescribed three weeks' rest and a heavy plastic walking boot. My father brought the boot home, tried it on, took two steps, and said, "There's no way I'm gonna be able to work in this." Next, he removed the boot and dropped it in the trash.

"What're you gonna do?" I asked.

His answer: "Tape up the toe, eat a few extra ibuprofens, get through the shift." He didn't miss a day of work.

And it's not just him. It's all of us. Working through pain is just part of working at McSorley's, to the point that "Get through the shift" belongs in the canon of essential bar maxims. Working through everyday aches and pains or ailments like the flu is so common that the staff won't even bother bringing it up with each other, although the constant passing around of a communal ibuprofen bottle hints at our shared burden. Yet as much as we ignore our agonies and injuries, the wear and tear that comes with working at McSorley's is no joke. The mere act of being on your feet for a full shift will leave your legs rubbery and your back so stiff that by the time you're home, you'll strain to reach your bootlaces. Lying in bed after busy shifts, you'll feel a gentle throbbing in your hands as a memento of the cumulative tons of glass and ale they just finished moving. The next morning, when you wake up, those hands will be plumper than usual, and the swelling might prevent you from being able to make a fist. For the bartenders and runners, repeatedly jamming your hands into vats filled with water and bleach, water and industrial-strength dish soap, and just plain scalding water can cause ugly side effects. My first couple of months on the job, my hands molted, chapping and cracking and flaking off skin until a new, sturdier dermis emerged. Waiters have dragged freshly fractured ankles, swollen like volleyballs, through the McSorley's sawdust. Longtime pumpmen like Scott will strap themselves into layers of harnesses and back braces—things that look like they were designed for power lifters and strongman competitors—to ease the searing hurt of slipped disks and to prevent further injuries. Johnny Wadd had his infamous hernia, the one that made him look like he was hiding a possum under his belt, and he still managed to wield a push broom for an extra ten bucks before his night watchman shifts.

In just a few years of picking up extra shifts around McSorley's, I ended up with plenty of my own bar scars and macho boasts. One Sunday afternoon in spring 2011, I was due at work by 3 p.m. and biking up Smith Street in Brooklyn after grabbing lunch with a friend in Sunset Park. In the bike lane, I noticed a brown station wagon I'd been pedaling beside starting to drift in my direction. It kept veering toward me, and at the moment I realized the car wasn't going to stop, I started screaming "HEY! HEY! HEY! FUCK! FUCK! FUCK!" until the side door was on top of my leg. I pounded the passenger-side window with my fist once before the car knocked me off-balance and I shot off the frame, airborne, and went skidding across the sidewalk on my shins and forearms. My mind was all panic and adrenaline, just a screeching surge of fight or flight, and my only instinct was to get up and pat down my body for broken bones. Meanwhile, the driver of the station wagon had pulled over and picked up my bike, while a handful of pedestrians ran over to help.

"Sorry, dude, it's totally my fault," the guy said, in the same tone you might use if you'd stepped on someone's foot in the subway. "I wasn't paying attention. It looks like your bike isn't messed up, though, so that's good. Are you okay? Can I buy you a coffee or something?"

I was too freaked out to process how batshit insane the driver's response was. He'd just run me off the road. If I hadn't been wearing a helmet or if I hadn't been lucky enough to land the way I had, the guy could have been looking at lawsuits, manslaughter—all kinds of life-ruining consequences. But as soon as I determined that I probably wasn't seriously injured, my only thought was to get away from the crowd as fast as I could. A woman ran across the street, yelling: "I saw the whole thing! He just ran into you!" I didn't know what to say to her or to anyone else, and so, like a complete idiot, I grabbed my bike from the driver and said, "I'm okay, I gotta get to work." I didn't get the driver's insurance information or his phone number. Didn't even note the license plate of the car that had run me off the road. I just jetted to McSorley's. Made it in time for my shift and started tending bar without telling anyone. It took a few hours before the adrenaline wore off and my head cleared and I was able to explain to Michael what had happened. My dad was due to start a shift in twenty minutes, and when I told Michael I hadn't thought to get any information from the driver, he shook his head and laughed: "Bart might kick your ass worse than that car did."

He was right. By the time my dad joined me behind the bar, my right ankle and hip had stiffened up and I was dragging my right side a half step behind the rest of me. I straightened out my gait, tried to sell it like I didn't have a limp, but after years of hobbling around on bad knees, there was no fooling my father. "What's wrong with you?" he asked after five minutes of watching me labor up and down the bar. When I told him about the accident, he didn't get pissed at me so much as he just became highly aggravated about everything. The thought of me getting badly hurt— and him being unable to prevent it—infuriated him. He cursed me for not getting the driver's information, cursed the driver he'd never met, cursed the city for being full of careless motorists and clueless pedestrians and slippery manholes and all manner of hazards that might endanger his son. Fortunately, this time I'd only been scratched and banged up. My ankle loosened up after a few days and my hip felt janky for about a month, but I wasn't injured, and when it was over I had a badass McSorley's story to share with the staff: *Oh yeah? Remember the time I got run over by a car on the way to the bar and made it to work twenty minutes early?*

The worst pain I worked through at McSorley's came as a result of basketball injuries. The day after an errant chest pass turned the middle knuckle on my pinkie finger into a swollen, purple gobstopper, I made it through a busy afternoon at the bar by only using the four good fingers on my left hand to grab five mugs at a time, then compensating with eight-mug handfuls on the right. About a year before the broken finger, during a Saturday pickup game, I jumped for a rebound and got flipped over when another player barreled into my legs, sending me headfirst to the hardwood like a human javelin. I separated my left shoulder in the fall and made the regrettable, stubborn decision not to give up my waiter shift the following day.

I anticipated a fairly calm Sunday at McSorley's and planned to work one-armed whenever possible. Using my injured left arm to write checks was no problem—it was just that I couldn't raise it above shoulder level, and any feeble attempt to extend it in front of me made the arm feel as if it were being wrenched out of the socket. So I would try to only carry mugs in my right hand. For orders greater than eight, rather than distributing them evenly, I'd carry eight in the right and two or four in the left. With a little luck, I might make it through a full seven hours without having to hold six or eight mugs in my gimp arm.

No such luck. Sundays are unpredictable. They're almost never as busy as prime weekend shifts, when everyone arrives at work knowing they're going to sweat and jostle and hump ale out onto the floor from start to finish. Some weeks, Sundays are dead. But just as often, Sunday afternoons and early evenings will really hum. A waiter might have a group at every table, with enough spillover for a decent standing-room crowd at the bar. The day I came to work with one good arm ended up being a humming Sunday. I found myself gritting my teeth through jolts of pain, my shoulder shrieking as I pressed my mug-filled left hand against my chest to put more of the ale's weight on my core. As long as I held my left arm close to my body, I could gut it out. The two times I had to lean over a table and reach out with both arms to deliver a large order, my entire left arm slipped out of alignment and went numb for a few minutes. I played off my accompanying yelps of pain like bursts of laughter, and by doing so I think I managed to avoid freaking out too many customers. I got through the shift.

During my years working at the bar, the guy who always seemed to show up with the most impressive injuries was Brendan Buggy's son Sean, a waiter in his midtwenties whose side gig in construction and love for BMX bike riding frequently had him nursing wounds that would have put almost anybody else out of commission. He showed up one Sunday with a giant rectangular bruise in the middle of his forehead, like someone had stamped a cell phone on it. "The fuck happened to you?" was the first thing every fellow employee asked Sean upon seeing him. "A brick fell on my head at a building site yesterday," he answered. Pretty much everyone he told cracked a joke in response, but the one that stuck and remains part of the story today belonged to McNamara: "Fell? You sure somebody didn't drop a brick on your ass?"

Another time, during a slow weeknight shift, I was filling in behind the taps while my dad grabbed a bite to eat. Sean was working as the back-room waiter. He ordered five light and five dark—worth $27.50 at the time—and after I poured it, I noticed him taking longer than usual to pay for a pretty routine order. I looked closer at him. His eyelids drooped low and he fumbled through his wad of cash like he couldn't figure out the right amount.

"You okay?" I asked.

"Yeah, man, I'm good," Sean said. "I was on my bike last night and some fucker in a pickup basically ran me over, so my head's all fuzzy, but I can get through the shift."

He leaned over the bar and pulled his shoulder-length brown hair apart to reveal a gooey patch of hair and blood on his scalp. "This is where I cracked my head on the sidewalk," he said. "How bad does it look?"

The wound needed to be cleaned, but it didn't look that serious. Sean, however, was in bad shape and probably still had a concussion. He handed me his entire stack of bills, I took $30 from it and handed it back to him with $2.50 change, and he left to serve his five and five, wobbling and drifting as he walked back toward the kitchen. When he came back to put in another order, I offered to come out from behind the bar so he could go home and rest or head to the hospital to get checked out, but he declined. "Nah, man," he said. "It's cool. It's quiet tonight. I can make it till one. Would rather get paid than miss a shift."

Sean's answer exposed the real reason he and the rest of

us worked through any kind of pain, illness, or injury that didn't leave us bedridden: the money. Set aside the macho culture among McSorley's employees that encouraged tough-guy clichés about walking off injuries and gutting out shifts. Making a buck mattered most. And while the old-school way that McSorley's operates—cash only, no register, light or dark—is part of the pub's charm, it also creates a workplace that can be pretty damn unforgiving. For part-time staff like Sean and I were back then, guys who took fill-in shifts on short notice, turning down work didn't seem like an option. It didn't matter if a car had just slammed you off your bike or if somebody had dropped a brick on your head, if the McSorley's call came and you turned it down, you worried that there might not be another call. My dad, as a full-time bartender with years of experience, had more security, but when he missed work, that day's shift pay might be deducted from his salary (not to mention the amount he'd lose in tips).

Don't show up, don't get paid. It's a way to make sure that McSorley's bartenders and waiters stay committed to the job. It's harsh, but it's worked for 163 years. It's why my father waited decades to get knee replacement surgeries, gobbling ibuprofen and cursing under his breath to manage the non-stop torment in his joints. It's also why, when he got his knees replaced—one in 2005, the other in 2007—he pushed through rehab at a breakneck pace and was back to pumping ale in five weeks. He'd seen guys leave McSorley's for operations and return a couple of months later to learn that they'd lost their most lucrative shifts. And he knew that every day he didn't make it to work, he was jeopardizing his livelihood.

*   *   *

Shrugging off acute appendicitis to finish a shift at McSorley's may have been my dad's peak moment of barroom
invincibility, but that brush with disaster took a lot out of
him. Before then, even though he was well into his sixties,
pumping ale and working on his feet had kept him in great
shape. He stood six foot three and weighed 195 pounds,
trim around the waist and sporting a pair of thick, ropy
forearms grown from thousands of nights spent holding
hundreds upon hundreds of mugs underneath the McSorley's taps.

Now, bringing him home from the hospital a few days
after his appendectomy, I'd never seen him look so old. Bed
rest had cost him some muscle tone. His skin looked grayer
than normal and drooped loose off his bones. His steps
were short, halting, and uncertain, as if he wasn't quite sure
his legs could hold up his frame. It would be another week
before he could return to the hospital and have the sutures
removed from his belly, and in the meantime every move-
ment produced a wince and a grimace. Sometimes, on the
walk from his bedroom on one end of our apartment to the
bathroom on the other, he'd have to stop in the middle and
sit at the kitchen table to gather his strength.

He didn't stay frail for long. A week after coming home,
right after getting his sutures removed, he was back at work,
and a week after that he looked to be at full strength. But
even after his recovery, I still couldn't shake the image of
him curled up and frozen in pain on a hospital bed, and
from then on I kept a closer eye on him before, during,
and after work. At McSorley's, he was still Bart. No signs of

slowing down or becoming weak, still performing every task behind the bar with intimidating efficiency. He was old enough to get into movies with the senior citizen discount, but still capable of pumping more ale in a seven-hour shift than barmen twenty or thirty years his junior. At home, though, his routine was changing. He slept later and took more naps. He'd sit down in the recliner chair in our living room to read a novel, then conk out with the book spread across his chest before turning a page. His labor stayed as physical as ever, and he could still handle the pace and the pain McSorley's demands of its employees, but it was taking longer and longer for him to recover between shifts. He kept a strict regimen of rest and gym sessions to maintain the strength and stamina the job required, and this schedule was taking over his life. He had less time to work on poems or to drive upstate for hunting and fishing trips. When he made time to do the things he loved, sometimes the energy wasn't there to enjoy them. He devoted his days off to recouping the strength he'd need to get through the next week, with little time for anything else.

We worked together one night a few months after his surgery. The bar was packed and we made good money from 6 p.m. till closing, charming extra tips out of customers who guessed that the two six-foot-three gentlemen bartenders with the same nose and the same way of leaning back with our arms folded across our chests were father and son. It was winter by then, and gusty single-digit temperatures made the bike ride home feel especially bitter. The cold was so severe that when I got inside our apartment, I realized that the legs of my ale- and water-soaked jeans had frozen into sheets of cardboard denim. I waited for my pants to thaw, threw on some sweats, and sank into the couch. My dad brought over a quart of strawberry ice cream and crumpled into the chair beside me. I was asleep by the time he turned on the TV.

A couple of hours later, I woke up. The TV was still on and so were the living room lights. I saw my dad snoring gently in the chair, a spoon on his chest riding the rise and fall of his breath. It looked like he'd conked out midbite, and a circular pink stain had formed on his sweatshirt beneath the spoon. In his left palm, somehow, he still held on to the quart container, which seemed ready to fall at any moment.

It was a peaceful image, the simple spoils of hard work and a job well done. But there was also something searing and heartbreaking about seeing my dad, this man I'd loved watching pump ale since I was a toddler, passed out and looking utterly shot, like he had nothing left to give. I took the spoon and the ice cream, put them away, and left him to sleep in the recliner. That night finally drove home the notion that my father's career at McSorley's—his life's work—was winding down.

I knew he'd be back to normal in the morning and that his actual retirement was still years away. It wasn't hard to imagine him holding on to a couple of slower shifts until he turned seventy-five. Maybe even eighty. My only hope was that he'd be able to walk away whenever he was ready, and that he wouldn't stay long enough to let the bar take everything. There was nothing wrong with the work guys like Frank the Slob or Johnny Wadd did at McSorley's, peeling onions and staying overnight, because there wasn't much else for them to do. But I didn't want to see my dad enter that phase of the barman's life cycle. You could argue that there's a sweet-sad romance to that fate—my father, giving his body to McSorley's until he was completely, eternally spent. The poet in him might appreciate an image like that. But my dad has always been the hero of my story, and when the time comes for him to hang up his apron, I want to see him ride off into the sunset.

CHAPTER 12

Wishbones

THROUGHOUT MY LIFE AROUND McSORLEY'S, there was no
piece of the bar more sacred than the World War I wishbones. Other artifacts are more valuable, like the original
April 1865 wanted poster for John Wilkes Booth, "THE MUR-
DERER"; a signed letter that President Franklin Delano Roosevelt sent to McSorley's from the White House; the
Pulitzer-winning photograph of Babe Ruth's final curtain
call; Harry Houdini's handcuffs; and an original sketch by
Thomas Nast, the Gilded Age political cartoonist who
helped bring down New York's corrupt Tammany Hall
regime. Who knows, the wishbones might be worth even
less than McSorley's gray waiters' jackets, which part-time
employees occasionally swiped to sell on eBay for better
than fifty bucks a pop. But it never mattered what the bones
were worth, because according to tradition, no one could
touch them, let alone put them up for sale.

No McSorley's object was revered quite like the wishbones. There were about twenty of them, all turkey bones except for one curved duck bone, dangling above the bartop from the frame of a gas lamp that hadn't been used since electricity brought lightbulbs to McSorley's in the 1930s. When I was a kid, the bones were sheathed in an inch of dust, as if feathers of ash had grown back around what was left of the birds. In a bar where everything was old, from the scarred tables to the potbelly stove to the nineteenth-century icebox, the wishbones appeared downright ancient. For dust to grow that thick on top of those little bits of skeleton, they had to have been left untouched for almost a hundred years. They looked otherworldly, so much so that when tourists would visit McSorley's after reading about the wishbones in guidebooks, they would often march right up to the taps, glance at the dusty inverted Vs hanging above them, and then ask, "So where are the wishbones?" When the customers were informed that they were looking at them, their jaws would drop. Not only were the wishbones a stunning sight, but there was quiet grace and comfort in the notion that even in New York—where change is a sprint, not a march; where hustle is bred into the populace; and where the landscape of the city is repeatedly torn down, rebuilt, and transformed—those wishbones could remain in the same place, protected and still, long enough for that dust to accrue.

The beauty of those wishbones, although astounding, was no match for the story of how they came to hang above the bar. In 1917, shortly after Thanksgiving, a group of East Village locals came to McSorley's. Back then, the bar was run by Bill McSorley, Old John's son. The men were regulars, and in a matter of days they'd be shipping out to Europe to fight in the First World War. It was a going-away party, one last night of drinking and storytelling before they boarded a transatlantic freighter to head into combat and then, possibly, into the afterlife. Before Bill closed up that night, each of the men hung a turkey wishbone on the gas lamp for good luck. (Except for the one fellow whose Thanksgiving feast apparently had duck as its centerpiece. He left the stubby, curved misfit amid all the long, angular turkey bones, and eighty years later it would still hang there, puzzling drinkers and leading them to ask, "What's wrong with the one on the end?")

After the war, the men who survived came back to McSorley's. Each soldier took down one of the bones, a sign that his wish had been granted. The bones that remained belonged to the guys who never made it, and to honor their sacrifice, no one had been allowed to touch the bones since then.

I loved listening to my father tell the story of the wishbones. Whenever I could, I'd cling to his words, following along as he hit every note, sometimes speaking in a solemn tone that softened as the story reached its heartbreaking end, sometimes favoring a matter-of-fact style that let the bones themselves supply the drama. No matter how he delivered it, his rapt customers would be frozen, awash in awe as they gawked at the bones and realized that they were standing in the exact spot where the young soldiers had stood generations before them, standing in the footprints of those men who had raised a final toast to New York and their loved ones before leaving to give their lives in the Great War.

When my dad was in a good mood, he might continue,

pointing me out in the bar and telling the customers that his son, Rafe, was named after his great-grandfather, a World War I veteran named Raphael Eagan, who was wounded and awarded the Purple Heart for his conduct during the Battle of the Hindenburg Line. Then he'd weave in how the wishbones grounded McSorley's long tradition of being a place where servicemen could honor their fallen comrades. He'd point to the refurbished artillery shell that had been fired on D-Day at Omaha Beach and tilt his head in the direction of Vietnam War dog tags wrapped around various tchotchkes behind the bar. Years later, this progression would grow to include commemorative patches and engine company helmets displayed in memory of firefighters and police officers who died in the World Trade Center on 9/11.

As patrons listened to the wishbone story, I could watch the emotion build inside them. They usually didn't cry, but they'd turn reverent and grave. They were moved. Sometimes, emotion would get the better of people and they'd reach up to touch the wishbones, to pinch a chunk of dust and rub that history between their fingers. And that's when my father and every other McSorley's employee in sight would scream, "DON'T TOUCH!"

It's part of that sixth sense McSorley's workers have. The same way that Scott and Michael and Teresa could look at fifty clean mugs spread in front of them and pick out the one with a lipstick smudge, the same way my dad could feel a phony ten-dollar bill the moment it touched his fingertips, and the same way I learned to echolocate cracked handles on mugs, just about every bar employee could anticipate a hand reaching up toward the wishbones. At that point, it had been ingrained in us to do everything in our power to protect the wishbones. Fortunately, that duty has never gotten violent, but many of the guys at the bar wouldn't hesitate to push someone out of the way or snatch a hand out of the air to preserve the bones. Thankfully, a stern command just about always got the job done: "HEY, PAL! YOU WANNA TOUCH THAT? YOU'RE FUCKING WITH THE MEMORY OF SOLDIERS WHO DIED IN WORLD WAR ONE."

When I came of age and started picking up shifts at McSorley's, first during the spring of 2006, around the time of my mother's death, and then later, on and off for about five years between 2008 and 2015, I loved telling customers about the wishbones in front of my father. The first few times, he made a show of not paying attention to what I was saying, but I could see him watching from the corner of his eye, occasionally nodding as I hit my marks. I didn't have the confidence to deadpan it like he sometimes did; I always took a deep breath, put a sober look on my face, and attempted to convey gravitas. To be honest, though, I don't think the delivery mattered. That was the bounty of McSorley's—whether you were a foul-mouthed Irish crank or an overeager twentysomething trying to sound like his bartender dad, patrons loved the stories because they loved the bar.

Whenever I got through the whole story and whatever follow-up questions people had without needing to ask my father for a clarification, I felt like I'd just aced a midterm. It was another sign that I wasn't just a poser whose dad worked the taps. The respect I could command from customers while sharing the bar's most poignant story was proof that I wasn't only learning the mechanics of the job. Working at McSorley's meant more than just being fit and strong and coordinated enough to serve ale in a madhouse for seven hours at a time. The lifers I looked up to, employees like Brendan and Timmy, Scott and Michael, Teresa and Pepe, and my dad, they all knew how to perform McSorley's. They possessed distinct styles of relating to customers and spinning bar tales that felt heightened and authentic at the same time. When I started to find my McSorley's voice, I knew I belonged.

But just as I felt myself coming into my own, things began to change around the bar. The cost of living in Manhattan had risen to such exorbitant heights that the McSorley's crowd seemed to lose its identity. I had grown up listening to my dad say that people from all walks of life drank at the bar: cops and mobsters; movie stars and neighborhood bums; tourists from all over the world; every race and ethnicity you could find in the city; Wall Street suits and broke college students. But the heart of the place, he'd always add, was the working crowd: subway conductors, librarians, construction hard-hat types, teachers, Parks Department employees, school janitors. "That's the way it's supposed to be," he'd say, pointing to the menu for proof. "The place serves two ales for five bucks and four-dollar ham sandwiches—what else do you expect?"

By 2010 or 2011, rents were so high that the working crowd seemed awfully scarce in Lower Manhattan. Sure, there were stragglers who clung to apartments through rent control or lucky bastards like my dad and me who were grandfathered in. We'd owned our apartment for decades, since my mother bought it with the man she married and divorced before meeting my father, back when our block consisted of little more than loading docks and shipping depots. There was no way we'd be able to afford the place in the current market. But besides outliers like us, everyone my dad saw moving into the downtown neighborhoods where he'd lived for nearly his entire adult life had big money: investment bankers, hedge fund folks, corporate lawyers, consultants of this or that nonsense. The working crowd still drank, but they appeared to be spending less of their time and money in Manhattan and at McSorley's.

Foreign tourists were becoming the backbone of the business. And hey, as long as they bought food and drink, there wasn't much reason to complain. My dad never missed an opportunity to flex some broken *español* on visitors from Spain or Chile, and he turned European customers' resistance to tipping into a biting new catchphrase. Whenever he got stiffed, he'd call out, "FBI, Jim! FBI here! They're only leaving fingerprints!" Seconds later, calls would come back from the waiters: "No *Federales*! Ship 'em! Ship the maggots!" But when half the tables inside McSorley's on an average weeknight have Lonely Planet guides open on them, the place feels a little bit less like part of a neighborhood and instead starts to resemble a gimmick. Were we genuine McSorley's barmen? Or just historical reenactors playing dress-up in a tourist trap? "I don't know, Jim," my dad would grumble intermittently, sometimes at work and sometimes just sitting at our kitchen table. "Feels like the whole business is changing."

My dad might be the most paranoid man on the planet. He's been warning me to prepare for the day he drops dead from a heart attack since I was in second grade. He spiced up my first live Yankees game with a warning that gang members would be waiting to slit my throat if I went to the bathroom alone. He wished me well on my first day of riding the subway to high school with this reminder: "Don't make eye contact with anyone. If you lock eyes with the wrong person, they'll take a blade out and turn your face into a jigsaw puzzle." None of those things occurred. Likewise, although the changes at McSorley's did seem to mirror larger social changes in the city, business was still healthy and the bar remained true to its roots.

Then the city started fucking with the wishbones.

In July 2010 Mayor Michael Bloomberg announced a new citywide program of annual health inspections at New York restaurants and bars. Similar initiatives had been popular in Los Angeles and other major cities around the country. After passing a random inspection, the business would be assigned a letter grade to be displayed in the window for customers. That way, diners and drinkers could spot an A or B grade and feel confident that the food handling and preparation processes had been vetted and approved by a city agency whose sole concern was safety.

As public policy, the inspection plan seemed sound. It was standard-fare technocrat governance from a billionaire businessman mayor who promised to apply private-sector methods to improve New York's quality of life. When I arrived to work a Saturday shithouse gig a few days after Bloomberg unveiled the plan, however, the McSorley's staff was worried about how it could affect the business.

Richie the King, the back-room waiter, smirked at the idea of enforcing modern cleanliness codes on a bar where, to the best of everyone's ability, the place operated like it was still the early 1900s, and where an element of preserved griminess was part of the draw. "This is McSorley's, for Chrissake," Richie griped. "People come here 'cause it's old and dirty. What if they come in and tell us to stop putting sawdust down?"

"I guess this means hash is off the menu," cracked McNamara, who was filling in as the front-room waiter. "No more dog food—the hipsters will riot!"

Teresa, who was working the bar with my dad, calmed everyone down. "Relax, guys," she told the group. "Whenever the inspectors come, we'll deal with it. If they ask us to change things, we'll fix it. It's no big deal." She reminded us that we weren't just working in a bar but in a beloved New York institution. Bloomberg himself had visited McSorley's to make peace with the city's Irish community in March 2010, after he'd offended them by calling St. Patrick's Day an "excuse for drunks to start drinking earlier in the day." (I happened to be filling in the night of Bloomberg's courtesy call, and he posed for a picture behind the bar with me and Teresa, which now hangs on the back-room wall.) The city wasn't going to be unreasonable with us, Teresa said. The even keel was one of Teresa's trademark moves, and coming from the owner's daughter, it put everyone at ease and let us settle into the day's work.

Six months later, when the inspectors finally showed up, the city's team of two decided to hit McSorley's at nine thirty on a Friday night. The place was jammed, with a line stretched down the block and the staff in no mood to stop working and answer questions from a couple of two-bit bureaucrats. The waiters and bartenders held it together, gave the duo all they needed, and then resumed fueling the mob. I came in for another shithouse gig the next morning, and the staff was buzzing about the inspectors' list of infractions:

- A couple of blocks of cheddar were being stored in the icebox behind the bar, where the temperature was two degrees above the legal limit.

  Okay, just leave the cheese downstairs and the chefs will have to walk a few extra steps to replenish the supply.

- Dust was observed on some ledges behind the bar.

  No shit. Only on some ledges? They ever hear about the wishbones?

- A fly was observed in the kitchen during business hours.

  What the hell did these dimwits want? Is the chef supposed to put everything down at the busiest hour of the night, when he's got fifteen burgers on the grill, to shoo away a fly? We didn't make the fly! So what there's a fly? A fly could be anyplace, anytime.

- Two rodent droppings were found in the basement.

  Really? Two droppings? In the basement! They're really gonna say that the food in our kitchen could get contaminated by a stale mouse turd a full story below?

The staff gripes were two-pronged. First, who was the city kidding? McSorley's was a couple of years shy of its 160th birthday when Bloomberg's inspection policy kicked in — did they think a bar that old wasn't going to have a few cobwebs in the corners? Second, we took pride in the way we ran the bar, and history and experience told us we were doing it right. McSorley's operating procedures had been fine-tuned over generations. More technology would likely only take up space behind the bar, slow down service, and cut our profits. And furthermore, McSorley's health record was fine. Some of our cooks might have been bad enough to have James Beard rolling in his grave, but their food wouldn't have been responsible for putting that fat sucker six feet under. Our chefs' sins were almost always related to overcooked food—burger patties that felt like they'd been treated at a vulcanizing shop, boiled veggies turned into waterlogged mush, and slices of steak that could take ten minutes to chew into swallowable morsels. This wasn't fine dining, but it wasn't likely to get anyone sick, and the rest of the menu consisted of idiot-proof ingredients like cold cuts, cheddar cheese, raw onions, liverwurst, and canned chili and hash.

In my time working at McSorley's, I can't recall a single complaint that bar food had made a patron sick. More significantly, in the lifetime's worth of bar stories I'd heard from my father, food poisoning never came up. The way the bar functioned might have been outdated compared to other New York establishments, but it worked for our specific business and our customers. The city's new inspection regime felt to us like it wasn't nudging McSorley's toward sounder practices, but rather creating an arbitrary list of violations, assessing a fine, returning a couple of weeks later to make sure the bar had addressed the infractions, and then assigning us our passing grade.

As fate would have it, a health inspection didn't end up giving McSorley's its first major nudge away from tradition in recent years. Instead, that push came via a rambunctious kitty and a frivolous lawsuit. When McSorley's got Minnie, a new kitten, in 2010, it had been around fifteen years since the bar had found a widely adored cat. The previous one had been Sawdust, the tabby whose death in 1995 inspired Gene Hall's sweet elegy. McSorley's always had cats, though, and the two that inhabited the bar in the period between Sawdust and Minnie were a skittish brother-sister pair notable for their blimplike obesity and for the time one of the chefs puked on one of them. We cared for those sad little waddlers until they expired, and maybe a month later someone brought in Minnie.

Minnie was a darling: Her gray coat blended into tiny white booties at her paws, she had incandescent sapphire eyes, and she would have spent entire days rolling and playing in the sawdust if we would have let her. But city laws prohibited restaurants from keeping pets on the premises, and the McSorley's compromise was to banish Minnie to the basement during business hours and only let her into the bar before and after closing. But Pepe, the weekday manager, adored Minnie from the moment she popped out of the little cardboard box in which she'd been carried to the bar. During slow Monday and Tuesday mornings, he'd steal as much extra time with her as he could, scratching her belly on the bar and supposedly coaxing her to perch on his shoulder while he pumped ale. (I never saw this occur, and the image carries a distinct whiff of bar story poetic license.)

There was little harm in this—customers generally loved Minnie, and health inspectors were unlikely to arrive first thing in the morning. Then one day, as Minnie zipped around the bar, soaking up attention from the handful of

early-bird patrons, a woman in the back room started playing with her and wound up getting scratched. None of the
people who witnessed the incident thought much of it, and
the injury didn't seem severe, but a couple of weeks later we
learned that the woman had filed a lawsuit claiming that
the cat had "mauled" her. It was a joke, one that the *New
York Post* saw fit to put on its cover, which showed an ador-
able picture of Minnie, rolled over on her back with the
headline: IS THIS THE FACE OF A KILLER?

From what I heard, the lawsuit ended in some token settlement, but the publicity brought a call from the health
department. If it was true that McSorley's was keeping a cat
on the premises, it would have to be removed, and there
would be serious consequences if future health inspections
found we had ignored this recommendation. Minnie had to
go—Pepe ended up adopting her. But for the first time in
my life and the first time in more than a century, McSorley's
had no cats.

Maybe it was an omen. When our next inspection came
around, the unthinkable happened. One of the city inspectors pointed up and said that the thick dust clinging to the
wishbones presented a health hazard. What if a clump fell
off and landed in someone's mug of ale? This wasn't a new
concern for us, nor was the solution difficult: We'd apolo-
gize and pour them a new mug. Even if the inspector didn't
know the story of the wishbones, couldn't he tell just by
looking that they were special? That they must have been
left untouched for a reason?

This inspector arrived on a Saturday night in April 2011,
during a predictable crush of customers, and nobody working had time to educate the guy on the wishbones' meaning

or to talk him out of his decision to write up the violation. Let the guy do his job, then figure out a way to save the wishbones later. That was the plan.

I was scheduled to work Sunday and Monday night with my dad that week, and when we arrived at the bar a few minutes past five thirty on Sunday, Michael, who was finishing up his waiter shift, filled us in on the controversy and the options being weighed. Michael said he thought we could detach the gas lamp and wishbones and move them back from the bar to make it all but impossible for falling dust to land in a customer's drink. My dad said he could call Dan Barry, the *New York Times* columnist who'd written about the wishbones in 2004. But even though public sympathy would surely side with McSorley's in the dispute, using the press to pick a fight with City Hall wasn't worth the risk. Municipal employees like police, fire inspectors, probably even the food safety inspectors, seemed willing to give McSorley's favorable treatment because of the bar's venerable status and because a lot of them drank there. We always made a point of treating them to a round of ale on the house or free burgers. They liked the place. Out of respect for their service and because it was good for business, we wanted to keep it that way.

I suggested we build a sneeze guard–style shield and suspend it so that plexiglass would cover the areas immediately in front of and below the wishbones. If that wasn't enough, we could encase the entire gas lamp, including the bones, and either leave it suspended in place or find some new spot to display them. The ideal solution involved keeping the turkey bones where they were, but if that proved impossible, there had to be some way for us to keep them and the dust intact.

We batted ideas back and forth all night. Of all the outcomes we discussed, the one we didn't consider was to abide by the health department's command and clean off the dust. For me, that was inconceivable. One of the first McSorley's lessons my father had ever taught me, on the first day he brought me to work, was never to touch the wishbones — to respect the memory of those soldiers. I bet my father wasn't quite as naïve as I was that night, but he seemed equally convinced that McSorley's and the city could find an acceptable compromise on how to preserve the bones without exposing customers to any perilous snowflakes of dust. We closed up, tucked Johnny Wadd into the row of back-room chairs he used as a bed, and went home with the full expectation that when we came back for work the following night, we'd be returning to the same McSorley's.

Nope. That Monday we biked to the bar, like always, around 5:30 p.m. When we stepped through the swinging doors and into the front room, the day waiter, Shane, was waiting for us, pointing up at the gas lamp and shaking his head in disapproval. The turkey bones were still there, but they were naked. For the first time in my life, I saw the actual bones beneath all that dust.

"No." It was the only word I could muster. I was stupefied.

"Did you have to do it?" my father asked.

"Thank God, no," Shane said. He explained that after we closed up and left Sunday night, Matty came to McSorley's, the bar he'd owned since 1977, and did something he never thought he'd have to do. Rather than get into a protracted dispute with the city about how to preserve the dust, he decided his only recourse was to clean the wishbones. But he knew more than anyone how much that dust meant to the bar, and he couldn't bring himself to assign the task to an employee. So he drove in from Queens around three on Monday morning, rang the buzzer to get Johnny out of bed, and began the delicate work of removing each wishbone, one by one, wiping off the dust, and hanging it back in the same spot.

After he'd cleaned them all, it seemed like a sacrilege to toss away the dust, a potent symbol of the ninety-three years that generations of McSorley's bartenders, waiters, and customers had spent honoring those fallen soldiers. We would continue honoring them, of course, just not in the same way. Matty swept the dust into a Ziploc bag, sealed it, and took it home to Queens for safekeeping. Since my father and I had closed up just an hour or two before Matty arrived to shoulder his grim burden, that meant we were two of the very last people to see the wishbones the way I'd expected them to be forever—coated in dust.

I didn't expect to feel so rattled when the wishbones were dusted. I'd spent the first twenty-nine years of my life believing that the slightest graze against that dust was tantamount to desecrating the graves of the soldiers who'd hung the bones, and then over the course of one weekend that idea was turned on its head and discarded. I couldn't accept that. The dust on those bones was one of the bar's most profound symbols. That near-century of accumulated grit allowed us to literally see the soldiers' wishes to survive the war and make it home safely. To me, it suggested that even when a dream doesn't come true, it can live on to inspire others in ways that the person who made it could never imagine. In this case, their dreams hung in the McSorley's air, ennobling the laughter and song and drunkenness of the bar and reminding us to enjoy every precious moment.

The dust also mattered as a bit of lore that felt as if it couldn't have existed anywhere in the city besides the pub Old John opened in 1854. Another bar could hang a bunch of wishbones, but there was no shortcut to coating them with ninety-three years of dust. To see McSorley's lose such a distinctive piece of its history was heartbreaking, and it stoked a familiar sadness that had sat in my gut throughout my twenties, as the New York I grew up in was being erased and replaced around me.

Zito's, the Italian bakery on Bleecker Street that made the whole-wheat bread I ate nearly every day as a boy, had closed in the mid-2000s. When I walked around the downtown neighborhoods of my childhood, every corner seemed to represent the ghost of a long-gone storefront I'd once known. The deli on Seventeenth Street that had always seemed to have a back table full of construction workers sipping tall-boy cans of cheap beer was now a gourmet sandwich shop. The Chinese restaurant where I'd lunched with high school friends on half days had become a TGI Fridays. The places I associated with my formative years, the neighborhood shops that made New York my home, were gone or disappearing, and the city that was growing to replace them felt foreign to me. Here I was, a native New Yorker, unsure whether I still belonged in this town.

McSorley's should have been a bulwark against these feelings. Joseph Mitchell, the great *New Yorker* writer who profiled the bar in 1940, remained a regular until his death in 1996 precisely because McSorley's timeless nature allowed him to recapture a sense of the New York he loved. In

Thomas Kunkel's 2015 biography of Mitchell, *Man in Profile*, the author quotes from an entry in Mitchell's journal that describes a visit to McSorley's in the seventies:

McSorley's, middle of the afternoon, sit at [a] table in the back and have a few mugs of ale and escape for a while from the feeling that the world is out of control and about to come to an end.

He's right. McSorley's has the power to transport any of us to whatever New York era feels most like home. That's because it doesn't matter if a person first ordered two and two in 1967 or 2000, or if it takes two weeks or thirty years for that customer to come back. Whenever he returns, McSorley's will be the same.

That was what nagged me about the wishbones in 2011 — it was the first time I witnessed McSorley's succumb to change, and that sacred dust was never coming back. The bar had lost a crucial part of its identity. And if we could allow ourselves to break the promise never to touch the turkey bones, why believe in the story behind them at all? As Dan Barry noted in his 2004 *Times* column, there's no physical evidence that dates the bones to 1917. Inside McSorley's, the story is true because that's how it was passed down between generations of bartenders, from John Smith to Matty to my dad to Scott and Teresa and so on.

But if we trace the story back to John Smith, whose version included the vow to protect the wishbones, and that vow could be abandoned, why should we put any faith in the rest of the legend?

That first Monday night after the bones were dusted, I began the shift with my mind spinning, full of doubt and recriminations. I imagined a near future where the city had changed so dramatically that even though McSorley's remained intact, it no longer felt special. We'd still be there, serving ale and making a living, but we'd be more like actors at a Renaissance Faire than genuine barmen. McSorley's authenticity was a product of continuity—stories, work practices, and customs that started with Old John in 1854 and remained alive in today's staff. Losing the dust off the World War I wishbones was a blow to that continuity.

About forty-five minutes into the night, a couple of NYU students walked up to the bar from the back room. "Sorry," one of them said, to get my attention. "Can you tell us about the wishbones?"

Oh, shit. I looked to my father for guidance. How was I supposed to spin the ending? All he gave me was a shrug. "Don't ask me, Jimbo," he said. "Not my problem."

So I pointed to the smooth, dustless wishbones above our heads and started from the beginning: *Well, it was 1917. A group of local guys, regulars at the bar, planned to have a going-away party here at McSorley's. . . .* I stuck with the script all the way till the end, only it was no longer the end.

. . . The dust was an inch thick all around. For ninety-three years, nobody had been allowed to touch the wishbones. We would smack customers' hands out of the air if they reached up. And it was like that until—well, you guys aren't gonna believe this—until last night.

The twist had the NYU guys hooked. It had me hooked, too. I felt a rush, realizing that I was helping to unspool a new chapter of the bar's oral history.

No kidding, guys. The city health inspectors came in Saturday and ordered us to get rid of the dust, and because the owner knew it would've broken any of our hearts to clean the wishbones, he snuck in here after closing, without telling anyone, and did it himself. Gotta respect him for stepping up like that.

They were rapt. My concern that the wishbones would lose their power to inspire after being dusted couldn't have been more wrong. And as I recounted the careful attention Matty had paid to cleaning the bones one by one and making sure each was returned to its former spot on the gas lamp, I gained a greater appreciation for the sacrifice he'd made on behalf of his staff. McSorley's was his life's work, just like it was my dad's and Pepe's and everyone else's. It must have torn a hole in Matty's conscience to clean those wishbones, and he'd spared us that pain. And his decision to preserve all the dust and take it home with him was a touching act of reverence, worthy of the dreams those soldiers left on the gas lamp in 1917.

All of a sudden, a shift that had started with me feeling devastated and forecasting the eventual decline of McSorley's once-great Ale House had flipped into an emotional high. I'd never felt prouder to work for Matty, never felt prouder to be a tiny patch in McSorley's timeless fabric.

CHAPTER 13

Sandy

IN THE SPRAWLING HISTORY OF McSorley's—the hundreds
of men and women who've worked at the bar, the generations of drinkers who've ordered a round—I'm no more
than a blip. This is the pub where Abraham Lincoln stood
on Peter Cooper's chair in 1860 and appealed to everyday
New Yorkers to make him the sixteenth president of the
United States. It's where John Sloan observed and painted
saloon life. It's where Dylan Thomas got out of line and got
eighty-sixed. Hell, it's the home of a watershed moment for
the women's rights movement, thanks to the court decision
that forced McSorley's to finally open its doors to female
customers in 1970.

My overall contribution to the bar could be summed up
like this: "Helped keep the place running for a couple of
hundred nights over the course of about five years." Out of
163 years of continuous operation (and counting), that's

bupkes. So even though that half decade and two hundred or so fill-in shifts were a lifelong dream come true for me, perhaps the most noteworthy thing I can say about my bartending days was that I worked the last shift before the longest shutdown in McSorley's history—the night in 2012 when Hurricane Sandy blasted New York, caused thirty-two billion dollars in damage, and plunged Lower Manhattan into darkness.

That four-day power outage wound up doing what no other event—not even Prohibition—could do to McSorley's for a sustained period: keep the bar closed. Since Matty asked my father to start working Sundays in 1979, McSorley's has only been closed to the public on Christmas and Thanksgiving. When blizzards buried New York under several feet of snow in 1996 and 2010, the bar still opened at 11 a.m. and closed at 1 a.m. After Al Qaeda brought down the Twin Towers on September 11, 2001, when New Yorkers were shell-shocked and city officials banned travel below Fourteenth Street for everyone except downtown residents and people on official business, McSorley's remained open. And we would have kept serving ale right through Sandy and in the storm's aftermath, too, but the blackout stopped us. The ale lines, plastic tubes that draw booze from the kegs in the basement and carry it upstairs to the taps, rely on electric power. With no juice, there was no way to fill the mugs, and for a few days McSorley's became like a body with no blood.

But this isn't about that handful of days, the only time in New York's last century and a half when you couldn't saunter through the swinging doors at 15 East Seventh Street and order two light ales and a small cheddar plate. It's about the night before, the most unforgettable shift of my McSorley's career, and working it with my dad.

*   *   *

Sandy hit New York on Monday, October 29, but bitter-cold rain and umbrella-shredding winds had already arrived in the city by Sunday. That night, Scott and Michael hopped on the phone to plan the bar's staffing during the storm. By then, the severe conditions and the repeated warnings about flooding and hurricane-strength winds had been enough to convince us that most New Yorkers would stay home Monday evening. The previous year, the city had hunkered down for Hurricane Irene, and when the storm veered away from New York, the false alarm turned into an accidental holiday, with drinkers who'd been excused from work mobbing McSorley's to celebrate. It was pretty clear that wouldn't be the case during Sandy, so Scott and Michael decided that my dad and I would run McSorley's as a bare-bones two-man crew the way we'd done for the Super Bowl. Much of the staff lived in Queens and would risk being stuck in Manhattan if the storm caused road closures. Shane and Timmy lived upstairs from McSorley's, and Michael's apartment was a couple of blocks down Seventh Street—if the predictions turned out to be wrong and the bar got crowded, they'd be able to provide reinforcements. Barring that, however, it would be just the Bartholomew boys, with my dad on the bar while I waited tables and ran a limited kitchen.

Monday afternoon, all it took was a quick glance out the window to know that we wouldn't be able to bike to work. On the street corner, we could see a stop sign vibrating furiously in the wind. If we rode out there on bicycles, it looked like neither of us would last three blocks before getting blown off our seats. So we started gearing up to walk through the hurricane. Forget umbrellas, the only option was to layer up thermal undershirts under our raincoats and pull the hoods tight over our heads. We each carried a full change of clothes in our backpacks—T-shirts, socks, underwear, jeans, and white dress shirts, double-wrapped in plastic bags. The walk across town would soak us to the bone, but at least we'd have a dry change of clothes once we got to McSorley's.

Since my father has thirty-seven years on me, he left the apartment ten minutes earlier. For a sixty-seven-year-old with two bionic knees, he was in fantastic shape (and going on seventy-two, he still is), but I was a few steps faster than him and gave him the head start. Plus, for reasons that are purely idiosyncratic, he preferred a route that zigzagged northeast from Houston Street to LaGuardia Place to Fourth Street and then finally up the Bowery, while I insisted on slicing diagonally through Washington Square Park and then hooking around Astor Place for a walk that included fewer stoplights but spat me out one block north of the bar. Besides, in the middle of a brewing hurricane, with rain hammering down on our hoods and wind howling all around us, this wasn't the time for a father-son walk. This was weather for a solo trek that would chill a man's bones and test his mettle.

I'm laying it on thick with the prove-your-manhood stuff. We were really just walking across downtown Manhattan in a bad rainstorm. But that's the McSorley's influence, the impulse to build a story out of anything, perhaps so you can tell it later at the bar but also because it livens up the way we think about our day-to-day lives. The answer to "What'd you do today?" isn't "I walked to work and served drinks." It's "A goddamn taxi ran a red light and almost killed me on the way to the bar, then Pepe had me hump mugs up from the basement all morning until it got busy, and I had to tell a couple of Hells Angels to put their bowie knives away and stop carving up the tables, and I didn't even have time to get a bowl of soup out of the kitchen for lunch." Both accounts could describe a normal day at McSorley's, so why not go with the more exciting version?

From our third-story window, I watched my dad step out into the rain, wipe the fog off his glasses, and tie a scarf around his face like a balaclava. He put his head down and leaned into the wind, his bright yellow jacket flapping hard against his back. Later, when I faced that same wind, it felt like a wet slap in the face. On my way to the bar, I passed downtown landmarks that had undergone eerie transformations in the storm. The West Fourth Street basketball courts, where I used to spend summers clinging to the chain link fence and watching tournaments, had been whipped into a sunken garden, with a parquet of fall leaves plastered to the blacktop and severed branches of nearby trees stuck in the backboards. The chessboard tables at the southwest corner of Washington Square Park were for once empty of speed-chess hustlers and dudes whispering "Yo, big man, got trees, got coke, got weed." In the thirty-five minutes it took to walk to McSorley's, I counted only three other pedestrians out in the rain. It was the neighborhood where I'd spent most of my life, but on this day it looked like nothing I'd ever seen before.

When I reached McSorley's, I entered the front room with a few slow, deliberate stomps to shake the water off my boots. My dad was standing next to the potbelly stove with his belt unbuckled and his pants undone, in the process of tucking in his work shirt. This was a sure sign that business was dead—that there were so few customers that my old man didn't feel the need to duck into the kitchen or the men's room to fix his shirt and pants. I headed back to the kitchen to change into my spare clothes, and when I returned to the front room it was empty except for my father, Michael, and Shane, the two of whom said they'd poured less than half a keg of ale all day (a paltry amount). If projections that the storm would strengthen overnight proved true, our chances of getting a surprise rush at some point were probably nil.

Michael and Shane lingered after the shift change, and our conversation turned to whether the hurricane would knock out power in parts of Manhattan, as city officials had warned it might. In case it did happen, Michael had bought a couple of dozen tall red candles and placed them in two plastic bags on top of the bar. My father had read about the coming storm surge, the likelihood of flooding on blocks near the Hudson and East Rivers, and the chances that the weather could affect Con Edison's substations and transformers: "There's gonna be a blackout."

I didn't believe it. I could remember too many times when the city had overstated warnings about danger and damage coming from all sorts of natural and man-made hazards: Atlantic hurricanes; winter blizzards; "nor'easter" snowstorms; bird flu; swine flu; even Halloween 1997, when the NYPD and Mayor Rudy Giuliani urged high school students to stay off the streets because a New York offshoot of the Bloods gang was planning to slash the faces of innocent pedestrians as part of a mass initiation. That Halloween ended up being the safest in decades, and those flus never affected anyone I knew. Half the time, it seemed, the storms didn't even arrive. When they did hit, they were often less severe than predicted, and the worst effects of the biggest, baddest weather events that hit New York never seemed that bad. So what if the financial markets couldn't open for a day or if school was canceled and the city lost money? It never touched me.

I knew Hurricane Sandy was nasty—I'd just walked through it. That was the thing, though. If my dad and I could put our heads down and trudge through the storm, how could it manage to knock out power and force McSorley's to close? I knew this was awful logic—what did our ability to walk across town have to do with the power grid? But I didn't need logic to trust what I'd known as long as I'd been alive: that McSorley's would stay open through damn near anything, and that my dad would be there, pumping lights and darks. There was nothing more reliable in my world, and that had been true ever since I was a toddler standing in the front room on Saturday mornings and craning my neck to watch my dad pour on the other side of the bar. Broken toes and a burst appendix hadn't stopped him in the past, and as far as I was concerned, neither would this storm. We would make it to the end of the shift.

"You really think we'll have to close early?" I asked.

"Jimbo, the question is when, not if," my dad said.

Michael chimed in: "Well, if it happens, we'll come back and have a drink before you go home." Then he and Shane left to get dinner, and it was just my dad and me left inside McSorley's to work and to wait.

"Where's the hurricane crowd?"

A young couple had walked over from their apartment in Alphabet City and couldn't believe they were the only customers inside McSorley's. "I've never seen it like this before," the woman whispered to her husband.

They'd stopped by McSorley's the previous year, when Hurricane Irene wound up bypassing the city, and they'd expected to find another raucous mob looking to take advantage of a day off work during Sandy. "In case you guys didn't notice," my dad said, "the storm actually hit us this time."

The couple stayed long enough for a few rounds, and I volunteered to fire up the grill, turn on the deep fryer, and cook them burgers and fries, since I had nothing better to do. While I played around in the kitchen, my dad pointed out little bits of wall trivia that customers rarely get to see during normal business hours: *You see that faded broadsheet by the thermostat? That's the London* Times *from 1815. If you look close you can see it has a report of Napoleon's decision to engage the British Army at Waterloo.... Yeah, that's a bunch of us with Charlie Sheen in the back. My son—the guy cooking your burgers, if you didn't notice—was crazy about the* Young Guns *movies with Sheen and Estevez back then....See the American flag framed above us right here? Count the stars. Only forty-eight. It went up before Hawaii and Alaska became states.*

By the time I'd finished cooking the burgers, a couple of larger groups had shown up and claimed tables—just gangs of four or five friends from the neighborhood who'd gotten tired of waiting out the hurricane in their apartments and wandered out to see what was open. My dad poured their ale, and after I'd dropped the mugs off on their tables I went back into the kitchen to toss together a couple of cheese plates on the house. While the customers watched local news coverage of the storm on the back-room TV, my dad and I wandered to the front of the bar to watch the street. A wire garbage can had blown over on the corner of Taras Shevchenko Place, a single-block street that runs between Sixth and Seventh Streets next to St. George's Church and a Cooper Union architecture school building. The wind spun the trash can in wide circles like a stunt driver doing donuts in an empty parking lot, and every thirty seconds a piece of cardboard would fly past the window. Long stretches would pass without us seeing a car or pedestrian moving about in the street.

"Nasty," I said. "What's the weirdest thing about this?"

My dad thought it over: "No taxis. It's like a different city."

Just then, a Chinese-food deliveryman struggled by on a bicycle. Every ten feet he'd have to take his feet off the pedals and plant them on the concrete to prevent a fall. Rain kept blowing sideways into his face. Near the corner his tire slipped on a manhole cover and he nearly wiped out. "Well, Jim," my dad said, "I guess some poor mofos out there got it worse than us tonight."

While we chuckled over the deliveryman's plight, a hunched figure scurried past the window and through the front door. It was Johnny Wadd, with a sweatshirt draped over his head and a black plastic bag in one hand. "Quit laughing at me, you two," Johnny said. He sat down at a window table and started rifling through the bag, which he liked to call his "purse." Its contents never varied: Luden's cough drops, cherry flavor; a couple of nubby half-smoked cigarettes he'd scrounged off the sidewalk; lotto tickets; and a battery-powered AM/FM radio. "Are they still gonna pick the numbers tonight?" he asked of no one in particular.

"Johnny, look outside," my dad said. "The city's got bigger problems. By the time they're supposed to draw the numbers there'll probably be a blackout."

"That's why I brought the radio," Johnny said. "Say, do you have any batteries back there? I should get some fresh ones in case the power blows and we gotta hear the news."

"Johnny, you whore, you got some balls under that hernia," my dad said, tossing him a couple of AAs from behind the bar. "You bring that thing every day. You want to con me out of some batteries, just say so."

"Go fuck yourself, Bart," Johnny said with a knowing smirk. "This is what I get for trying to help around here."

Then, out of nowhere, we heard a violent crash outside. It sounded like a building had collapsed somewhere down the block. We all jerked our heads in the direction of the noise and scanned the street for damage. I had caught a glimpse of something from the corner of my eye—like a giant wooden outhouse falling from the sky and splattering on the sidewalk. But that didn't make any sense. Where would an outhouse come from? Against my dad's wishes, I slipped out the front door to get a clearer look. Across the street, on the sidewalk in front of the Cooper Union building, was a pile of splintered two-by-fours and bent metal brackets, all scattered like pickup sticks. When I spotted a piece of what had been the structure's conical roof, the puzzle came together in my head.

"Looks like a water tower blew off one of the buildings on that block," I told Johnny and my dad once I got back inside, dabbing the rain off my face with a bar rag.

"*Jesus*," my dad said. "I'm not walking home through that. If it stays this bad, we're having a sleepover here with Johnny."

*   *   *

For the next hour or so, everyone in the bar seemed on edge. Sandy showed no signs of letting up; objects that don't normally defy gravity kept blowing by, airborne in the street; someone stepped inside the bar just to caution anyone who had planned to head outside to stay away from Fifth Street and the Bowery, where glass windowpanes had gone flying off the upper stories of the Standard Hotel. The nose-diving water tower put a scare into me, my father, Johnny, and the handful of customers still inside McSorley's. At that moment, no one seemed totally confident that the night would end without some measure of disaster.

Yet the lights stayed on and we kept serving light and dark ale whenever folks were ready for another round. During lulls in the downpour, I'd talk myself into believing we'd make it through the night without losing power, but then the rain and wind would pick up again and it would feel like we were all cooped up in the bar, waiting for something to snap.

And then, a few minutes after 8:30 p.m., we heard a swift, sharp crack, followed by darkness.

"WHOAAAAA!" The dozen or so customers in the back room whooped and clapped. It was the crescendo we'd been waiting for. Of course, none of us knew that the climax had been literally explosive—fifteen blocks away, a Con Ed substation near Fourteenth Street and the East River had blown up and plunged Lower Manhattan into untempered night. The battery-powered emergency flood lamps above the side door leading to the tenement hallway came to life, and the pale fluorescent bulbs lit the back room like a ghostly campsite.

The customers at two tables asked to settle their bills so they could head home and make sure their apartments were secure. The last remaining group looked at me and my father: "Can we just keep drinking?"

I looked at my dad and shrugged. *What do you want to do?* "The emergency lights will last a half hour, maybe forty-five minutes," he said. "Finish your ales, then we'll sell you guys a round of bottles, and after that you should probably take off." He handed me a flashlight and told me to check out the kitchen. I made sure the gas line was closed and that the door and gate leading to the alley behind the bar were locked. My dad was in the front room, lighting candles in a row down the bar, asking Johnny if he was okay, and throwing the bolt lock across the front door just in case the blackout brought out people looking for trouble. I grabbed a marker and scrawled CLOSED — STORM on a sheet of paper, then taped it in the front window. My father got Johnny's radio, found a station that was broadcasting news about the hurricane, and put it in the middle of the bar so the sound would carry.

"I told you we were gonna need it!" Johnny snapped, infusing his voice with more *neener-neener-neener* than I'd heard since grade school.

"Yeah, Johnny, you're a real hero," my dad told him. He ambled up to the taps, pulled each one forward as if he were going to pour, and confirmed that they couldn't draw ale up from the kegs. "Yep," he chirped, "party's over."

I collected the leftover empty mugs and asked the guys in the back if they still wanted bottles (before the bar's brewery stopped bottling McSorley's Ale in 2014, we always kept a few six-packs of the light behind the bar). "Hell yeah we want 'em," one customer said. "Nothing to do but get drunk now." I pulled a sixer out of the icebox, popped off the caps, and dropped it on their table.

These fellows weren't alone in their impulse to drink once the electricity blew. About fifteen minutes after the lights went out — long enough for folks in the neighborhood to look out their windows and decide that the city wasn't going to erupt in riots — the pay phone next to the window table started ringing off the hook with callers wanting to know if we were open. The moment downtown went dark was like catharsis, the breaking point New Yorkers were waiting for, and once it came, people were ready for a drink. But would any place be open during a blackout in the middle of a hurricane? McSorley's was the first bar that came to mind for dozens of would-be revelers that night, and their back-to-back calls drove Johnny nuts. (He was laid out, dozing on the chairs underneath the pay phone.)

"Leave it off the hook!" he wailed. "Please! I'm trying to sleep."

"Hey, numbnuts," my dad piped up. "That's the only working phone we got right now. Why don't you pick up that big ol' wad of yours, stand up, and lay your lazy ass down by the stove." Johnny muttered and grumbled, swept his belongings into his plastic bag, and then groaned and shuffled his way to the other table.

The pay phone rang again, and I answered, expecting to tell another customer that no, there was no more ale to serve, so McSorley's would be closed until further notice. But this time it was Matty on the other end, checking in from his home in Queens. I told him we were all fine and passed the phone to my dad. "Hey, Matt," he said. "Yeah, it was quiet all night. Some damage on the block but nothing close to us. Johnny's good, he's with us. Crazy thing is that if we had any way to stay open, we'd probably get some action right now.... Uh-huh, Murphy's Law. That's McSorley's, right?"

Michael and Shane showed up around nine, just as the guys in the back were finishing their bottles and settling their tab. Five minutes later we had McSorley's to ourselves, and about five minutes after that the emergency lights went kaput. We lit a couple of candles and took them over to the big round table near the potbelly stove. Johnny was a couple of feet away, stretched out on the chairs lined against the wall, right where Sawdust the cat had loved to sleep.

I brought a mug and a can of ginger ale for my dad, plus two clean empties for Michael and Shane, who came with Irish whiskey and a few bottles of wine, plus another six-pack of McSorley's from the icebox. At first we talked about the storm. Michael and Shane had heard about the Con Ed explosion via text messages from friends outside the city, who had seen TV footage of the substation consumed in a flash of green light. We all assumed—incorrectly, as it turned out—that power would be restored within twenty-four hours. We marveled at the notion that hardly anything in history had managed to stop us and the generations of McSorley's employees before us from coming to work, and that the next morning, for the first time in as long as anyone could remember, the bar would stay closed past 11 a.m. on a weekday that wasn't Christmas or Thanksgiving.

Before long, our conversation turned to bar stories. This

might have happened under any circumstances, but the storm beating against the windows and the candle-lit darkness inside made McSorley's as timeless and elemental as we'd ever seen it. My dad said he couldn't believe that it had been more than forty years since he'd accidentally swindled Doc Zory out of a Friday waiter shift to work his first night at the bar. "It feels like I've been around that long, I guess," he explained. "I'm just not sure when I turned into such an old fucker." Michael joked that my dad was already old twenty years ago, when Michael came to New York from Ireland and began working at McSorley's.

I asked if anyone had any idea where Katz, the former night watchman, was during the hurricane, and Michael said Katz had an apartment way out in Brooklyn, somewhere near Canarsie or the Flatlands. This led into the story of how Katz got banned from McSorley's. After the night when he'd showed up and spent most of the Super Bowl kvetching at Mel Gibson the dolphin, Katz had become increasingly unhinged. He started arriving at the bar early in the day and waiting around till closing to begin his overnight shift, which might not have been a problem if he hadn't also become bolder and creepier than ever in his interactions with customers. It was one thing for Katz to come fifteen minutes before last call and point his voodoo hex at customers who needed to finish up and leave anyway. But now he was camping out at the window tables during the lunch rush and using his schizoid anti-Semitic ventriloquist act with the stuffed dolphin to scare away customers who tried to share space with him. This cost the bar money, and it wasn't long before Pepe eighty-sixed him permanently and Katz was told not to come back for his overnight shifts.

"Remember, that's not even the best part," my dad added. "The week after Katz got the boot, he rented a white SUV on a Friday night and had it drive around the block over and over again for an hour. Every time it would pass the bar, the truck would slow down, and Katz would lean out the window. Crazy bastard had a white shirt wrapped around his head like a turban, waving a towel in one hand, drunk as a skunk and yelling, 'I got a bomb, I got a bomb, I got a bomb!' Then that high-pitched, squealing cackle of his. I wasn't here but McNamara said it was the funniest thing he ever saw." (Katz's exile lasted about three years. He eventually made amends with Pepe and is currently allowed back inside McSorley's, although he's no longer one of the bar's night watchmen.)

Johnny sat up in his chair: "I was out there with him. I almost popped my hernia laughing at that fruitcake. But still, the funniest thing I seen here was the night you had Rafe tossing those grates into the Dumpster."

That was my cue. I jumped in to explain to Michael and Shane how one night a couple of winters ago we'd noticed that a construction crew had moved one of those bus-length open trash containers across the street from the bar. For us, this meant a chance to finally dispose of a stack of heavy, rusted grates that had been part of the kitchen's old grease exhaust system. Normal city trash pickups wouldn't take this kind of waste, so we waited for the right opportunity to get rid of the grates, and the Dumpster was it. A few minutes after 1 a.m., once we'd gotten all the customers out, my dad told me to drag the grates out from the alley and heave them into the Dumpster. Johnny was around that night and he crossed the street with me to keep lookout, since officially we weren't supposed to be adding our trash to the

SANDY

contractor's private Dumpster. The wall of the container was around eight feet high and the grates weighed about thirty pounds each. I crouched down, sprang up with my knees, and used my momentum to loft the first grate over my head and into the Dumpster. No problem—three more to go. On the second grate, though, right after it cleared the wall, a homeless man leapt from the Dumpster onto the pavement in front of me.

"Holy shit!" I shrieked. I was so startled that I cocked a grate back to swat the guy if necessary.

"Man, I was sleeping in there," the homeless man said, sounding plaintive and disappointed before running down the block. Meanwhile, Johnny was doubled over, crying with laughter.

"Oh, that was the best," he gasped. "I can't even breathe. You looked like you shat your pants. Oh, that was good. I need to sit down."

When I finished the story, Johnny was once again in stitches, sucking air between joyous complaints that he might laugh himself to death. Once he settled down, my father asked Michael if he'd heard anything about the plan my dad had recently floated to juggle the schedule and allow him to reduce his workweek to four shifts instead of five. "Matt say anything about the shift change? What about Teresa or Scottie?" my dad said. If it went through, he said, he thought he could keep working at McSorley's well into his seventies, slowly scaling back from four shifts to two as the years passed. That was better than retirement, he said, since we'd never gone on family vacations or road trips and he just spent his days off upstate. He owned a lakeside cabin a couple of hours northwest of the city, where he liked to hunt and fish and read and watch sunsets and thunderstorms out on the water.

"As long as I can stand through a shift," my dad reasoned, "I might as well show up a couple times a week, keep myself in half-decent shape, and make a buck."

Before we knew it, a couple of hours had passed. Michael and Shane had killed both bottles of wine, and I'd just about polished off the McSorley's bottles. Johnny was zonked out with a bar rag covering his face, his chest heaving gently as he emitted wheezy little snores. It was almost midnight and the hurricane had finally quieted down. The wind was still strong enough to rattle the aluminum parking signs on the sidewalk, but the rain had slowed to a drizzle. My dad stood up to take a leak, and when he came back from the men's room, he tapped me on the shoulder. "Whaddya think?" he said. "Wanna take our chances out there and see if we still have a home on the other side of town?"

"Fuck it," I said. "Let's walk."

Michael and Shane said they'd stay behind. Some friends from the neighborhood were due to come over, keep them company, and play card games by candlelight while they killed what was left of the whiskey. Eventually, Michael would head down the street to his place and Shane would sleep upstairs in his apartment and then come down to check on Johnny in the morning. We had no clue the blackout would go on for three more nights and figured we'd all be back on normal work schedules by Wednesday. (Instead, McSorley's didn't reopen till Friday.) We all shook hands, Michael and Shane wished us luck, and my dad and I wandered into the night.

When we reached the corner, the view up Third Avenue was spellbinding: Manhattan with no lights. We could make out the gray geometry of the street plunging into the horizon between an endless stretch of looming apartment buildings and skyscrapers. We started down the Bowery but got turned back by a poncho-clad policeman at the corner of Fifth Street. Apparently, there was still some concern about glass falling from the hotel.

"What are you guys doing out right now?" the officer said, a touch of anger in his voice. "It's not playtime. People can get hurt."

"We're from McSorley's," my dad said, knowing that a name-drop of the bar would put the officer at ease. "Just trying to get home after work."

"McSorley's, no kidding," the officer said. "I used to go in there before I was even allowed to drink. You know Scott and Brendan? I fuckin' love those guys—they always take care of our crew from the Ninth. So which way you headed?"

"Trying to get across town," I answered. "Greenwich Street, a couple blocks below Houston."

"Well, don't come this way unless you want to catch a shard of glass in your neck," he said. "You're probably safest walking up to Ninth and going west from there. Haven't heard of any problems up that way."

We thanked him, told him to stay safe, and headed back toward Ninth Street. No cars were out—among other reasons, the lack of working stoplights encouraged motorists to stay away. So we walked right down the middle of the street, far from the sidewalks in case the blustery winds knocked anything off a building as we passed. Also, staying in the middle of the street gave us plenty of options to head the other way if someone stepped out of the shadows and we didn't like the looks of him.

Maybe it sounds ridiculous for two six-foot-three men to

worry about getting jumped in a part of Manhattan that's among the safest and wealthiest chunks of land on the planet, but both my dad and I had lived through the days when getting mugged wasn't rare in any part of New York. I'd been robbed twice by the time I was fourteen, and my dad used to carry a military baton to swat away would-be assailants while he biked home from McSorley's. Even though the city had changed, we'd never been able to let go of certain street-smart precautions.

At every avenue, we couldn't help but stop and marvel at the stretches of murky, lightless metropolis. We never saw such pure night—not anywhere in the five boroughs, at least—and it made the city seem raw and wild and a little bit scary. But there was also something spiritual in the quiet of that night, a once-in-a-lifetime moment to feel the city asleep.

When was the last time New York had been this silent? Would Old John McSorley have felt anything like this? Probably not—the East Village and Lower East Side of the late nineteenth century were a teeming mosaic of immigrant neighborhoods, an overcrowded melting pot at the point of boiling over. But Old John had built the bar that 150 years later would teach me how to appreciate tranquility on empty Tuesday nights and desolate Super Bowl Sundays, when the best way to get through a shift was to let my mind wander until it was lost.

I got to thinking that the bar had formed the values that mattered most to me and the traits that made up the core of my being. After withstanding the all-day rush of Paddy's Day, I knew I could keep my cool in the midst of any chaos. I could power through all sorts of pain—broken fingers, separated shoulders, car-on-bike collisions—and still finish a job. I could survive the anguish of watching my mother die with the strength of the bar behind me. I knew I could go out anywhere in the world, come back to New York at any time, and still have a home, a place where people have known me since I was just a phrase — "Little Bart," as my father wrote in the McSorley's logbook the month I was born. Matty, Teresa, Scott, Michael, Pepe, Richie the King, Brendan — they'd all seen me grow from tyke to man.

To have that kind of history is rare in any place. To have it amid the constant churn of New York City is almost unheard of. In my city, McSorley's Old Ale House may not have literally been around forever, but it feels about as permanent as anything gets. And knowing that I come from the same stock as a place with such staying power, that some chunk of me is cut from the same cloth as Old John McSorley, his son Bill, John Smith, and the entire 163-year-old lineage of McSorley's bartenders, waiters, chefs, and hangers-on — well, it's hard to describe precisely how that makes me feel. It's like having an anchor; as long as the bar is there, I'll never be adrift.

All this was blazing through my mind as my dad and I turned the corner down Seventh Avenue and headed south for the last few blocks before we reached home. It occurred to me that all the strengths I had gleaned from McSorley's also happened to be virtues that I saw in my father. Was it the bar that had made me? Or was it my dad? To me, there was no difference.

At the corner of Houston and Varick Streets, he slung his arm around my shoulder. "Hey, bunghead," he said. "I love you."

Acknowledgments

Before everything else, I have to thank the owners and staff of McSorley's Old Ale House. Without you and the bar this book wouldn't exist and neither would I, at least not the person I am today. To Matthew Maher and his family, Teresa Maher and Gregory de la Haba, Scott and Annie and Sean Pullman, and Maeve McNamara; to Richie Buggy, Richie Walsh, Brendan Buggy, Shane Buggy, and Sean Buggy; to Michael Brannigan, Pepe Zwaryczuk, Timmy Whelan, Allan McLafferty, and Mike McNamara; to Mary Moylan, Jerry, Carolina, and Enrique; to Kevin Bielinksi and Coach, Schultz and Motz, Marty and Jerry; Bill and Phil, Mike Mele Jr and Pete De Adamo; to Tommy Lloyd, Tommy Nolan, Pete Farnan, Tom Fuller, Pete Drum, Kevin Noone, Bill Wander, and John Mahoney; to the generations of McSorley bartenders who came before us; to Bart. Thank you for allowing me to work alongside you; thank you for permitting me to write this book; thank you for raising me. As proud as I am to have the opportunity to publish our story, it's hard to shake the feeling that I'm less deserving than any of you to tell it. I hope that you'll forgive all the wonderful details I wasn't able to fit into these pages and that you'll find what I did manage to include true to our experience.

It's no exaggeration to say that this book would not have

made it to publication without the support, encouragement, and hard work of many others besides myself. I owe an immense debt of gratitude to my editor, John Parsley, as well as Reagan Arthur at Little, Brown and Company, for their commitment to this project—there were times when it was on the ropes, and their patience and confidence in me allowed me to finish. Malin von Euler-Hogan, Michael Noon, and Gaby Mongelli provided additional help in the editing process that proved invaluable. And I never would have gotten to square one without my agent, Mollie Glick, who believed in me and stuck with me even when I thought she might be crazy to do so.

The other side of my life in recent years was spent at the website *Grantland,* where I had a dream job of assigning, editing, and sometimes writing the kind of in-depth sports and pop-culture narrative journalism that inspired me to pursue writing in the first place. Of course, no one deserves more thanks for creating that opportunity than the site's creator, Bill Simmons.

A number of my former colleagues at *Grantland* encouraged me to reach the end of this book at times when I thought it might be impossible, and that support meant the world to me. To Bryan Curtis, Jordan Ritter Conn, Mark Titus, David Shoemaker, Jay Caspian Kang, Dan Fierman, Jonathan Abrams, Wesley Morris, Louisa Thomas, Megan Creydt, Joe Fuentes, Harlan Endelman, Jim Cunningham, David Cho, Elise Craig, Brian Phillips, Holly Anderson, Max Cea, Amos Barshad, Jason Concepcion, Danny Chau, Corban Goble, Kirk Goldsberry, Jonah Keri, Sarah Larimer, Zach Lowe, David Jacoby, Ryan O'Hanlon, Rany Jazayerli, Robert Mays, Mike Philbrick, Monica Schroeder, and Craig Gaines: Thanks for rooting for me. And to many other coworkers: You gave me such powerful motivation to complete this book, and I hope to someday return the favor.

During several of the moments when I felt as if I'd never find the time to write this book, encouragement from close friends, mentors, and acquaintances nudged me forward and prevented me from giving up. Those small "just finish the damn thing" talks added up to something very powerful for me, and the long, probably incomplete list of people I'd like to thank for their encouragement includes: From the worlds of boxing and ESPN, Brian Campbell, William Dettloff, Eric Raskin, James Foley, Nicole Duva, Peter Nelson, Andres Ferrari, Max Kellerman, Kevin Arnovitz, Henry Abbott, Jackie MacMullan, and Baxter Holmes; Charles Whitaker, Patrick Michels, and Georgi Derluguian from Northwestern; Ted Ross, Ben Austen, Paul Ford, Stacey Clarkson, Rafil Kroll-Zaidi, Rachel Kaadzi-Ghansah, and Tommy Craggs from the extended *Harper's* family; PBA and Manila-based friends like Rob Reyes, Tim Cone, Jeffrey Cariaso, Ravi Chulani, Matt Makalintal, Darvin Tuason, Sev Sarmenta, Mico Halili, Tony dela Cruz, Carlo Pamintuan, Chuck Araneta, Polo Bustamante, Jinno Rufino, Mohan Gumatay, Nikko Ramos, Jimmy Alapag, Chot Reyes, Alex Cabagnot, Becca Dizon, Ryan Guzman, Mike Huang, Kathy Yap-Huang, Banjo Albano, Jutes Templo, Dindin Moreno, Mike Villar, Laurel Fantauzzo, Julia Nebrija, and many, many more.

To Ricardo Bernard, with whom I've remained best friends for the past decade despite both of us bouncing around between four continents, thanks for always keeping that connection alive and for telling me in no uncertain terms, way back in the day, that I had to write this book. And to our other close friends Nnamdi Igbokwe and Ed

Brown, I feel you always checking for me, and it means the world.

To Caroline de Vera, thank you for putting up with me disappearing in the middle of the night and sequestering myself on three-day Amtrak trips to push through till the end of the writing process. I love you and I hope to be cleaning out your Tupperwares for the rest of my days.

Finally, to my dad, Geoffrey Bartholomew: This is the second time you get referenced in these acknowledgments, but why the hell not since you've inspired every page of this book. I can't believe I get to say that I wrote a book about how much I love my father and how proud I am to be his son. Thank you for everything.

About the Author

RAFE BARTHOLOMEW is the author of *Pacific Rims*. His writing has appeared in *Grantland, Slate,* the *New York Times,* the *Chicago Reader, Deadspin,* and other leading online and print publications. His stories have twice been honored in the *Best American Sports Writing* series.